Made in Brooklyn

Artists, Hipsters, Makers, Gentrifiers

Made in Brooklyn

Artists, Hipsters, Makers, Gentrifiers

Amanda Wasielewski

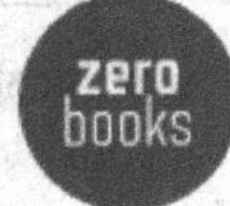

Winchester, UK
Washington, USA

First published by Zero Books, 2018
Zero Books is an imprint of John Hunt Publishing Ltd., No. 3 East Street,
Alresford, Hampshire SO24 9EE, UK
office1@jhpbooks.net
www.johnhuntpublishing.com
www.zero-books.net

For distributor details and how to order please visit the 'Ordering' section on our website.

Text copyright: Amanda Wasielewski 2017

ISBN: 978 1 78535 658 2
978 1 78535 659 9 (ebook)
Library of Congress Control Number: 2017930559

The rights of Amanda Wasielewski as author have been asserted in accordance with the Copyright, Designs and Patents Act 1988.

A CIP catalogue record for this book is available from the British Library.

Design: Stuart Davies

Contents

About Amanda Wasielewski

Amanda Wasielewski is a Lecturer in Media Studies at the University of Amsterdam in the Netherlands. She has previously taught Modern Art History and Architectural History at Lehman College and City College of New York and is a practicing artist whose work has been exhibited internationally. She currently lives in Stockholm and Amsterdam.

Acknowledgements

I would first and foremost like to thank Prof. Marta Gutman for her mentorship and support throughout my research for this book. Her encouragement and enthusiasm were invaluable. I would also like to thank the Bushwick arts pioneers who agreed to be interviewed, including Thomas Burr Dodd and Kevin Lindamood. Thanks, as well, to Igal Nassima and Jo-Anne Hyun of 319 Scholes who invited me to work in their co-working space, which gave me firsthand experience of maker culture in Morgantown. I would like to thank my doctoral advisor Prof. David Joselit for his continued support of my research. Special thanks to my family and Katie Sullivan for their support, and to Chelsea Haines, Leila Harris, Jenny Sarathy, and Johanna Sluiter for their time in the trenches with me. Finally, thank you to Agri Ismail for going above and beyond the call of duty and being my best and most dedicated editor and supporter.

For Agri Ismail

Introduction

On New Year's Eve 2008, I visited the industrial hinterland around the Morgan Avenue subway station in Brooklyn for the first time. I ended up there totally by chance after a last-minute change of plans: an art school friend from London, where I was living at the time, also happened to be in New York and invited me along to a friend's warehouse party that night. Sandwiched between the Brooklyn neighborhoods of Williamsburg and Bushwick (and usually included in the latter), this tract of hulking industrial property, cracked pavements, and creative types had already become a playground for hipsters and artists by the time I showed up there, although it appeared wholly desolate to me at the time – the only sign of life I detected was a lone kebab shop on Bogart Street. Many of the other establishments in the area, I learned later, were well-disguised within their surroundings. Throughout the night, my friends and I were ushered through a series of former industrial buildings with warren-like mazes of makeshift rooms and lofted beds, each creating their own little version of bohemian utopia.

As a tourist, I was somewhat oblivious to my geographic location at the time, not realizing where I had been until four years later when, while planning a move to New York, this already-infamous artist neighborhood popped up on my radar. In May 2012, Hrag Vartanian, the founder of Bushwick-centric art blog *Hyperallergic*, indicated that Bushwick was, by that point, somewhat past its trend-setting prime in an article titled, "Is Ridgewood Breaking Away from the Bushwick Scene?"[1] I read, with interest, how artist-led gentrification was spilling over the border into Ridgewood, Queens, which was trying to eke out its own individual identity apart from its neighbor. Intrigued by the unravelling narrative of the neighborhood and looking to find live/work studio space, I arrived in Morgantown (a nickname for the area around the Morgan Avenue subway) in 2012. I was, of course, decidedly late to the party.

Located on the far northeastern edge of Brooklyn and not exactly commuter-friendly, Bushwick must have seemed like an unlikely candidate for a real estate bonanza just a decade before. When I moved to the area, many of the three-story brick row houses had crumbling moldings and collapsing front steps, and the distinctive wood-frame buildings of the area, coated with vinyl siding and ringed with chain-linked fences, remained rundown. Despite its persistently gritty aesthetic, many of the neighborhood's crowded, dimly-lit bodegas and the auto repair shops had recently been replaced by a smattering of yoga studios, bars, health food shops, and newly-built luxury apartment buildings with underground parking garages. The streets were still littered with broken glass in many places and there were quite a few remaining industrial operations, but the professional graffiti murals dotting the shopfronts, replacing informal graffiti, marked the neighborhood's transitional period. Young artists, who had been in the area for only about a decade, were increasingly finding it hard to cope with higher rents.

In the 1970s and '80s, Bushwick was primarily an African-American and Latino neighborhood that had faced economic downturn in the wake of deindustrialization. Before artists began moving into the industrial warehouse space just north of Bushwick around 1999, the neighborhood was perhaps best known for riots during the July 1977 blackout and, before that, as an industrial hub and beer-brewing center. The artists who came after, many of whom were priced out of Williamsburg in the late '90s and early '00s, formed a new artist enclave there, perhaps hoping it was far enough from Manhattan to avoid the kind of gentrification that Williamsburg had seen. The allure of a creative community, however, outweighed geographic distance and, soon, Bushwick was the new cool neighborhood that 20-somethings flocked to.

In 2013, artists William Powhida and Jules de Balincourt invited artists in the neighborhood to organize and brainstorm possible strategies to avoid being priced out of the rapidly gentrifying area.[2] On June 20th, the "Stay in Bushwick" meeting was held at a venue called Starr Space, located in a large garage-type building at 309 Starr Street; it was one of the older Bushwick artist establishments and had formerly been an experimental theater and art space, so it was an appropriate venue to mourn the passing of one era of gentrification into the next.[3] Those present at the meeting discussed a proposed project by Read Property Group LLC to rezone the former site of the Rheingold Brewery, which was seen as a grand-scale attempt to capitalize on and essentially change the artistic character of the neighorhood.[4] Unknowingly, however, the organizers of the meeting scheduled their gathering the same night as a community board meeting on the rezoning plans, symbolically re-enforcing the separation of artists from the larger community.[5]

Powhida's proposal to avoid displacement of the artistic community, outlined in a document titled "The Yellow Building," suggested collectively purchasing a building in the area and using it as a co-operative studio space. He argued that this solution, "… poses a stewardship model based on collective need within the capitalist market system. Private property and ownership are not abolished, but the terms are modified to provide a way around the decision making of an individual owner or developer."[6] The idea of forming artist co-operatives, however, struck attendees and commentators at the meeting as neither a radically new nor a particularly effective way to maintain the whole of Bushwick as an artist enclave. When those present at the gathering brought up the neighborhood's Latino residents and their right to remain, they were met with resignation by de Balincourt, who said, "Gentrification is – like, that's just the history of New York. I don't think you can stop that."[7] It seems that the artistic community had grown weary of the constantly shifting urban landscape and deeply cynical in the process. Idealism and issues of social justice have been increasingly pushed to one side, weighed down by the inevitability of speculation in the real estate market and the struggle to survive neighborhood change.

The Bushwick creative scene first began in the industrial area of Morgantown, officially called the East Williamsburg In-Place Industrial Park (EWIPIP), and spread southward through the neighborhood. The EWIPIP is roughly bounded by the Brooklyn-Queens Expressway to the north, Flushing Avenue to the south, Newtown Creek to the east and Bushwick Avenue to the west. Though the area had been home to a mix of light and heavy manufacturing facilities since the 19th century, artists did not move there until the late 1990s when many of them migrated from neighboring Williamsburg, where prices were rapidly rising on similar property. The newly colonized subsection of the EWIPIP around the Morgan Avenue subway station was later nicknamed Morgantown, a name that some residents associate with property development and gentrification. I refer to this neighborhood as Morgantown precisely because of its connotations of capitalist growth and investment, which are, in many ways, the founding principles of anchoring institutions in the neighborhood. I also use it as a way to separate the development of the industrial part of Bushwick from the largely residential character of the neighborhood south of Flushing Avenue. This smaller zone of the EWIPIP is, according to my estimation, bordered by Grand Street to the north, Flushing Avenue to the south, Stewart Avenue to the east and Bushwick Avenue to the west. The main concentration of activity in the area centers around the stretch of Bogart Street near the second entrance to the Morgan Avenue subway, where I first emerged into this undercover bohemia in 2008.[8]

The Makers Of Morgantown

Thomas Burr Dodd is the founder of Brooklyn Fire Proof (BFP), an organization housed in a loft building near Morgan that rents studio space for artists, events, and musicians, and operated a bar and café until late 2014. He was briefly the object of Powhida's disapproval in a 2009 piece in which he labeled Burr Dodd's spaces as "criminally overpriced."[9] Burr Dodd was upset by Powhida's characterization, saying, "I was devastated by that. I felt like I had failed."[10] BFP is an example of a new, more entrepreneurial model of artistic activity in Morgantown, and, as such, comes into conflict with older models of artist-run spaces. In comparison to BFP and other art organizations in the area, Powhida's vision of co-operative artists' spaces seems both wonderfully idealistic and hopelessly anachronistic.

Indeed, since the mid-2000s, a new philosophy has taken root: where artist neighborhoods once tended to be left-wing and communal, they are now outward-looking and entrepreneurial. This book charts the ways in which the character of this artist neighborhood, Morgantown, differs from those that came before such as SoHo and Williamsburg and argues that the people who settled this area were artist-entrepreneurs who aided in the rise of the Maker Movement over the last ten years. The movement, which has been broadly feted as the future of business and labor, is characterized by informal, experimental, peer-led learning of unconventional or niche skill sets, often dealing with customized electronics or traditional craft. Growing out of DIY (do-it-yourself) culture and electronic hacking, the term "maker" was popularized by *MAKE* magazine (founded in 2005), Cory Doctorow (writer for *Boing Boing* and author of the 2009 novel *Makers*), and Chris Anderson of *Wired* magazine.[11]

"Maker" describes a variety of self-motivated, creative individuals in professions such as design, programming, architecture, filmmaking, music and dance. The creative freelancer, often young, ambitious and urban, is the quintessential maker. Makers value creativity as well as business innovation and are forged in "incubators" and "co-working spaces," places where equipment and ideas are shared, often for a membership fee, and maker culture unites artistic and market-driven objectives. Makers bear an uncanny resemblance to Richard Florida's conceptualization of the "creative class" and the Maker Movement's acolytes are often dismissively labeled "hipsters."[12] Tech entrepreneurs like Steve Jobs and Mark Zuckerberg are, consequently, the patron saints of the Maker Movement in that they were innovators who earned their fortunes through groundbreaking use of new technology rather than spending years climbing up the corporate ladder. The maker does not want to keep her ideas within an elite sphere or clique but rather has ambitions to bring her product to as large an audience as possible.

Either unconcerned with or having given up on attaining a certain status in the art world, the most recent generation of art school graduates is increasingly concerned with making an impact online. The ultimate accomplishment, in many ways, is producing an article, web project or video that goes viral. Fueled by sites like *Instructables* (instructables.com), *Boing Boing* (boingboing.net), *Wired* magazine (wired.com), *Hackaday* (hackaday.com), *MAKE* (makezine.com), and many others, the drive for unique, viral hits and entrepreneurial success stories motivates makers. With the advent of digitally-enabled, programmable production tools like 3D printers, laser cutters, CNC (computer numerical control), and 3D scanners, network culture and the Web 2.0 model have entered the physical realm. While tech writers often praise the culture of "sharing" fostered online, this type of sharing is often more akin to self-promotion, broadcast, advertising, and marketing of either oneself or one's products. The sharing economy only serves the purpose of defining one's tastes in opposition to everyone else's rather than fostering any genuine community, and the endlessly modifiable nature of digital content may, instead, promote a sense of alienation.

Gentrification (Hipster Remix)

At the core of the Maker Movement is the remix paradigm, within which artists in Morgantown preempted potential outside developers – at least for the time being – and embraced their role as DIY business entrepreneurs. As I detail in Chapter 4, the long and complicated history of artist spaces, residences, and galleries throughout the city elicits a number of broad generalizations and trends: artists seek out large, cheap spaces; they often settle in areas that are ethnically and economically different from their own upbringings or education levels; and artistic activity changes the nature of business in the neighborhoods in which they reside. It has long been a truism that plentiful, cheap space was a sufficient explanation for artistic activity in disinvested or poor neighborhoods.

The "frontier" of gentrification eloquently theorized by Neil Smith in the 1980s and '90s in relation to the Lower East Side continues to push further and further out along the L subway line into Brooklyn in the 2000s.[13] This eastward push began from Smith's gentrifying Lower East Side, which was rebranded as the East Village post-gentrification.[14] By the 1980s, the East Village was enmeshed in passionate debates over artists' role in gentrification, as the industrial space of SoHo was no longer a cheap, viable option for artists to live and work. Williamsburg's industrial waterfront, only one subway stop across the East River, beckoned to those looking for large, cheap studio space. By 2005, the city of New York had rezoned the Williamsburg waterfront area for real estate development and high-rise luxury condominiums quickly sprang up.[15] An artist community was once again displaced by evictions, rent increases, and the push of wealthy professionals into the neighborhood.[16] Once again the creative "pioneers" picked up and moved deeper into Brooklyn, settling around Morgantown. This time, however, the creatives who colonized the area were well aware that they might soon be displaced and many sought to insulate themselves from being pushed out.

As detailed in Chapter 6, the pioneers of Morgantown were attracted to the authenticity they perceived in the roughness, decay, and danger of the area. Surviving these elements is a badge of honor among early residents, who describe an anarchic, disinvested area with packs of feral dogs roaming the streets, regular car fires, and heroin addicts squatting stairwells. The Morgantown pioneers also participated in the anarchy, treating the empty industrial buildings as their personal playgrounds, setting off fireworks from rooftops with impunity and throwing huge warehouse rave parties. Gentrification in Morgantown has, since that time, proceeded quickly. By 2015, the neighborhood was home to a variety of high-end restaurants like Blanca and Momo Sushi Shack and cafés like Swallow Café and Newtown. The blue-chip art gallery Luhring Augustine came to the area in 2012, bringing wealthy art collectors far into the depths of industrial Brooklyn.[17]

Morgantown is known as a "hipster" neighborhood, filled with young people hunting for individualized culture. The original hipsters were a beat-era, white, urban subculture in 1950s who appropriated black culture, particularly in their manner of speaking and in their choice of music.[18] Hipsters today are stereotyped in a slightly different way: young, fickle culture snobs who are oblivious of their class privilege and live only to please themselves with twee affectations and an interest in niche consumer products. Both the old hipster and the new hipster are, thus, seen as inauthentic poseurs. As I argue in Chapter 1, the new hipster is a product of the sharing economy and the prosumer model that is present in the Maker Movement and among self-described makers. "Hipster" is not only universally negative but has become a kind of urban boogieman, like "yuppies" were in the '80s and '90s. The same people derided as "hipsters", however, are happy to call themselves makers. Both hipsters and makers are defined by their interest in DIY creative pursuits. The stigmatization of hipsters and the freelance model of labor that prosumer tools and sharing have fostered are connected. Increasingly, young people in creative professions work from their laptops on a gig-by-gig basis, lacking job security or basic benefits. A hipster sitting in a café on her laptop in the middle of the weekday may look like a frivolous trust-fund kid but she is most likely working hard to scrape together freelance assignments, sold on the idea that this way of working gives her more freedom and choice in her lifestyle and career. Her employers, meanwhile, have no responsibilities to provide her with workspace, equipment, or benefits.

Visual artists in the 1970s and 80s in New York could support themselves, as well as pay rent on a studio and apartment, by working a part-time job and still have plenty of time to make their work. Since that time, the cost of living and rents in the city have pushed creative professionals further and further outside of Manhattan, chasing cheaper rents. The visual artists and other creatives living in Morgantown saw the swift gentrification of Williamsburg firsthand in the late 1990s/early 2000s. These artists and creatives were presented with the choice of either seizing the area for themselves or falling prey to developers in the near future.

The ideology of creativity within the Maker Movement emphasizes a universality of creative potential and experience. In doing so, it fails to recognize the importance of difference in processes of urban change and the organization of labor. This point has been explored by Christina Dunbar-Hester, who writes:

> ... some women and people of color might encounter barriers to sharing in the same affective pleasure in technical

making experienced by many white men. This represents not only difficulty for egalitarian technical projects, but points to the limits of "universalist" discourse more generally: universalism all but depends on glossing over differences in power, access, and status among different groups.[19]

The arguments made throughout this book are primarily concerned with issues around social and economic class within the Maker Movement and in Morgantown, but race, gender, and sexuality also interact in complex ways. The public face of urban change in Brooklyn has been primarily young, affluent, and white, replacing long-standing ethnic and racial identities of neighborhoods and changing the character of local businesses. Ethnic diversity is not completely absent from the process of gentrification, however: some of the first entrepreneurs in a gentrifying neighborhood are often children who grew up in the neighborhood and have been able to gain a foothold in the middle class. Several examples of this type of local gentrification in Bushwick are detailed in Chapter 4. This is not to say that residents of the neighborhood are the primary driving force of gentrification, but they are not wholly excluded from it either. Having already equated makers, hipsters, and gentrifiers in this chapter, it appears that all three are, at least in the public imaginary, primarily white and middle or upper class.

While non-white racial and ethnic groups are often visibly marginalized within gentrifying urban neighborhoods and are positioned in opposition to white hipsters in popular accounts, it is less clear how gender and sexual difference come into play. To start with, gays and lesbians have historically been harbingers of gentrification just as often as artists have been. Both artists and LGBTQ individuals have built communities in urban areas, motivated by both elective and forced seclusion from more intolerant, conservative locations. Simultaneously, many of the artists and LGBTQ individuals who move into poor and working class neighborhoods are white and from middle-class families, but have not, for the obvious reasons, historically chosen to live in neighborhoods of other white, middle-class people. The topic of this book is primarily artist-led gentrification, not LGBTQ-led gentrification, but, of course, these groups are not mutually exclusive. Gay people have traditionally been part of artist neighborhoods like Williamsburg and Bushwick in Brooklyn, or, historically, the West Village or Chelsea in Manhattan. Granted, not every gay neighborhood is an artist neighborhood. One Brooklyn example of LGBTQ-led urban change can be found in Park Slope, where lesbian women were some of the earliest white, middle-class people to move (back) to the neighborhood and begin gentrifying historic brownstones in the area in the '80s. It is now one of the most expensive and desirable neighborhoods in the city.[20]

The place of women in the Maker Movement or hipster neighborhoods is even less clear. Certainly, both the Maker Movement and urban gentrification mirror society in that women are often relegated to less prominent or powerful roles. Due to the fact that the Maker Movement has grown out of male-dominated computing and STEM disciplines, there has been a concerted effort to promote the movement to women, particularly young girls.[21] The egalitarian message of the movement states that *everyone* is a maker, boy or girl, and that all children should be encouraged to play with building and constructing toys like Lego and littleBits.

In gentrifying neighborhoods, men often assume roles of power because of their greater autonomy within society at large. As detailed in Chapter 5, the first reported residents of Morgantown were exclusively young men. Women have historically been taught to fear for their bodily safety in urban environments, even in wealthier neighborhoods, and this fear may be one of the reasons women were less likely to be the first to live in abandoned, high crime, or disinvested neighborhoods.

This is not to say, however, that women are not quick to follow in the wake of male gentrifiers, assuming the same sort of postures that the men do with regards to their "rough" but "authentic" neighborhoods. While artist-led gentrification since the 1950s has followed many of the same patterns over the years, including the desire to live in a more authentic (and less homogenized environment), both hipster culture and the Maker Movement have ushered in a new phase in gentrification where the adversarial relationship between subculture and mainstream has largely dissolved. In the United States, people across the income spectrum identify as and aspire to be middle class (regardless of what their actual socio-economic status is) because belonging to the middle class has long been part of the American Dream.[22]

The pioneering creative institutions of Morgantown were the art studio and event spaces OfficeOps to the south and Brooklyn Fire Proof to the east, the residential McKibbin Lofts to the west, Roberta's Pizza at the center, and the co-working space 3rd Ward to the north (which closed in October 2013). These key sites reflect the DIY entrepreneurial outlook of the Maker Movement, so Morgantown was, from its very inception, infused with the maker philosophy. At the center of the movement is a new model of labor and development facilitated by new techniques to create and produce within network culture. Architecture/media theorist Kazys Varnelis writes, "If appropriation was the key aspect of postmodernism, network culture almost absent-mindedly uses remix as its dominant form."[23] The remix paradigm is the foundation of the Maker Movement and the tool with which artists in Morgantown preempted potential outside developers and embraced their role as DIY business entrepreneurs.

The McKibbin lofts are two massive daylight factory buildings across the street from one another that have long housed incoming creative young people in Morgantown. The units of these buildings are often divided into six or seven small rooms in a ramshackle, DIY manner, and have a reputation for being unkempt, infested with bedbugs, and frequently hosting wild parties. OfficeOps provides a combination of studio space, apartments, and rental spaces for weddings and events.[24] Brooklyn Fire Proof (BFP) also provides art studio space as well as larger unit rentals for other creative projects or events.[25] OfficeOps and BFP were, in many ways, monetizing the way artists have occupied former industrial property in the past. Those that buy into these spaces are no longer getting a deal on cheap space, as artists were in SoHo or Williamsburg, but rather buying into the aesthetic that their forebears had popularized.

3rd Ward, however, presented a striking new way of organizing artists' studios and creative space in former industrial neighborhoods like Morgantown. More than any other organization in the area, 3rd Ward paved the way for the transition of the creative professional from artist to maker. Opening in 2005, 3rd Ward provided studios, workshops, and courses for a membership fee. It was a quintessential maker space. While the art students who founded 3rd Ward did not have a clear business model for how they would ultimately manage or monetize their operations, they had endless expansionist ambitions. 3rd Ward started out hosting club nights and providing studio space, but they were quick to branch out into new spaces in other cities, pop-up locations elsewhere in New York, and other real estate and financial investments. Ultimately, 3rd Ward expanded too quickly and, in 2013, was dramatically shut down overnight, leaving many of those involved in the organization without paychecks, studios or refunds on courses, as I detail in Chapter 5.

The opening of Roberta's pizza restaurant in 2008 marked a turning point for the neighborhood and its entrepreneurs. In many ways, Roberta's made Morgantown a destination: suddenly Manhattanites were making the journey out to the edge of Brooklyn to wait in line for one of the restaurant's famous artisanal pizzas. The year Roberta's opened ushered in a period of consolidation and formalization of the area. With the arrival of Roberta's, Morgantown was no longer an untamed wasteland but had become a desirable and amenable place to live and work. Bogart Street in Morgantown is now post-frontier – it is buzzing with activity night and day. Spaces to live and work in the area are desirable and expensive, and costs are rising all along the length of Bushwick. In Roberta's or Momo's on Bogart Street, young European tourists and moonlighting Manhattanites are easy to spot. Despite the dramatic downfall of 3rd Ward, many of the original artist-entrepreneurs are still flourishing in the area. It will take another few decades to see whether the maker model of development produces a different outcome than SoHo or Williamsburg, but the model itself is already recognizably different. The interest of Roberta's, OfficeOps, and Brooklyn Fire Proof in sustainability, environmentalism, and ethical urban living already sets these businesses apart from traditional gentrifiers. The makers of Morgantown may prove themselves to be wolves in sheep's clothing or they may, despite the neighborhood's naysayers, change the nature of gentrification and ameliorate at least some of its brutality and upheaval.

Art Student Living

This book aims to provide a foundational critique of the Maker Movement in general as well as highlight the specific impact of the movement on Morgantown, which was the epicenter of hipster/maker culture in New York City between roughly 2000–2015. My interest in artist-led gentrification started when I lived in London between 2005 and 2010, studying art first at Goldsmiths College, living in New Cross/Peckham, and then the Slade School of Fine Art at UCL, living in Finsbury Park and Green Lanes. I watched as my artist friends and I moved through the city, occupying one gentrifying neighborhood after another in quick succession. When I left London in 2010 for a two-year art residency in Amsterdam, I saw how my friends in London continued to push further and further eastward outside of the rapidly gentrifying East End and Hackney. While in Amsterdam, I learned about the history of Dutch squatting and how artistic activities flourished in these occupied spaces. About a month after I arrived in the Netherlands, in October 2010, squatting was officially banned, ending a century of toleration of the practice. In 2012, at the conclusion of my residency in Amsterdam, I moved to New York to begin a doctoral program. In the run-up to the move, I knew that I wanted to find a live/work space so I could continue to work on my art practice while pursuing my academic research. It did not take me long to decide to move to Morgantown, as Williamsburg and East Williamsburg were already well beyond my budget.

The resulting analysis, therefore, is a conglomeration of ethnography from the time I spent living in the neighborhood, academic research that draws from my background in art history, and a more journalistic account of the recent changes in the neighborhood. Although I grew up in and spent the majority of my undergraduate education in Chicago, where I first took an interest in artist-led gentrification and urban change, I was unprepared for the differences between the New York art scene and the British or European equivalents I had grown accustomed to while I was abroad.

When I arrived in Morgantown in 2012, I saw a lot of sublets in loft spaces that were dingy and dark, including rooms in the McKibbin lofts that had no windows or space for a bed and often no walls or doorway. They were also shockingly expensive. I ended up finding a place in a building on the corner of Johnson and Stewart Avenues – the fourth floor of 75 Stewart. 538 Johnson, the address of the other side of the same building, contained more live/work studios, one of which contained a huge half-pipe for skateboarding. It was, in many ways, a fantasy of bohemian living. The loft dwellers of the building communicated via a joint Facebook group, where people mostly detailed an endless list of issues with plumbing, trash disposal, vandalism from unruly parties, and conflicts with the building management and the Fire Department. My bedroom and workspace, surrounded by windows in the corner of the building, was lofted above the main living room of our unit and I shared the unit with two other people, the leaseholder, who was a woodworker and freelance designer, and a Danish photographer. There was a separate walled-off area for a bed and studio and I paid $1100 per month for the space, not including an extra $150 a month for bills and private trash collection (our building was not serviced by the city, as it was not a legal residence).

Unbeknownst to me, the building's residents were facing possible eviction when I moved in and I very quickly became acquainted with New York's rules and regulations for occupying industrial property. The leaseholder had lived in the space for eight years and, given the popularity and price of loft spaces, it naively never occurred to me that we could be evicted for illegally living in the property. At that time, the building was not under the protection of the Loft Law, which was designed to protect artists living in industrial properties from eviction. Many tenants, including my leaseholder roommate, objected to the provisions of the law, which would have meant tearing down the homemade multistoried constructions we were occupying and bringing the unit up to fire safety code.[26] In September and October of that year, the Fire Department and building inspectors visited us multiple times, and each time a message went out on the Facebook group warning others not to let them into the building. By the end of October, we were sure that an eviction notice was imminent, and a group of leaseholders in the building were meeting with Loft Law advocates and lawyers to try to come to some consensus on what should be done. Luckily, one of the other tenants had a contact in the Department of Buildings who tipped us off that the eviction notice would arrive on the 30th of October. We had only twenty-four hours to get a Loft Law application in, which would allow us to stay in our homes. On the night of the 29th of October, Hurricane Sandy hit New York. The Fire Department was, as a result, busy with more urgent matters that week, and we managed to get our application in before being evicted.

I remained at 75 Stewart through the following May, although we were still under threat of Fire Department intervention. During that time, the rate of new restaurants and bars popping up in the neighborhood was increasing at a rapid rate. Friends who lived in Manhattan would travel out to Morgantown to eat at Roberta's pizza or visit the bars on Wyckoff in Bushwick. I had been struck, when I arrived, at how desolate Morgantown still seemed and was surprised to see so many working factories and industrial shops in operation, given the now hip reputation of the area. From my building I could see a scrap metal yard on Stewart, where a large machine would crush cars and then stack them up in tall heaps, a slick of oil blackening the sidewalk and street in front of it. In May 2015, it was announced that the site of the metal scrap shop would be turned into a 9-story luxury hotel.[27] The first three floors of my building housed a print shop and the halls would regularly be filled with a pungent chemical smell. Across the street, a former feather factory had recently been renovated into artists' studios and galleries.[28] Around the corner on Harrison Place, foul smells and chemical runoff emanated from a food factory, and, across the street, next to the scrap metal shop, the upper floors of Global King Inc. and Peking Food Products Corp. at 47 Stewart housed artists in residence, announced by the A.I.R. signs on the doors.

After moving out of 75 Stewart, I sought cheaper rents further south in Bushwick, as many other artists and students were doing at the time. I moved south of Myrtle Avenue at Putnam and Irving Avenues to an apartment building where the landlord seemed to be actively seeking my demographic –

young, white – in a largely Latino neighborhood. Our middle-aged neighbor downstairs, who had lived in the building for thirty years, suspected that the landlord was trying to force her out by purposely sabotaging our boiler in winter and refusing to make any repairs on the building, including providing lighting for the hallways or a closed door to the roof. Needless to say, she was not overjoyed to see three twenty-something white girls move in upstairs. Meanwhile, I sought a separate art studio space back in Morgantown.

Finding affordable studio space was next to impossible. I viewed one studio in Brooklyn Fire Proof that was approximately 300 square feet shared between six people that would have cost me $250 per month, but there was hardly any room to move with that many people crowded in it. A friend suggested trying out 319 Scholes, a co-working space where I could get a desk for $350 per month. The space promised access to a laser cutter and 3D printer, and everyone in the studio was working primarily on computer-based projects. I decided to give it a try but was surprised to find that the others working at 319 Scholes were not like the artists I was familiar with in London or Amsterdam. All of those working in the space were actively engaged in commercial projects: one made high-production-value video work for corporate clients, two of the others worked on interactive displays for Lacoste's store windows, another was engaged in freelance animation projects, and yet another was creating super high-res visualizations to project on the side of buildings for the opening of a condominium complex in Williamsburg. At the same time, they were engaged with their own smaller-scale projects in the studio that they hoped to gain funding for via Kickstarter, corporate partnership, or with money earned through freelance gigs. I realized that I was now part of a maker space.

Every day, new maker spaces or incubators are popping up in Morgantown. The popular press around the Maker Movement heralds the return of "industry" to formerly industrial areas like this one, but, as I will argue in this book, the movement is not bringing industrial manufacturing back to these areas but rather transforming them into tech-industry enclaves. Artists in New York can no longer afford to live and work with the income from part-time or unskilled jobs and have therefore turned to design and tech jobs in the freelance economy. I realized during my time at 319 Scholes that perhaps "artist" is an occupation left behind in the twentieth century, that artists now are increasingly becoming makers. These artist-entrepreneurs must hustle constantly for recognition, funding, visibility, and, most importantly, to make a living in an increasingly individualistic capitalist economy. In the 1980s and '90s, neoliberal political factions worked to dismantle the National Endowment for the Arts (NEA) and succeeded in seriously curtailing public funding for the arts in the United States. Far-right-wing politicians and activists have continued to push for the abolition and defunding of what little money remains for the NEA.[29] Artists are, therefore, often left with corporate sponsorship or Kickstarters as the only viable way to continue making the work they make.

The Maker Movement has generated a lot of enthusiasm and excitement in both the business world and academia over the last decade, but there are many issues within the movement that must be addressed with a critical lens in order to situate it in changing urban geographies, notably formerly industrial neighborhoods. This book is, therefore, divided into two parts: the first part deals with the Maker Movement itself and its historical antecedents and development, and the second part addresses its effect on urban spaces and the Morgantown neighborhood specifically. The Maker Movement is not just changing business, work, and leisure but also urbanism and the nature of artistic practice.

Part I
The Maker Movement

Chapter 1

The Maker Movement

In 2005, Dale Dougherty, co-founder of O'Reilly Media, coined the phrase "Maker Movement" to describe the recent trend towards personalized, computer-aided do-it-yourself (DIY) projects. Evolving from the hacking and computer programing clubs of previous decades, communities of DIY enthusiasts were increasingly connecting online and meeting up in workshops called "co-working spaces," "incubators" or "hackerspaces."[1] Dougherty hoped to consolidate and capitalize on the trend by launching *Make* magazine as well as organizing a series of auxiliary "maker" events, workshops, and fairs.[2] While Apple, Google, and Facebook dominated the mainstream media in the '00s, the staff of *Wired* magazine and O'Reilly Media – including Dougherty – were operating in the background, continually creating the narrative around technological trends. These two organizations have, in fact, been defining business on the Internet since the early 1990s. Drawing from his previous experience in branding technology trends, Dougherty expanded and popularized the Maker Movement around the world over the subsequent decade.

The Maker Movement was not the first turning point in Internet culture that Dougherty pinpointed and labeled; he also coined the term "Web 2.0" in 2003. The phrase was designed to attract investment back to the Internet after the dot-com bubble burst in 2000, positioning the new model of platform-based web business as inherently different from the goods-and-content-producing sites of the '90s. Web 2.0 sites no longer depended on distribution, warehouses, goods or products but, instead, offered user-driven content creation and social media (sites like Facebook, Flickr, YouTube in the '00s). Unlike early net business, the Web 2.0 model took the responsibility for content creation out of the hands of the business itself. Web 2.0 businesses simply build a fun, attractive, and useful platform to draw in users, who would then create value for the product through voluntary labor. The labor of users is harnessed in the name of entertainment and these sites are positioned as free services. Users might assume that the content they create on a website that they enjoy would not constitute unpaid labor. As Guy Debord noted in the 1960s, however, leisure is an insidious form of alienated labor.[3] Organized leisure activities allow business interests to seize control of free time in order to extract excess productive labor from workers. According to Debord, the entertaining nature of these activities – or, the spectacle – distracts us from this condition.

The Maker Movement was the next step beyond Web 2.0. While Web 2.0 facilitated rapid online exchange of digital products such as music, films, images, and text, the Maker Movement promises to do the same for physical goods. The world of things can now be scanned, designed and otherwise recorded into a digital file that can then be shared and printed out again on a 3D printer or cut with a computer-enabled laser cutter. The Maker Movement, like Web 2.0, is powered by user-driven content. Maker Movement proponents claim that, for the first time, production is in the hands of consumers. The main distinction between the longer history of DIY and the Maker Movement lies in the use of new consumer-grade methods of production – 3D printers, laser cutters, CNC (computer numerical control) machines, etc. – that are becoming more accessible and affordable to non-specialist amateurs, allowing individual hobbyists to "manufacture" professional quality products more easily. The Maker Movement's fixation on manufacture is, however, a chimera. As I argue in Chapter 4, what the movement calls manufacture is simply the absorption of production under the banner of consumption. For example, consumer-grade 3D printers are very similar to desktop inkjet printers: they may facilitate small scale projects but are not equipped to manufacture industrial-scale products. The exercise of producing therefore becomes a leisure activity and another form of consumption. This is not to say, however, that some Maker Movement acolytes have not spun their DIY businesses into full-scale production or manufacturing businesses. These "Maker Pros", as the movement calls them, often find themselves treading a very traditional pathway to industrial production: as Maker Movement leaders readily admit, neither the maker's garage nor the maker space/incubator is equipped to deal with industrial-scale production. Therefore, many of these Maker Pros are manufacturing their products in Chinese factories.[4] Rickshaw Bags in San Francisco, one of the maker businesses profiled in Mu-Ming Tsai's documentary *Maker* (2014), positions itself somewhere between the industrial might of China and homegrown DIY. According to its founder and CEO Mark Dwight, all of the components of his bags are made in China and are then assembled and customized in a linear production chain at his workshop. Ironically, all of the women he staffs in the San Francisco shop are Chinese and he proudly claims Chinese is the first language of everyone there.[5]

Yet the movement's rhetoric seems to ignore the realities of maker production. Mark Hatch, CEO of a chain of maker spaces called TechShop, claims that the Maker Movement is reversing deindustrialization in the west: "Manufacturing is coming back, and urban centers have a place in the ecosystem."[6] Hatch describes a tantalizing utopia where every corner of the world can be self-sufficient, no longer tied to large corporate production methods in distant countries or forced to rely on *old* industrial methods. The ideology of the Maker Movement, which revolves around egalitarian access to tools and the transformative powers of creativity, is married to free market capitalism, which works aggressively against fair distribution of wealth and equal opportunity. The contradictions between the ideology and the market are rectified through a techno-utopianism that promises deliverance through new technology.

Maker Movement Pros often begin their work in maker spaces like TechShop, where they prototype their products. After a certain amount of investment is secured, they move their manufacturing to Asia. While the Maker Movement claims that it is bringing manufacturing back to the United States and western Europe, it has done nothing to remedy the loss of well-paid working class jobs in old centers of production. The movement revolves around empowering individuals to build their own products with new consumer-grade tools, but the truth is that these tools and workshops will never equal the industrial power available overseas. In any case, the very idea of "professional makers" is antithetical to maker rhetoric, which posits that we are all makers and technology will soon enable us to manufacture everything we need locally.

The Maker Movement's biggest promoters, including Dale Dougherty and *Wired* magazine's former editor Chris Anderson, claim that we have entered a new era of industrialization. The "New Industrial Revolution" they promise will put manufacture and production in the hands of everyone. It is not surprising, therefore, that the issue of American versus Chinese labor is left unaddressed. For Andrew Huang, an open source hardware designer and entrepreneur, utilizing Chinese industry is inevitable (as it is for many Western corporations). He has even moved his center of operations to China, explaining, "Very often I'm asked if it's really necessary to go to Asia – why not just operate out of the US? Aren't emails and conference calls good enough… I guess this is possible, but would you hire an agent to shop for dinner or buy clothes for you?"[7] Successful members of the Maker Movement have, so far, relied on the same globalized system of industrial manufacturing that other corporate entities utilize.

Chris Anderson, editor of *Wired* from 2001–2012, was one of the earliest promoters of the Maker Movement. He left the magazine to pursue his own maker business as CEO of 3D Robotics Inc., a company specializing in DIY drones. His 2012 book *Makers* outlines the ideology of the movement and can be found on the shelves behind nearly every interviewee in Tsai's *Maker* documentary. As Anderson enthusiastically proclaims, the impact that network culture had on immaterial information in the "realm of bits" is crossing over into the world of real things thanks to programmable production equipment.[8] He writes, "… the digital revolution has now reached the workshop, the lair of Real Stuff, and there it may have its greatest impact yet."[9] Anderson's writing on the Maker Movement builds on his 2006 book *The Long Tail*, in which he writes that new digital tools have allowed more people to consume and produce their own digital content and share it online.[10]

In the 1990s, software was developed to allow a wider base of consumers to do professional video editing, photo manipulation, music recording, desktop publishing, etc., and the Internet made it possible to share those creations online. The "long tail" is a term for the statistical trailing off a distribution curve along an asymptote and was adopted by Anderson to describe the way in which users of digital technology are able to create and share content on the Internet, satisfying increasingly personalized and individualized tastes and interests. He uses the example of digital music, claiming that people no longer listen to all the same Top 40 songs because, with a quick Internet search, they can now find the music of a niche independent artist just as easily as they can find songs from a studio-backed pop artist. This leads, according to Anderson, to a greater diversity of digital content available.[11] In the past, groups of young people – both in the mainstream and in subcultures – were united as a community by a certain body of music they all shared. Now, each individual can curate his or her own eclectic collection of music from the most obscure to the most popular. According to Anderson, this trend is both good for consumers and good for musicians. Popular music is, of course, still around and there are still hit songs that large groups of people identify with, but we have moved to a more individualistic model of consumption in music, leisure, and fashion.

Anderson predicts that the ability to modify and 3D print a vast archive of real world products will similarly lead to the long tail of things, created by modifying and remixing digital objects instead of immaterial digital content like music or video. While tech writers often praise the culture of "sharing" fostered online, I would argue that, by this definition, sharing only serves the purpose of defining one's tastes in opposition to everyone else's rather than fostering any genuine community. People need common identities as well as personalized tastes. A utopia of infinite consumer choice and customizability may, therefore, create alienation, as people strive to distance themselves from each other and cultivate increasingly individual identities. Young adults of the millennial generation, many of whom are derogatorily called hipsters, have grown up in this remix culture. Unlike past generations, which were largely united by the same music and fashions, millennials have curated individual tastes, which has led to accusations in the press of extreme individualism and exceptionalism.[12]

As a counterpoint to Anderson's long tail, Kevin Kelly, founding editor of *Wired* and former editor of the *Whole Earth Review*, developed the theory of the "1,000 True Fans." In a 2008 blog post, Kelly outlines how any artist can survive in the "long tail" by cultivating a group of one thousand die-hard enthusiasts who will buy absolutely everything the artist puts out. According to Kelly, "The genius of the True Fan model is that the fans are able to move an artist away from the edges of the long tail to a degree larger than their numbers indicate. They can do this in three ways: by purchasing more per person, by spending directly so the creator keeps more per sale, and by enabling new models of support."[13] The new models of support that Kelly describes include websites like Fundable, just one of a myriad of crowd-funding websites that rely on friends, family, and fans to finance an idea or product. Kickstarter was founded in 2009 (a year after the blogpost appeared) and is perhaps the most famous of the crowdfunding platforms. It is a Maker Movement staple and is often pegged as a way to "democratize" financing, cutting out big bureaucratic entities like banks and governments (with their security checks, rules, and regulations).

The term crowdfunding grew out of the vogue in the mid-'00s for the labor practice of crowdsourcing, a way to alleviate the costs of full-time employees in lieu of freelancers. Crowdsourcing works in a variety of ways, but it fundamentally involves soliciting something (ideas, designs, or, in the case of Amazon's Mechanical Turk, tiny tedious data processing jobs that humans still do better than computer software) from the pool of people on the Internet, sometimes with the offer of a payday for the selected entry and sometimes even for free. Unsurprisingly, the term "crowdsourcing" came out of a conversation between two *Wired* staffers, Jeff Howe and Mark Robinson. Howe described the phenomenon as like "outsourcing the crowd" or crowdsourcing. Although he coined the term half in jest, Howe brought the concept of crowdsourcing to print in a June 2006 article, where he outlined the system of harnessing cheap (or free) labor:

> For the last decade or so, companies have been looking overseas, to India or China, for cheap labor... Technological advances in everything from product design software to digital video cameras are breaking down the cost barriers that once separated amateurs from professionals... The labor isn't always free, but it costs a lot less than paying traditional employees. It's not outsourcing; it's crowdsourcing.[14]

Howe essentially describes crowdsourcing in the creative industries as a means for companies to circumvent professional designers, coders, artists, etc., in favor of skilled amateurs or would-be professionals just starting out in their chosen field. The availability of accessible consumer tools like Adobe Photoshop or Apple Final Cut Pro has created a surplus of capable and available producers willing to work for little or no money, saving companies the money they would have otherwise paid professionals.[15]

The term "crowdfunding" followed closely on the heels of crowdsourcing in August 2006, and was coined by Michael Sullivan in text accompanying the launch of his Fundavlog project, an ill-fated Internet funding scheme for video bloggers.[16] The crowdfunding industry is now swarming with different funding portals, the most famous of which is Kickstarter. Other sites such as Indiegogo, GoFundMe, YouCaring, and Fundrise now serve a variety of purposes, such as filmmaking, retail products, charity, and even real estate, and adopted different models of "rewarding" the investors in each project, from simple thank you notes to the product itself (when the work is completed). Kickstarter backers are increasingly finding, however, that the money they pledge is more of a donation than an investment.

For Maker Movement start-up companies, crowdfunding, like crowdsourcing, is pegged as a way to get something for nothing. Over and over again, Maker Movement enthusiasts describe Kickstarter as a democratizing force, allowing those that cannot procure bank loans, venture capitalist funding or other revenue sources the opportunity to get the money they need to start their business. Mark Hatch writes:

> Online crowdsourcing really changes the fundamentals for financing products. It democratizes access to capital in a way we haven't seen since the Glass-Steagall act of 1933 made it illegal to advertise for investors. But this is even better, for

the artists are not selling stock, they are reselling products or projects and as such aren't giving up a piece of their companies.[17]

Although Hatch tries to soften the message by referring to Kickstarter companies as "artists" (and, therefore, emphasizing the individual rather than the business entity), the advantage of the Kickstarter model of funding, like crowdsourcing in general, lies entirely with the company soliciting financing. Investors in Kickstarter projects typically get no equity, no share in the company and no guarantee that the product *idea* they support will produce the product they want (or any product at all, even).

In an interview in Tsai's *Maker* film, Danae Ringelmann, co-founder of Indiegogo, claims that crowdfunding is creating a market-driven meritocracy and that "people are voting with their dollar."[18] Hatch makes a similar argument, stating, "This platform helps to prove or disprove whether it is a good project or not by whether enough money was raised to fund the project."[19] These statements, on one hand, highlight the persistence of centuries-old theories about the "invisible hand" of market forces, which are seen as part of the natural order and thus should be left to operate in an unmediated way.[20] On a deeper level, though, Kickstarter funders are relying almost entirely on blind trust, on the strength of an idea, and, often, a flashy video. While anti-regulation CEOs like Hatch may rail against the antidemocratic nature of traditional vetting processes (which allow only those with strong financial profiles to acquire loans and funding through banks or venture capitalists), these rules exist to protect the investors, who often want some share or stake in the business. The Kickstarter model does not force businesses to provide any background checks or guarantee that users will see a return on their investment.

Instead, Kickstarter funders normally sign up for nominal rewards like movie tickets or posters, which amounts to, essentially, a donation to the project. For products, funders often pay an amount that will count as a pre-sale purchase for the item that will be delivered to the financer once it's put into production. On some level, users who donate money know the risks they are undertaking and the amount of money they put up for each campaign is often relatively small, but a great number of people are taken in by the techno-utopian rhetoric of "being part of a community" and "being in on the ground floor" of exciting new technology and, so, never consider the possibility that they are being exploited. As Kickstarter co-founder Chris Adler says in *Maker*, crowdfunding provides "more art for more people," which references Chris Anderson's long tail of content production. The allure of more products, with more customized features, which align more directly with each consumer's curated individuality, is undeniable. One again, though, this curated individuality produces a culture that values uniqueness over community.

The reality, however, is that many Kickstarter projects have failed and even been accused of fraud. There are numerous examples to be found online, bearing all the hallmarks of an unchecked system. In 2014, a video gaming company called Playdek started a Kickstarter campaign, promising a sequel to a beloved game that would be designed in the spirit of the original role-playing game format (RPG). After raising $660,000, Playdek floundered and the game was delayed for several years afterward. While the Kickstarter investors were disappointed with the delays, they were outraged at the updated description of the game that appeared in a September 2015 timeline for a late 2016 release of the game, which was no longer an RPG and bore no likeness whatsoever to the game they were originally promised.[21] Other projects like the ZUta labs printer, which raised $511,662 and promised a portable tiny robot printer that would skate across the surface of a paper and print a document on the go, and the Lima file sharing dongle, which raised $80,346 and promised to sync up all devices into one centralized system, were mired by technical difficulties for years as producing the technology they promised turned out to be more difficult than they expected. In response to some of these disasters, Kickstarter has, since 2012, implemented its own rules and regulations for fundees, including a mandate that designers have to demonstrate a working prototype of their product. In 2015, Kickstarter also started a forum called Campus where users can discuss the reliability and trustworthiness of various companies soliciting funding.[22] The true believers in *laissez faire* capitalism may cry foul at such limits to freedom, but regulation has always gone hand in hand with capitalist growth. These regulations may, in fact, allow more money to be made, as more users are reassured that their donations are going to a trustworthy designer.

Despite these minor precautions, exaggeration and overstated promises are still rampant in the world of Kickstarter campaigning. One game developer, Peter Molyneux of 22Cans, was at the center of several funding scandals after overpromising on Kickstarter. He blamed the platform for his company's failure to deliver the promised products, stating:

There's this overwhelming urge to over-promise because it's such a harsh rule: if you're one penny short of your target then you don't get it. And of course in this instance, the behavior is incredibly destructive, which is "Christ, we've only got 10 days to go and we've got to make £100,000, for fuck's sake, let's just say anything." So I'm not sure I would do that again.[23]

While a growing number of media outlets have devoted space to these Kickstarter failures, the Maker Movement has maintained its belief in the utopian project of crowdfunding. With claims of democracy and meritocracy, it plays well into the technologically-infused brand of libertarianism that permeates the movement.

As more crowdfunding sites enter the market, it is inevitable that more regulation and checks will be instituted. This may mean that the small-time maker can no longer feasibly compete against the larger companies that are raising money on the platform, but, in light of the bad press, new rules are necessary for the survival of Kickstarter and other crowdfunding sites.

Critical Making and Materialism

In recent years, an offshoot of the Maker Movement has formed around the term "critical making," rejecting the shallow, business-minded approach of O'Reilly Media and maker entrepreneurship. Academics in information technology, engineering, and the social sciences as well as defectors from *Make*-sponsored fairs have joined together to form a Maker Movement faction that is pro-maker on an ideological and intellectual level but suspicious of both corporate and government involvement in the movement. Critical making often reframes DIY as DIWO (do-it-with-others) and DIT (do-it-together), emphasizing the practice of collaborative learning.[24]

Coined by Matt Ratto, the term "critical making" is a combination of critical thinking and thinking-through-making. Ratto writes, "… critical making is an elision of two typically disconnected modes of engagement in the world – 'critical thinking', often considered as abstract, explicit, linguistically-based, internal and cognitively individualistic; and 'making', typically understood as material, tacit, embodied, external and community-oriented."[25] Through critical making, Ratto promotes a form of learning that moves away from text and language-based critical reasoning and toward a way of researching and learning that is hands-on and intuitive, a method of learning-by-doing. Ratto has performed several experiments in maker-based research around the thesis that a hands-on maker project would foster a deeper knowledge than a discussion would. One project had participants at a conference build a "bristlebot," a robot that would move along a surface using a vibrating toothbrush. The project aimed to spark a discussion amongst participants on the value of distance learning and, perhaps, change their positions on the topic. A second project utilized "flwrs," programmed electronic flowers that communicated and interacted with one another in a variety of ways, to explore the concept of the "walled garden" of the Internet, i.e. the consequences of protected or closed off spaces online.[26] The former is described as a failure because participants failed to change their minds about distance-based learning. Ratto deemed the latter a success, however, as it instigated a lively discussion.

While it is clear that Ratto's critical making experiments have a powerful demonstrative and pedagogical function, as well as the ability to spark debates, their usefulness in higher level research is unclear. These critical making demos do not take away the need for text-based argumentation but rather serve as a pedagogical tool to start a conversation. In describing the need to move away from text-based learning, Ratto borrows art historian David Peters Corbett's term "textual doppelgangers," which is used to describe the textual replacement for a work of art that historians use to analyze the artwork in lieu of the work itself.[27] Ratto describes reading this text, and thinking, "Aha! Here seemed to be the 'earth' in our current geocentric model of criticality and technology – too much of a dependency on textuality and language."[28] Unfortunately, Ratto's demonstrations are also representations that stand in for real-world social scenarios or interactions with technology and so, just like textual descriptions, are merely stand-ins to be analyzed rather than something closer to the thing itself. Both text-based description and participation in the demo can be useful ways to think about a larger problem, but they are, nevertheless, both descriptions/representations of the real world that are at least one step removed from it.

The trend toward critical making has dovetailed significantly with the recent transdisciplinary interest in Bruno Latour's Actor-Network Theory (ANT), Speculative Realism, Object-Oriented Ontology, and investigations of materiality under the heading of New Materialisms.[29] While the Maker Movement does not engage with some of the more esoteric philosophy that New Materialisms does, both sides claim to take a "view from below," an understanding apart from the over-intellectualized abstractions and theories that enforce a top-down hierarchy on knowledge and obscure the essential material quality of the world. New Materialisms and the Maker Movement both claim to have open, egalitarian positions, where actions are collaborative, and both have fostered a renewed utopianism in technology discourse that is reminiscent of the optimism around the Internet in the mid-1990s. Many intellectuals at the time heralded the advent of the Internet as the dawn of a new open and democratic age, thinking that it would be a kind of digital commune where everyone would have a voice and power structures would be dismantled. As writers such as Richard Barbrook and Andy Cameron realized early on, however, the Internet was already being driven by a capitalist impulse coming out of California.[30]

The Maker Movement and New Materialism have also both fostered a kind of Romanticism, detailed in Chapter 2, or primitivism that positions making as a way to get in touch with humanity's native state and reach a kind of transcendental fulfilment beyond the subject. On the topic of New Materialisms, Patricia Falguières writes, "But ultimately art, as a form of making, has always been an experience of decentering the subject... artists intended to renew ties with an 'archaic' regime of art that the academic institution and its doctrinal apparatus had not been able to entirely eclipse ever since the seventeenth century: a regime where making is a mode of knowledge, a 'disposition to produce equipped with logos.'"[31] The focus on material animism in New Materialisms discourse often serves the purpose of anthropomorphizing the material world rather than, as intended, decentering human subjectivity.

New Materialisms has been positioned as a key theoretical framework for describing the influence of the Maker Movement on the contemporary art world. The activities of these artist-makers spawned the Post-Internet movement, in which artists utilize digitally-enabled tools (like 3D printers or laser-cutters) to make paintings, sculptures, animations and other objects. While this movement succeeded in bringing artists who explicitly reference and work with Internet culture into the center of the contemporary art world, the conflation of these practices with New Materialisms has been viewed with suspicion in some quarters. Avoiding the technophobic critiques that have plagued digital media artists since the 1980s, some critics and commentators have questioned the branding of these artists in light of New Materialisms discourse. Armen Avanessian writes, "In short, there have been a great many efforts that have led at the very least to successfully establishing a new, young, fresh generation of artists in a global market... Same old sculptures – this time 3D printed? Yet more decorative paintings with some new industrial colors or maybe on synthetic materials? This is pretty much the impression one gathers when following some quite fruitless debates about post-internet art."[32] D. Graham Burnett, meanwhile, compares New Materialism to one of the darlings of the Maker Movement, Etsy, a website where craftspeople can sell their wares. Burnett writes, "And who doesn't love 'material culture'? Why it's almost like Etsy! Like Etsy kissed by *philosophy*. What could be better? The more dematerialized and etherealized our consumerism becomes, the more sweetly nostalgic an emphasis on actual medium-sized dry goods. They are, after all, something like the Real Presence of late capitalism."[33] Critical writers in both New Materialisms and critical making have wondered if Marxism and democracy are being sold back to us in some kind of convenient capitalist package – that, somehow, Materialisms is just being materialistic (in the colloquial sense, i.e. consumerist) and making is just a new form of leisure consumption (i.e. nothing revolutionary or participatory at all).

Many of the participants in critical making buy into the same rhetoric and ideology of making found in the corporate world. While they critique some surface elements of *Make* magazine and the consumer culture of the Maker Movement, they rarely question the underlying premise that making is the best way of learning and that the text-based learning favored by academia is a lesser substitution. Besides researchers like Ratto, many others joined the critical making wing of the Maker Movement after Dale Dougherty announced in 2012 that DARPA (the Defense Advanced Research Projects Agency) would be funding a maker program for high school students.[34] In April of that year, Mitch Altman, a high-profile participant in Maker Faires, announced he would no longer participate on account of the DARPA funding, stating, "Hackerspaces are not about the money. They are about exploring and doing what one loves. Once we start accepting money from organizations that do not share our goals, then what kind of self-censorship are we willing to make in order to increase our liklihood [sic] of getting more of that grant money?"[35] Tim O'Reilly fired back at Altman on the comment thread, arguing:

Yes, DARPA wants to see more scientists and engineers in our society, but that's the extent of the military aspect of this project. I think it's great that DARPA wants to fund science education. I'd much rather have them doing that than funding weapons research. Your notion that this is a secret recruiting scheme for weapons research is… well, indication of a lack of critical thinking. By your reasoning, you should also stop any association with any science or technology university, because (gasp) they too receive DARPA funding (or other military funding) for some of their research. I hope you're

> also stopping using GPS-enabled maps and directions – or for
> that matter, the Internet...[36]

As O'Reilly implies, Altman and others opposed to the DARPA funding may be in denial about the involvement of the government in funding technology. Or, they may represent a belated backlash against Maker Media, Inc. Nevertheless, the move on the part of Maker Media prompted an exodus from official Make events.

While talking to Altman about his withdrawal from Maker Faires in the wake of the DARPA controversy, Garnet Hertz came up with the idea to create a series of critical making zines.[37] Within the series many of the writers make salient points about the role of class and leisure, consumption, and, of course, the involvement and interest of the military-industry complex in the Maker Movement. Similarly, writers in *DIY Citizenship*, a book of essays on critical making co-edited by Ratto and Megan Boler, critique *Make* magazine from feminist, leftist and antigovernment perspectives.[38] Neither of these publications, however, question the reactionary tendency to romanticize hands-on learning or the effects of the Maker Movement on cities and the models of labor it creates. Meanwhile, people around the world pursuing the Maker Movement dream are often young and working in the gig economy as creative freelancers.[39] Members of this demographic are, however, rarely viewed with compassion or understanding because they are often dismissively labelled "hipsters." This urban type, which has been maligned and misunderstood for years, deserves a closer look.

Makers or Hipsters?

Freelance "creative" workers in the neoliberal economy, the millennial generation who grew up inhabiting the personalized culture of the "long tail" of consumerism online, the young interlopers in gentrifying neighborhoods like Bushwick, and, now, the makers of the "New Industrial Revolution" are all overlapping categories that come together under one highly charged term: hipsters. The rise of neo-hipster culture began roughly around 1999 and underwent several stylistic changes over the years. Hipsters are defined in many ways, most often as arrogant, over-privileged gentrifiers who are constantly chasing a more underground, unknown element of culture to identify with. A whimsical, nostalgic, or twee sensibility accompanies the cultural scavenging of hipsters, who embrace old technology and fashions as readily as new ones.

The perceived snobbery of this hipster stance is simply the result of the "long tail" that Chris Anderson first trumpeted in 2004. Online culture and the proliferation of consumer choices have fostered a generation of young people who have no dominant pop culture or subculture to adhere to. The desire to excavate fashions and remix disparate styles was facilitated by the first round of tool for makers – the software that allows consumers to edit video, photos, and music into an endless array of permutations. This computing and software revolution helped young people create their own personalized media that is tailored to each individual's exact taste. It is a wonder that anyone is confused or surprised by the hipster search for authenticity and individuality: this is the lifestyle that *Wired*, *Make* and the tech industry at large are actively promoting today. By definition, hipsters tend to seek out greater and greater forms of individual consumption. They do so because the nature of Internet-enabled capitalism enables and encourages this behavior.

At the same time, there is, of course, a certain homogeneity to the fashion and dress sense of hipsters – otherwise they could not be labeled as a cohesive group. Like the "fast fashion" stores they shop at, young people's fashion choices change quickly but briefly assume global homogeneity. Kids from Tokyo, Santiago, and LA can all wear similar offerings from international brands like H&M. People all over the world look to the same social media accounts and celebrities for fashion inspiration. As with other subcultural groups such as hippies, punks, goths, etc., however, the external cohesiveness is only really meaningful in that it points to the values that group embodies. While older people may wring their hands at the fashion choices of the young with each and every passing generation, and while fashion choices often have symbolic meaning, they are never as important as what the group itself represents. Perhaps the reason that the term "hipster" has outlived a variety of external stylings, unlike hippies, punks, and goths, has had more to do with the fact that "hipster" stands for an extreme manifestation of individuality facilitated by the Internet.

Another well-worn observation about hipster culture is that the hipster is always seeking out authenticity and originality. This Sisyphean search is the driving force of hipsters' fickle churn through newer and newer (or older and older) styles and fashions, which, once popular enough, are no longer authentic and original. Underlying this quest for authenticity is the terrifying truth that it no longer exists. Or, rather, it no longer exists because it never existed in the first place, except as a general feeling that it is absent from the modern world. We can only define authenticity and originality as those things we have lost, now that the world seems so *in*authentic and *un*original. Authenticity is defined in relation to nostalgia for a time before mechanical and digital reproduction (never mind that the printed word is very old indeed). The rate of change is astonishing: in the past fifteen years, hipsters have exhausted the fashion of nearly every decade of the twentieth century and have, unbelievably, moved on to fashions from the *nineteenth* century such as suspenders, waistcoats, long beards, etc.

The original use of the term "hipster" derives from the 1950s, which referred to Beat-era urban dwellers who, according to Norman Mailer's oft-cited 1957 essay "The White Negro: Superficial Reflections on the Hipster," embraced black culture, particularly in their manner of speaking and in their choice of music.[40] The quest for authenticity is something that both the Beat hipster and the contemporary hipster share. Both groups often look to marginalized or lower class groups as more real or authentic. The contemporary use of the term "hipster" for young, urban dwellers, often from white, middle-class suburban upbringings, it is speculated, came from a brief resurgence of fifties-style beatnik fashion in the mid to late '90s: black turtlenecks, goatees, berets, etc.[41] This phase of fashion, however, is largely forgotten in favor of the hipster aesthetic that followed.

The first wave of what is now known as hipster culture arose in the early '00s and was marked by a nostalgic and ironic stance toward culture, embracing a 1970s/80s-era working class white suburban aesthetic: wood paneling, trucker hats, little league T-shirts, cheap beer like PBR and cheap cigarettes like Parliaments. Some have seen the fashion at that time for Polaroid cameras and Girl Scout/little league T-shirts as an obsession with childhood and a need to continually reclaim the lost artifacts of youth. The "millennial" generation is seen as particularly fixated on childhood, which helps re-enforce the stereotype that they are immature and unable to face adult realities. I would argue, however, that the origins of this childhood nostalgia lie not necessarily in childhood itself but in a desire to recapture elements of the way life was before the Internet, complete with its technology and fashions. Many of this era's young people, born between 1980 and 1995, remember a "simpler" time before widespread computer and Internet usage, and it just so happens to have coincided with their early childhood. (The nostalgic childlike aesthetic is exemplified by the films of Wes Anderson, like *The Royal Tenenbaums* (2001) or the more recent *Moonrise Kingdom* (2012), as well as the wildly popular indie film *Napoleon Dynamite* (2004).)

Beyond simple nostalgia, however, some have seen the trappings of early hipster style as an appropriation of working class whiteness, a fetishization of the marginalized people known as "white trash" or "trailer trash." Just as the hipsters of the 1950s exotified black culture and saw it as more authentic or real, appropriating the aesthetics of the white working class allowed urban-dwelling middle-class whites from roughly 2001–2005 to discard the trappings of their white bourgeoisie upbringings and feel a part of an exotic underclass. While a few elements of this phase of hipster style have remained, an amateur anthropologist looking for hipsters in urban areas today would find hipsters looking a bit different. Despite very marked changes in external styling of hipsters between 2000 and 2015, the term has remained because the essential attitude and posture toward culture has remained relatively stable since that time: hipsters are defined by their individualized appropriation and remix of culture, which necessitates change.

The television sketch comedy show *Portlandia*, which began in 2011, has skewered many of the tropes of hipster culture and other alternative lifestyles found in Portland, Oregon. The pilot of the show opens with a musical skit called, "The Dream of the '90s is Alive in Portland," which shows how slacker lifestyles, flannel shirts, tattooing, and environmentalism still live on in Portland. Describing, essentially, the stereotype of the hipster, actor Fred Armisen says, "Remember when people were content to be unambitious, sleep til eleven, hang out with their friends... You had no occupations whatsoever except maybe working a couple of hours a week in a coffee shop."[42] A year later, *Portlandia* skewered the changing hipster fashion by releasing a second musical number called, "The Dream of the 1890s is Alive in Portland," which shows bearded young men home-brewing beer, wearing suspenders, making homemade sausages and a variety of old-time activities. Capturing the more recent phase of hipsterdom, Armisen says, "In Portland, people raise their own chickens and cure their own meats."[43] Between 2012 and 2015, hipsters and their hangouts could be identified by fashion styles that recall a rural, woodsman aesthetic. Long beards, flannel or checked shirts, taxidermy animals, deer antlers, and other animal-related paraphernalia abound. As the *Portlandia* skit points to, however, the hipster of today blends seamlessly with Maker culture: homebrew beer, hand-chipped ice, and home curing or pickling food are all part of the do-it-yourself ethos of the Maker Movement. The negative connotations of this

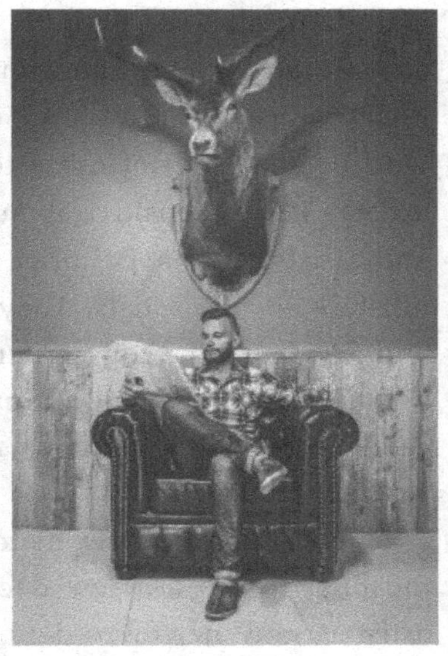

word "hipster" can easily be assuaged if we replace it with "maker," and indeed, makers and hipsters are one and the same.

The transformation of urban space in the era of hipsters/makers has meant that the physical space itself has been appropriated and remixed. The post-industrial aesthetic is now firmly fashionable, so much so that buildings without an industrial heritage readily adopt this aesthetic. Sharon Zukin discusses the perceived authenticity of post-industrial cities in her book *Naked City*, arguing that dirt and grit were transformed into commodities in neighborhoods like Williamsburg. She writes, "And suddenly you see that this projection of your own self-image on the shabby chic streets is exactly what the marketing theorists expect authenticity to be: a sympathetic vibe between consumers and the objects of their desire."[44] Hipsters, thus, simultaneously consume and appropriate disinvested urban areas.

While the term "hipster" is universally derogatory, much like the term "yuppie" was for the '80s and '90s, people of this demographic readily embrace the term maker. Ann Fensterstock, in her history of art neighborhoods in New York, conflates "hipster" and "yuppie," and, indeed, they may share many attributes in common such as a middle-class upbringing and a high level of education.[45] Unlike yuppies, however, the hipster type emerges from artistic communities, and the art world – made up of those that think of themselves as "true" artists – is very sensitive about any comparison between hipsters and artists. Dayna Tortorici states, "Almost by definition, real hipsters are *not* artists. They're curators and critics, re-mixers and designers, the copywriters and 'prosumers' who trail in the artists' wake."[46] I would argue, that hipsters *would* have been called artists if the term artist had remained stable for the last two hundred years.

The term "artist" seems to have been sapped of its broader meaning in the last few decades, or, at least, ghettoized: the artist is now narrowly defined as a participant in the global contemporary art world. "True" artists, therefore, bristle when the word "artist" is applied more broadly, particularly when artists are lumped together with hipsters. As argued above, maker is the positive label for the same type of person negatively described as a hipster. Artists, too, have not remained immune to the Maker Movement, as my analysis in the following chapters will show. Looking to the contemporary art world, curators are increasingly taking center stage as the creative stars of the field while artists themselves are often also working as curators. Curators and critics (and hipsters) have largely replaced the monolithic category of artists today. Artists have become makers and have, like yuppies in previous generations, embraced business and the opportunities for wealth that come along with it. At the same time, artists/hipsters/makers are different than their yuppie predecessors in that they consume and produce in a manner that mirrors the development of digital technology from the late '90s to the present.

The hipster is a digital native, a remixer, and a maker. While the first flush of hipster culture was roughly between 1999 and 2004, the term and its type have not gone away. In 2009, Brooklyn-based literary magazine *n+1* held a panel on the hipster phenomenon at the New School titled "What *was* the hipster?" which was followed by a book reflecting on the proceedings.[47] Why has the term not died out? Because the model of how we use technology has remained relatively stable between 1999 and 2015, or, perhaps more accurately, this model has grown in power and scope since the late '90s, with more and more tools for creation and sharing now available. The Maker Movement is simply a continuation of the DIY consumerism ushered in by the Internet and computer software in the late '90s. Whereas once hipsters could define their individual identity through music, photography, and video, now they can remix the physical world. If the hipster moment is to end, it would have to come about concurrent to the end of prosumption. Youth culture has subscribed wholeheartedly to Chris Anderson's "long tail," of consumption and the young people of today tailor their tastes individually. According to Rob Horning, "The hipster, then, is the bogeyman who keeps us from becoming too settled in our identity, keeps us moving forward into new fashions, keeps us consuming more 'creatively' and discovering new things that haven't become lame or hipster."[48] Put another way, the hipster is the supreme acolyte of the long tail model of consumption: nothing that gains any kind of popularity can truly be authentic and individual anymore, so he or she must constantly search for new sources of individuality. This leads the hipsters to mine the past, the present, and the foreign in their endeavors to curate themselves.

The connection between hipster and maker comes down to an interest in DIY creative pursuits. The cultural presence of the hipster who makes craft beer, participates in a knitting group, or raises chickens has become a cliché, but it fits very well into the ethos of the Maker Movement. Part of the rationale for hipster backlash is that hipsters are perceived as "trust fund kids" and gentrifiers. They are seen as hypocritical in that they usually hold progressive political beliefs but do nothing to combat social inequalities in the urban environments they inhabit. They are seen as frivolous culture snobs, moving from trend to trend, constantly in search of a more obscure band or item of vintage clothing. Many hipsters are involved in creative industries like fine art, music, dance and design, which increasingly utilize new software and gadgets. Hipsters involved in these fields, therefore, are likely to take on freelance jobs that allow them flexible or remote working arrangements. The proliferation of Wi-Fi enabled coffee shops in hipster neighborhoods are filled with freelancers on laptops, perhaps feeding the notion that hipsters "don't work" or are surviving solely on money from their parents.

Creative disciplines have evolved with new technology in two ways, which have changed the nature of labor for young people in New York City and elsewhere. One common definition/criticism of hipsters is that they don't make anything themselves – they are not artists but rather curators or critics. What detractors seem to have missed in this characterization is that curating or remixing a set of critically approved items *is* what passes for creation in the Post-Internet world (and, certainly, in the Maker Movement). As noted, new software tools have led to the so-called "prosumer," the combination of producer and consumer. Video editing, special effects, 3D animation, photograph editing/altering, and other software tools that had formerly been accessible only to professionals are now readily available to consumers so that the prosumer can simultaneously produce and consume content. Web 2.0 sites like Facebook, Twitter, Instagram and YouTube allow users to both share and view content.

In addition to these new software tools, ubiquitous Internet connections allow more people to work remotely. While this has been covered extensively in popular business books, which praise the flexibility and creative outlets available today, this shifting nature of work has given rise to the niche pursuits of the Maker Movement. Despite all the praise heaped on this new model of labor, the freelance lifestyle is rife with insecurity. Freelancers' jobs and pay can fluctuate wildly from month to month and they may lack healthcare and other benefits a full-time salaried job would provide. While hipsters or makers may look cynically opportunistic in terms of business ventures, they are facing the realities of survival in a freelance creative economy.

Creativity and Class

The cost-prohibitive nature of art school BFAs and MFAs needed for advancement in the art world, the enormous costs of workspaces in major art centers, the globalization of commercial galleries, and other factors mean that very few (if any) artists are able to work part-time minimum wage jobs and still have ample time for art-making. A minimum wage worker is compelled to spend the majority of his or her time struggling to make enough to pay rent and odd jobs are rarely a viable option. Luckily, many aspiring artists are now familiar with software tools that they can use in lucrative freelance jobs. Artists are, consequentially, now multipurpose, multi-talented makers. Maker culture is an expression of creative energies that leaves the door open to commercial applications partly out of necessity but also with an eye to the entrepreneurial zeitgeist initiated by the tech industry. As Sophy Bot writes, "Those of us in Generation Y and younger grew up in a world that rewarded successful youth. We watched the dot-com boom turn our peers into millionaires…"[49] In other words, young people are looking to the tech industry and its promise of success under the age of 30.

Increased cost of living and rents throughout New York City have pushed creative professionals further and further outside of the city center since the 1970s. Brooklyn has built a reputation over the last twenty years as the most trendy New York borough, and living in some areas of Brooklyn is now more expensive and desirable than living in Manhattan.[50] Brooklyn is undoubtedly the epicenter of maker culture in New York, known for its artists, DIY enthusiasm and niche foodie culture. The neighborhood around the Morgan Avenue stop on the L line in North Brooklyn, a formerly industrial area that was colonized by artists in the 2000s, was inhabited by increasing numbers of hipsters/makers/artists over the course of that decade. For the hipster/maker in Morgantown, having just witnessed the swift gentrification of neighboring Williamsburg in the late 1990s/early 2000s, the choice was clear: either seize the area for themselves or fall prey to developers in the near future. All of the early "settlers" in Morgantown started out as creative professionals in some capacity and transformed the area into the maker community it is today.

Richard Florida reconfigures the notion of social class in America in his widely criticized yet wildly influential book, *The Rise of the Creative Class*, which claims that old-fashioned class identifications are becoming obsolete in favor of a pure meritocracy of creativity. He has built a successful global consulting career on the thesis that cities will flourish if they can attract more creative people.[51] In a clever rhetorical flourish, Florida diffuses the potency of both "creativity" and "class" by reframing them: he expands the definition of creative work (typically thought of as those in the arts and design) to encompass nearly every (middle class) professional from engineers to lawyers to doctors and, like those in the Maker Movement, he claims that everyone is naturally creative.[52] In a variation on the American Dream myth, Florida writes that prosperity is as simple as harnessing the untapped creative potential every person has, ignoring other social and economic factors that might hinder or help a person's ability to follow a creative pathway.[53]

Florida's formulation of the creative class is indebted to the concept of the "creative city," coined by Charles Landry in the 1980s.[54] For Landry, creativity was the missing ingredient in urban planning and administration. Landry emphasized the need for imagination and a culture of creativity within city planning and governance, which would in turn encourage creativity to flourish within the city itself.[55] Florida and John

Howkins followed Landry in fleshing out the economic potential of creativity, as cities began to attract the middle and upper classes back to urban centers.[56] In these idealistic discussions of creativity, class is, at first, totally ignored, then swept aside, and, finally, rebranded (as in Florida's case). The Maker Movement has similarly repackaged myths of meritocracy and bootstraps neoliberalism in a package of techno-utopianism. Mark Hatch writes, in his *Maker Movement Manifesto,* "With access to the right kind of tools, you can experience your own industrial revolution in a matter of weeks. It's possible. It really happens."[57] A personal industrial revolution renders any semblance of class obsolete. This is rugged individualism at its most pure. In fact, Maker Movement acolytes will argue that the movement is actually creating a classless society.[58]

At the heart of the Maker Movement's self-help ethos is a failure to not only deal with class difference, but to accept anything less than a constant, all-encompassing life of labor for a maker (or a worker). Hatch describes a variety of people who had lost their jobs, laid off from other professions, slaving away in the TechShop maker space trying to make products that they could hawk themselves in lieu of any consistent or reliable employment.[59] He praises Florida's book in that it promotes a near constant state of labor, tapping into all the wasted "spare time" of workers:

The largest untapped resource on the planet is the spare time, creativity, and disposable income of the "creative class." As enumerated in Richard Florida's instant classic *The Rise of the Creative Class,* there are 40 million Americans in the creative class... their day jobs, if they still have them, are likely to be creative by their definition... These people are the front lines of the economy, working to make life happen. Many are focused on making it better, faster, and cheaper. That is what work is about. In a competitive economy, few get to rest on last year's accomplishments for long... I'm particularly interested in their "spare time," whether it's actually spare time or, having been recently laid off, between jobs "spare time."[60]

The Maker Movement, underneath the gloss of happy, creative lives, advocates the colonization of everyday life by capitalism. This kind of exploitation in the service of work, leisure and consumption was theorized by Henri Lefebvre and Guy Debord, and it ushers in the end of sleep predicted by art historian Jonathan Crary in his book 24/7.[61]

The desire to collect any spare time individuals may have and convert it into capital permeates the movement. In Tsai's *Makers* film, Tim O'Reilly talks about the way Dale Dougherty pitched him *Make* magazine (in the back of a cab). O'Reilly says, "Dale called it technology on your own time."[62] The movement openly celebrates the contingent, freelance nature of work in the twenty-first century, but, despite the market rationale for this mode of working, it does not produce the happy, free workers it claims to produce. Rather, it promotes a culture where workers are expected to constantly hustle for their wages, receiving none of the benefits of full-time employ.

Whether lured by the promise of creative fulfillment through making in your spare time or the fun ways you can connect with your friends on social media, corporations have perfected leisure technologies that make sure no amount of potential labor power is wasted. The driving force behind the tech industry has always been its utopian rhetoric, which derived in large part from its roots in the counterculture of the 1960s, which I address in depth in Chapter 3. The ideas around individual freedom and creativity that are promoted by the industry have much deeper roots, however, in the romantic movements in the nineteenth century. The phrases and sentiments now being used to promote the "New Industrial Revolution" in the Maker Movement are actually as old as modernism itself and the *original* Industrial Revolution.

Chapter 2

We Are All Romantics

In 2011, Maker Media Inc. CEO Dale Dougherty delivered a TED (Technology, Education, Design) talk on the Maker Movement, opening with the line: "We are all makers," a slogan that is also the subheading of *Make* magazine.[1] The phrase could easily be overlooked as corporate speak or the empowerment rhetoric of business leadership literature, but the underlying sentiment is, in fact, part of a longer history of aesthetic theory which positions creativity at the center of individual fulfilment. It speaks to a perceived *potential* in all humans to be makers (not just to make things but to participate in the process of making), and its origins are found in late-eighteenth and early-nineteenth-century Romantic philosophy. Building on this foundation, anti-industrial movements during the latter half of the nineteenth century also rallied around the notion of individual creativity as a basic human condition that was being stifled by modern industry: the Arts and Crafts movement attempted to put production back in the hands of individual craftspeople. The resurgence of romanticism in the counterculture of the 1960s and '70s also drew from these philosophical underpinnings. The Maker Movement, in turn, inherits this legacy.

In the Morgantown neighborhood of Brooklyn, a formerly industrial area around the Morgan Avenue subway stop, the Maker Movement has flourished, and young creative professionals, branded as hipsters, draw upon the philosophical heritage of these previous eras. Unlike their romantic predecessors, however, the Maker Movement offers more than mere resistance or reactionary solutions to the alienation of capitalist labor. The ideas that were once posed as resistance to free market capitalism are now used by people like Dougherty to support neoliberal models of business, couched in the utopian rhetoric of individuality, freedom, and personal fulfillment. New technology has been branded as a way to empower individual creative laborers, ignoring the increasing insecurity of workers in the freelance economy. Before dealing with the specific case of the Maker Movement in Morgantown, I will first address the origins of the movement in German Romanticism and trace its genesis through the last two hundred years. While the Maker Movement is, to a large extent, bounded by the conditions of our time and the current state of technological development, the values and idealism of the movement have direct ties to Romantic thought (and its echoes throughout the modern period). A clear trajectory can be drawn from Romanticism in the nineteenth century through the counterculture to the tech industry in the United States.

In 1979, Joseph Beuys famously said, "Everyone is an artist," indicating that all humans share a potential for creativity and imagination. The quote appeared in Beuys' definition of what he called Social Sculpture, where he positioned sculpture as an evolutionary process:

> **Social Sculpture**
> how we mould and shape
> the world in which we live:
> Sculpture as evolutionary process;
> **everyone is an artist**.[2]

Beuys sees the act of making as a mode of transmission. The objects artists create are therefore capable of affecting actual social change through a progressive societal dialogue. In other words, the act of making in the field of art is more than just the routinized production of isolated aesthetic products but rather a heroic means to liberate not just the individual maker but society as a whole, who participate in the dialogical act of making. Beuys' position provides one possible response to the conundrum faced by art critics at the time as to how to deal with sculpture's loss of autonomy in land art, minimalism, and process-based works.[3] The void left by the medium's former specificity within a purely *art pour l'art* context was filled with an appeal to the transcendent power of making.

Although Beuys was challenging the modernist definition of sculpture, the idea that "everyone is an artist" is one of the oldest in modernist thought. It is rooted primarily in German Romanticism of the late eighteenth and early nineteenth centuries. Building on the foundations laid by Immanuel Kant, who had placed aesthetics at the center of his philosophy, those that followed him, such as Johann Gottlieb Fichte, Friedrich Schiller, and Novalis, developed a series of philosophical positions around the power of creativity and imagination. English Romantic poets like Percy Bysshe Shelley, influenced by the Germans, also developed theories around creativity that were no less optimistic about its transformative effects on society. These ideas trickled through the nineteenth century in a variety of modernist movements: the Pre-Raphaelites, Arts and Crafts, Symbolists, and others.

The most notable resurgence of this brand of romanticism in the twentieth century came with the development of the counterculture in the 1960s, which sought a variety of ways to expand the human mind and tap into latent creativity. The early twentieth century had largely exhausted the Western public's enthusiasm for industrial and mechanistic production; two World Wars, Nazism, Fascism, Stalinism, and the dropping of the atomic bombs had seen to that. So, after a long hiatus from the First World War to the 1950s, romantic yearnings for greater individual freedom resurfaced. Discussing the origins of Joseph Beuys' countercultural statement, Thierry de Duve writes:

Rimbaud already said it and Novalis already thought it

long ago. The students of 1968, in Paris, in California, and gathered around Beuys in Düsseldorf, proclaimed it once again and wrote it on the walls. It always meant, and this since the German romantics: "power to the imagination." It has never become a reality, at least not in that sense... only those few, whom we stupidly call professional artists, know that in reality their vocation is to incarnate this unactualized potential.[4]

The ideals of the counterculture may have never come to fruition, but, for the tech industry, these ideals are enough to sustain a monstrously profitable industry. The romanticism of the counterculture evolved directly into Silicon Valley (and its global offshoots), which, in turn, produced the Maker Movement.

Like Joseph Beuys, Dale Dougherty believes in the liberating potential of an imaginative or creative act. In its contemporary manifestation, this line of thinking promises to solve all manner of societal issues, including urban redevelopment or "revitalization" in areas deemed impoverished or disinvested. The ideals of the counterculture have done little to build a more egalitarian urban environment: San Francisco and neighboring cities in the Santa Clara Valley regularly top lists of most expensive places to live in the United States (and the world). While the waves of gentrification have been good for property investors, lower income renters have been continually squeezed out of the market.[5] The group of young, tech-savvy urban residents formerly known as gentrifiers or yuppies has been infamously rebranded by Richard Florida as the "creative class," the vanguard who Florida claims are improving the fabric of society and urban centers through creativity.[6] The creative class, following the same mantra of creativity as the Maker Movement, is touted as a transformative and egalitarian influence on the urban environment, creating places of greater comfort, equality, and community. These improvements, however, are only making property and the cost of living more expensive, and, consequentially, the poor and working classes are continually moved further and further away from central areas of the city (or are forced to devote the majority of their wages to rent and scrape by on the rest).

Florida's definition of the creative class incorporates not only artists and creatives but a wide range of educated professionals (including most white-collar workers). Since its publication, his book has been widely criticized for its failure to address the negative effects of gentrification and social inequality, and his transition from academic to highly-paid urban consultant has been met with many a raised eyebrow. Florida's assertions that everyone is equally capable of unleashing creative potential ignores questions of access to education and free time. In his introduction to the revised version of his book, Florida addresses some of these criticisms, writing:

> That key thesis of my argument is as simple as it is basic: every human being is creative. That the Creative Class enjoys vast privileges is true, but to acknowledge that fact is not to endorse it. The essential task before us is to unleash the creative energies, talent, and potential of everyone – to build a society that acknowledges and nurtures the creativity of each and every human being. Creativity is truly a limitless resource; it is something we all share.[7]

Florida's point of view, therefore, echoes Dale Dougherty's statements on the Maker Movement. In an equation where we believe, on one hand, that "everyone is creative" and, on the other hand, that free market capitalism is the best system for our society, we can only reach the conclusion, as both Florida and the Maker Movement have, that creativity is a resource that needs to be tapped into and exploited for its wealth-creating potential. While the activities of the creative class and the Maker

Movement contradict, to some extent, the roots of their ideology in anti-capitalist modernism, the rhetoric of individualism at the core of romanticism is a powerful ally of free market capitalism. In the end, can the union of creativity and capital ever be as egalitarian and liberating as these cultural figures claim? As Thierry de Duve implies, the ideal of building a better society through individual creativity and imagination is a seductive but unrealizable dream.

In the spirit of maximizing the untapped potential of creativity, the Maker Movement has recast learning and sharing as pathways to wealth and individual fulfillment. "Learn" and "share" are values generally instilled in children from a young age, and are the earliest foundations of their education, starting in preschool. These seemingly innocuous words are heavily loaded, however, for the Maker Movement. The value we traditionally place on learning and sharing comes out of a left-wing modernist tradition that seeks to combat individualism with a renewed sense of communalism. These values and their connotations have, however, now been fully transformed into facets of capitalism in the context of the tech industry and are assimilated into the rhetoric of classic liberalism. For example, the tech industry considers corporations such as Uber and Airbnb to be part of the "sharing economy." They are car "sharing" and room "sharing" services respectively. In fact, these are large, profitable corporations that operate their services for fees and have little overheads, outsourcing all the risk to their gig economy workers. While there might have been some semblance of sharing in these corporations to begin with, i.e. users could "share" their cars or rooms in order to make extra money off temporarily unused assets, these companies have had less and less to do with sharing the more they have developed.

Mark Hatch's book *The Maker Movement Manifesto* echoes many of the sentiments of German Romantic philosophy, albeit with a decidedly positive outlook on free market capitalism and the benefits of an unregulated business landscape. One of the major tenets of the movement is sharing. He writes, "Sharing what you have made and what you know about making with others is the method by which a maker's feeling of wholeness is achieved."[8] Hatch's statement may as well have been cribbed directly from German Romantic philosophy. For Hatch, personal fulfillment is the primary goal of "making," but sharing is essential to individual fulfillment. At the end of the eighteenth century, the poet and philosopher Friedrich Schiller was also interested in ways to reunify the incomplete or fractured individual. Beauty, he asserts, following Kant, provides humanity with a means to achieve a sense of wholeness, which had been lost through modern culture's fragmentation and disciplinary specialization.[9] He writes, "… Beauty, which restores harmony in the tense man and energy in the languid man, and in this way, in accordance with its nature, brings back the condition of limitation to an absolute one and makes of Man a whole, complete in himself."[10] It is hardly surprising that Romantic thought turned toward the question of the wholeness of the human being at the beginning of the Industrial Revolution, a period when human faculties were continually alienated in capitalist production.

For the Maker Movement, the workshop (variously called a maker space, hackerspace, incubator, co-working space, etc.) is at the center of building a community. Mitch Altman, one of the makers featured in *Maker Pro* (although he has since parted ways with Maker Media), says, "People need community, and people need to express themselves creatively. Hackerspaces provide for these two deep human needs."[11] The ideal for the maker space is to operate in perfect balance between individual desires and community support. Indeed, it does seem that many maker spaces do operate in some equilibrium between individual goals and a sense of community. Mark Hatch writes, "It [the maker space] becomes a true community where people help one another, care for one another, and hang out and socialize. It becomes a true third place. A place that isn't home or work, but a place where one can unwind, relax, and pursue a passion with like-minded creative people."[12] Theorized by Ray Oldenburg in 1989, in the midst of its decline, the "third place" rarely exists as a nexus of community anymore.[13] Where once likeminded people gathered at a bar, a coffee shop, barber shop or elsewhere, now very few can claim to have such a place, the proverbial place "where everybody knows your name."

As I discuss in Chapter 4, the freelance economy has eroded these nexus points for the art world. While bars and hangouts are still plentiful in a neighborhood like Morgantown in Brooklyn, very few people are interacting with each other or meeting new people. Instead, most people are utilizing the free Wi-Fi and getting a bit of freelance work in. Likewise, as Hatch and others readily proclaim, the maker space is a place of work, not simple communal gathering. It is difficult, therefore, to see maker spaces as true third places, since the emphasis of the Maker Movement is primarily on creating or producing items to sell. The business-minded language of the movement always revolves around bootstraps, get-rich aspirationalism. Maker spaces, as Hatch and others readily proclaim, exist in order to capitalize on any excess productivity of the worker.[14]

When the Internet first became available to consumers in the 1990s, many were quick to herald the coming of the global village, theorized by Marshall McLuhan in the 1960s. During those early days of the Internet, techno-utopians talked endlessly about the digital commons or the global town square where we would foster a more egalitarian and democratic world in which everyone would have a stake and a voice. Today, with everyone online, this optimism has dissolved into dystopian fear: revenge porn, doxxing, swatting, the mob mentality of Twitter, and the activities of Anonymous are constantly disrupting any potential for a fair or democratic online discourse.[15] Early Internet users embraced the idea that their third place may be an online forum or chat room. Today, it is obvious that the Internet is no substitute for local community and, with the demise of traditional third places in the late '80s and the expansion of the Internet in the late '90s, we have had several decades without a fitting substitute. Thus, the Maker Movement is tapping into the desire for communal spaces where individuals can help one another and provide support. Many maker spaces provide this kind of community, but the underlying agenda of capitalizing on any potentially productive spare time is at odds with the romantic notion of community nurturing the individual.

Nevertheless, the ideals remain the same for both the Maker Movement and the German Romantic writers: personal fulfillment can only be achieved in relation to the effect individuals have on society through their creations. For Schiller, sharing one's creations is an essential component in achieving wholeness, and individual fulfillment can only truly be achieved within the context of society. He writes:

Not where Man hides himself troglodyte-fashion in caves, eternally individual and never finding humanity *outside himself*; nor where he moves nomadically in great hordes, eternally plural and never finding humanity *inside himself*; only where he dwells quietly in his own hut, communing with himself and, as soon as he issues from it, with the whole race – only then will her lovely bud unfold.[16]

Schiller's man cannot achieve individual wholeness and fulfillment if he never interacts with other human beings: he needs society. Any group of people in which the human is but an interchangeable cog in the social machine, who is not allowed to express any personal creativity or create for himself, is, by Schiller's calculation, not able to recognize his own humanity and therefore unable to find personal fulfillment in creative pursuits. Several of Schiller's contemporaries, similarly influenced by the philosophy of Fichte, asserted, as Beuys did in the 1960s, that the creative potential leading to this wholeness is naturally present in all human beings. Novalis wrote, "Almost every person is to a limited degree already an artist."[17] It is a sentiment he repeated several times in various forms: everyone is already an artist but must *learn* to tap into this latent creativity.[18]

Several writers in the critical making community voice ambivalence about the potential of DIY creative endeavors to liberate its practitioners in an educational setting. In their study of a DIY News Club, Jenson et al. write, "… we diverge from previous studies and present examples of how 'do-it-yourself' (DIY) culture can provide a much needed, inherently critical, hands-on learning experience, while also highlighting how as a process DIY does not necessarily challenge or evade systemic and structural limitations that contribute to the ongoing marginalization of young media makers."[19] Others in the critical making arena, on the other hand, wholeheartedly promote the notion that hands-on knowledge is the most natural and liberating way of learning. Bal et. al. write, "Maker culture has the potential to represent a cultural model that encourages individual citizens to construct their own social realities, connections, and material aspects of living, to take user generated production as acute individual self-determination, knowledge sharing, and community building."[20] In the Maker Movement, the act of sharing is the key to achieving harmony between the individual and the community, which was an idea shared by the Romantics.

Movement enthusiasts tout education and learning as the first step to achieving these goals, and the importance of hands-on learning is fervently discussed. In addition to sharing, Hatch lists learning as one of the key tenets of the movement.[21] He states, "Building a lifelong learning path ensures a rich and rewarding making life and, importantly, enables one to share."[22] Despite the emphasis on "sharing", the real benefit of learning described here is not cooperation so much as individual fulfillment. Sharing in this instance must be understood within the confines of the "sharing economy," a model of user-generated content creation where users "share" their creations or services on a platform that derives its value from this user-generated material. The sharing economy is undergirded by capitalist individualism.

The Maker Movement, like other similar idealist movements before it, celebrates hands-on learning and the trial-and-error method of invention. Maker Movement leaders share a disregard or even hostility toward academic or university-style educational systems. Mark Hatch writes:

I'll let the educators in this community help figure out why "project"-based learning seems to fit some learning styles better than others, but it certainly feels more natural. I always found the order we did things in physics class backward. Instead of being taught the formula for determining the ratio of the required output force to the input force and then trekking to the lab to see how a lever works, it makes more sense to first observe the lever in action and then learn the formula for it.[23]

Hatch has supporters from within academia as well as outside. While the Maker Movement is more prevalent in tech and design circles, academic disciplines like fine art and architecture have also embraced the maker ethos. In the field of anthropology, Tim Ingold sees making – learning through doing – as a way to revolutionize "the 4 As" of the academy: anthropology, archaeology, art, and architecture.[24] While he makes no direct reference to the Maker Movement as I have defined and described it here, his celebration of making bears many of the same romantic inclinations of the movement and he has sometimes been cited by proponents of Critical Making, the academic branch of the movement that has deemphasized the importance of creating new consumer products.[25] He argues that, "... in so far as they [anthropologists] continue to treat art as a compendium of works to be analysed, there can be no possibility of direct correspondence with the creative process that give rise to them."[26] Ingold proposes a model of anthropological study that eschews documentation and analysis in favor of learning through direct application of a process. He argues that, through making or doing, we enter into the activity we are trying to understand and, learning that activity through hands-on experimentation, we can achieve a much deeper and richer understanding of the object of study.

Ingold's theories on making often veer toward the reactionary and primitivist. He asserts that students should learn *with* the material or people they study, implying that the modern world has forgotten these hands-on methods of understanding. The process of making he describes is similar to the way children learn at a young age. The Saami people of northern Finland, uninitiated into Western analytical academia, are described as a people of ancient wisdom, having given the author the sage advice to "know for yourself."[27] Ingold simply puts a fresh face on the same old anti-modernist talking points, claiming we have lost our way through modernist analysis and specialization and that we will not truly understand art, architecture, or culture except through the creative process. This perspective echoes the primitivist positions of the nineteenth and early twentieth century that idealized works made by so-called primitive people – non-westerners, children, the indigenous, and the insane. Bal et al. imply that, because children often learn through trial and error, this is the most effective and natural way for all human beings to learn.[28] The child is presented as an innocent ideal that we should all follow in order to reclaim the innocence we have lost in the process of modernization. They write, "By tradition, the public elementary mass education system teaches students to follow nineteenth-century, middle-class values as well as industrial working protocols, which tend to dwarf their own belief system and notion of being, both key to self-determination."[29] Maker Movement writers are effectively still fighting against these nineteenth-century, middle-class values that arose during the Industrial Revolution with the utopian hope that new technology will finally deliver the creative ideal. Effectively, they believe that those working in the freelance and gig economy, by virtue of being creative workers, are less alienated and exploited than workers were in previous generations.

Subjected to the rationality of industrial modernism, modern thinkers created a myth that hands-on, trial-and-error modes of discovery are more natural or primal human behaviors and that rationality is an alien, inhuman force that drives us away from our native state. Expressing his skepticism of the scientific method of inquiry and education, Ingold states:

> *Human beings*, according to science, are a species of nature, yet to *be human* is to transcend that nature. It is this transcendent that both provides science with the platform for its observations and underwrites its claim to authority. The dilemma is that the conditions that enable scientists to *know*, at least according to official protocols, are such as to make it impossible for them to *be* in the very world of which they seek knowledge. It seems that we can only aspire to truth about this world by way of an emancipation that takes us from it and leaves us strangers to ourselves.[30]

The dominance of scientific epistemology over every aspect of modern life deserves to be interrogated and questioned, but it cannot simply be replaced by a nostalgic vision of learning by brute force.

The Maker Movement celebrates the trial-and-error method of learning because it feeds into the cult of heroic individualism and seems to give power back to the individual to understand

and control the world around her. The complex, collaborative nature of academic sciences and engineering push colorful stories of individual genius to the peripheries. While the return to hands-on learning gives the appearance of returning autonomy to the individual, the underlying structures of capital continue to function at increasingly complex levels beyond the ability of any individual to comprehend: for example, the computer-automated stock exchanges of the world. Eschewing collaboration or collective knowledge and theory in favor of trial-and-error experimentation creates the illusion that human beings still possess superior powers, not only in the hard to define realm of creativity, but in simple calculation, an area where computers have long outperformed the human mind.

With their focus on individual achievement, the hands-on methods of invention favored by the Maker Movement are ideologically compatible with the American Dream myth, which promises that simple self-reliance and hard work will deliver wealth, success, and happiness. An example of this can be found in the lionization of inventor Thomas Edison, whose tireless self-promotion and media presence guaranteed him a spot in the canon of American heroes. Edison embodied the American Dream in that he was a man who came from a humble background, had only a few months of formal schooling, and was able to make himself rich and famous through his hard work and creativity. Edison was also famous for his trial-and-error experimental methods, which meant that he had to fail often before finally hitting on a workable invention. In the tech industry, the cult of productive failure lives on. In his manifesto, Hatch cites Edison's fabled perseverance, saying, "Edison routinely failed thousands of times before discovering what he needed."[31] Matt Ratto, of critical making, also celebrates productive failure, saying, "My initial attempt to do this failed miserably, which let me know that I was on the right track."[32] While Edison's penchant for failure is legendary, his competition over electrical technology with the formally educated Serbian scientist and inventor Nikola Tesla at the end of the nineteenth century is the lesser-known story of the era and illustrates the divide between theory and practice.

Both Edison and Tesla were working on electric current (Tesla's alternating current won out over Edison's direct current) and various types of electric lighting. Edison is credited with the invention of the electric light bulb, while Tesla was working on neon and other illuminated neon gas light fixtures. Even though a large amount of public appreciation has been given back to Tesla recently, one of the reasons he fell into obscurity was his use of advanced theory and mathematical calculation, which was inaccessible to the public. Many of his inventions were well before their time and, as the sci-fi writer Arthur C. Clarke said, "Any sufficiently advanced technology is indistinguishable from magic."[33] In order to create his light bulb, Edison first created a media sensation by sending scouts all around the world to gather different metals that he would then try out one by one as light bulb filaments. Theoreticians like Tesla, meanwhile, were astonished at the wasted time and effort. The electrical resistance of these metals was known and recorded, and, therefore, could be calculated mathematically beforehand, making the task of collecting and trying out each one in the light bulb an enormous waste of time.[34]

The life of scientist and artist Frank Malina provides another example of how intertwined the trial-and-error method of invention is with American ideas of individualism. Malina was born in Texas and received his scientific training in rocket propulsion in the mid-1930s. Due to his preference for mathematical calculation, Malina was suspected of being a communist during the McCarthy era. Malina's son writes, "Informant No 11 claimed my father was a communist and had tried to delay the winning of the war. Informant No 11 asserted that my father insisted on doing too many experiments and mathematical calculations rather than just building and firing rockets."[35] For some, collaboration and calculation was perhaps antithetical to the individualistic narrative that dominated American politics at the time. Like Tesla before him, Malina fell victim to suspicion of his methods and was forced to move abroad, where he started making kinetic art and, eventually, founded the art and science journal *Leonardo*.

As Malina's case illustrates, the divide between theory and practice never really disappeared. Cold War research labs like MIT's AI lab were divided between planners and hackers, according to Steven Levy. The planners relied on theory and saw computers as a means to model the world around them while the hackers were primarily interested in tinkering with computing systems in a more open-ended way. At a time when a single computer had to be shared between multiple members of the lab, the planners tended to resent the tinkering of the hackers. Levy writes that conflicts emerged between the two groups, "Planners thought they were advancing true science. Hackers were blithely formulating their tidy, new-age philosophy based on free flow of information, decentralization, and computer democracy."[36] Makers are, both ideologically and in temperament, the direct descendants of the hackers.

Pure theory and calculation take away certain opportunities for chance occurrence and accidental discoveries that only hands-on tinkering can create, and humans do not base their behavior purely on analytical conclusions. Our machines are often, therefore, placed in opposition to ourselves in a human/robot dichotomy. The broad question of modernism has been whether humanity will subscribe to an individualistic or a mechanistic model. Building on Kant, philosophers of the late-eighteenth and early-nineteenth centuries were trying to draw together the empiricist and rationalist traditions which pitted independent thought (a kind of individual autonomy) versus sense- and environmentally-determined thought (a mechanistic model). Friedrich Schiller developed the term "play drive" in

On the Aesthetic Education of Man to describe the role that free play of imagination has as an intermediary between sensation and reason. The play drive responds to Kant's aesthetic theory and attempts to reassert a socially transformative role for art on Kantian terms. It is the creative faculty of the maker that bridges sensuousness and reason, feeling and understanding, and allows the human to realize her full potential and full humanness through the aesthetic experience.[37] A how-to book published by *Make* magazine describes a "Dark Age among Lego fans" where adults grow up and "decide they don't have time for the frivolity of toys."[38] The Maker Movement asks its followers to recapture that childlike, primal urge to play and experiment in a free form, hands-on way. While the emphasis on play is something makerism and Romanticism share, the end goal is vastly different. For makers, play is the route to innovation in the business sense and transforms modern society through capitalist progress rather than idealized democracy and transcendent beauty (though the concepts of democracy and beauty are often touted as the *real* goals of making). The how-to book *Maker Pro* explains that play and creativity can take a maker from an amateur to a pro. Financial remuneration turns the aimlessness of free play and creative inquiry into productive labor.

Art practice has followed a similar trajectory of professionalization. Before modernism, it was largely performed in service of society, though individual acclaim and creative expression were certainly present. In the modern era, acclaim and creative expression are seen as markers of genius, predicated on individuality and a system through which artists receive *credit* for their work (whatever form that credit takes: fame, societal status, etc.). Credit precedes the life of artworks as commodities, underwriting their existence before they pay dividends, therefore preserving the autonomy of artistic practice from the banal professionalism underlying it. Artists operate as brands insofar as their works are preceded by the value of their individual personae. The artwork is still valued for its "originality" in the market but, as artworks have increasingly become arbitrarily branded objects, the meaning of originality becomes equally arbitrary.[39] As better tools for mechanical reproducibility have arisen, the definition of originality has been stretched beyond its limit, extending the reach of the human hand in imitation of nature to the point of perfection. Artists of the twentieth century were left to question what originality could be, in light of new technology: does it lie in the conception of the work, manipulation of the materials, or within the form itself? The roots of this debate in Western art begin with Plato. The word poetry comes from the Greek root *poiein*, meaning "to make." According to Plato, poetry was the realm of true creation. Painting and drawing were inferior *techne* ("technique" or "technology") and therefore mere imitation. In *Republic*, one of the dialogues begins with the question, "And should we call a painter, too, a craftsman and maker of such a thing?" The respondent states, "Certainly not... In my view, the most reasonable thing to call him is this: he is an imitator of what the others are craftsmen of."[40] The distinction Plato makes between poetry and visual art continued to haunt aesthetics for centuries to come.

The Romantic poet Percy Bysshe Shelley draws on Plato's argument, as well as Philip Sydney's 1579 interpretation of it, in his "Defense of Poetry" (1821), reasserting the centrality of poetry to creation and unity.[41] Shelley writes, "A poet participates in the eternal, the infinite and the one; as far as relates to his conceptions, time and place and number are not."[42] Shelley's defense is a direct response to an essay published by Thomas Love Peacock in 1820, titled "The Four Ages of Poetry," in which Peacock calls the poet in modern times "a semi-barbarian in a civilized community." He states that poetry "can never make a philosopher, nor a statesman, nor in any class of life an useful or rational man."[43] Shelley's view is that the act of poetic creation or making is a force capable of unifying and transforming both the individual and society, while Peacock argues that, in societies governed by scientific rationalism, such as the industrialized countries of Europe at the beginning of the nineteenth century, the old model of poetry is a regressive force. Tim Ingold, in describing his anthropological method, takes up the Romantic position in the debate, claiming that science allows humans to know things about the world without being able to define themselves within that world.[44] Creativity essentially unlocks a kind of learning that develops on the inside and transforms the individual and, at the same time, the rest of society as well. In comparison to technological modernism, DIY makerism feels like a reactionary or conservative force against the dominant philosophy of our age: science.

The scientism of the modern era, taken for granted in the hard sciences as well as the humanities and social sciences, provides a model of understanding where the world around us is ripe for quantification and analysis. Romantic philosophy, and its celebration of sensuous experience, making and handcraft, instinctively pushes against the domination of scientism in all aspects of life. For writers at the beginning of the nineteenth century, it was poetry that offered liberation from the prison of quantifiable determinacy. For the Arts and Crafts movement of the latter half of that century, returning to handcraft and cottage industry was proposed as a means around the domination of scientism.

Arts and Crafts

The Arts and Crafts movement, which began in Britain in the 1850s and hit the peak of its popularity in both Britain and the United States between 1880 and 1914, has often been casually compared to the Maker Movement.[45] Dave Gauntlett, Professor at the University of Westminster, writes in *Maker Pro*:

One source of inspiration for me is the Arts and Crafts movement, which took off in the late nineteenth century, but was built upon a set of ideas that are still incredibly relevant. Emerging as a response to mass-produced goods, the Movement was all about the power of making distinctive, expressive things. A lovely bit of Arts and Crafts philosophy comes from John Ruskin, who expressed strong admiration for roughly-made, characterful things, such as the gargoyles on medieval cathedrals. Ruskin alienated himself from the Victorian art establishment with his passion for such quirky, unfinished, unprofessional things – but Ruskin's point was that these formal qualities are not what we should really value: the important thing is that you can see in the created object the spirit of a Maker who feels an urge to communicate, to express themselves, to say something or have an impact on others.[46]

While the emphasis of the Arts and Crafts movement was, indeed, on the loss of handicraft in the decorative arts during the Industrial Revolution, the ideology behind the movement was, particularly for Ruskin, rooted in Christian socialism. The movement looked back to the Gothic era as a purer, more humane time for the creation of decorative objects and described the alienation of the individual worker in terms of Christian morality. Unlike the Maker Movement, which fully embraces capitalist enterprise, the Arts and Crafts movement was, at least initially, anti-capitalist to its core. John Ruskin, an architect by training and the leading theorist of the Arts and Crafts movement, could not have made his position on the relationship between art and capital more clear, saying, "... beautiful things are useful to men because they are beautiful, and for the sake of their beauty only; and not to sell, or pawn – or, in any other way, turn into money."[47] The model of labor proposed by Arts and Crafts theorists was one of communal craft in a pastoral setting, echoing the love of nature and the countryside that was prevalent in British Romantic philosophy.

Like the Romantics, the Arts and Crafts movement lamented the fracturing of human faculties that had been perpetrated by the division of labor in industrial societies. They looked nostalgically back to pre-industrial times for inspiration on how to reform labor and improve the lives of the working class. John Ruskin wrote in 1853:

We have much studied and much perfected, of late, the great civilized invention of the division of labor; only we give it a false name. It is not, truly speaking, the labor that is divided; but the men: – Divided into mere segments of men – broken into small fragments and crumbs of life; so that all the little piece of intelligence that is left in a man is not enough to make a pin, or a nail, but exhausts itself in making the point of a pin, or the head of a nail.[48]

The Gothic period was seen as a time when laborers were free to express their creativity through their work, however imperfect the outcome may be. Reacting against European neoclassicism, Ruskin saw, in medieval architecture and decorative arts, a humanity that presented itself in its rawness and imperfection. Ruskin wrote that a man could either be a man, working with his hands, or a machine, working in a factory as an "animated tool", but not both. He states, "Men were not intended to work with the accuracy of tools, to be precise and perfect in all their actions."[49] Unlike the proponents of the Gothic Revival in England at the time, Ruskin wanted to return to not only the *style* of the Gothic but also to an idealized version of the working methods and craftsmanship of the pre-industrial era. One might extrapolate, then, that Ruskin would be rather troubled by the Maker Movement coupling his ideas to projects built with the precision of laser cutters and CNC machines.

The designer and writer William Morris, like Ruskin, also despised the pollution of nature and the degradation of labor he saw in industrial production. He believed, as Ruskin and the Romantics had, that every human being has the potential for imaginative, fulfilling labor. As a means to achieve social reform, Morris and Ruskin both championed the decorative arts, which were, within the academic systems, held in far lower esteem than painting or sculpture. Ruskin believed that the most beautiful artworks were those that were integrated into a particular location, as the sculpture was in Gothic cathedrals (what contemporary art historians might call site-specificity). Ruskin said, in a lecture delivered in Bradford, England, in 1859, "Get rid, then, at once of any idea of Decorative art being a degraded or a separate kind of art. Its nature or essence is simply its being fitted for a definite place; and, in that place, forming part of a great and harmonious whole, in companionship with other art... Portable art – independent of all place – is for the most part ignoble art."[50] This interest in the decorative arts and their contextual wholeness was directly opposed to contemporaneous theories of modern art that sought to keep art in a pure realm apart from the workings of everyday life and everyday people, called *art pour l'art* or "art for art's sake." Morris disparages the elitism of the philosophy of art for art's sake, writing, "This would be art cultivated professedly by a few, for a few... [it] has for its watchword a piece of slang that does not mean the harmless thing it seems to mean – art for art's sake. Its fore-doomed end must be, that art at last will seem too delicate a thing for even the hands of the initiated to touch..."[51] The Arts and Crafts movement, therefore, participated a long series of pendulum swings in modern art history between those that sought an integration of art and everyday life and those that hoped to keep art in a separate realm, unsullied by the everyday.

Morris believed that art was not for an elite few but rather for everyone, and, through art, society would be reformed and improved. One of the means by which this might be achieved, according to Morris and other Arts and Crafts thinkers, was through education and access to handcraft by both the low and high born. He wrote, "I do not want art for a few, any more than education for a few, or freedom for a few."[52] Morris saw art as a universal gift to all human beings, something that "all can share, that will elevate all."[53] Ruskin did not separate art from morality, politics, or religion, and saw the universal gift of art, that is the making of things, as the means by which humans may achieve Earthly happiness.[54]

Morris implemented his ideas in his famous Red House, designed in collaboration with architect Philip Webb in 1859 and situated in Bexleyheath outside of London. The Neo-Gothic home of the Morris family was also imagined as a workshop for his decorative arts company, Morris, Marshall, Faulkner & Co. (nicknamed "The Firm"), but, due to financial difficulties, the workshop never operated on those premises. Instead, the Firm produced a variety of decorative arts products – wallpaper, furniture, glass, metal-works, etc. – from their headquarters at 8 Red Lion Square in London. By 1875, Morris' ideal brotherhood of craftworkers had dissolved and he was operating under his name only, Morris & Co. For Morris, trying to operate a viable business during this period, integrating the Arts and Crafts model of work into a modern industrial society, became an unresolvable paradox. If workers were going to be making high-quality goods by hand, from start to finish, they would be so expensive and luxurious as to only be affordable for the upper classes. If working class people were to beautify their homes in the egalitarian ways promoted by Ruskin and Morris, the decorative products would have to be made, at least in part, by machine and through the division of labor. Morris claimed that he at least learned each process himself before setting workers to their tasks. After Morris' death in 1896, his designs were put into mass-production and the Arts and Crafts ethos was eroded to the status of style.

Perhaps the Maker Movement can learn something from the internal contradictions of the Arts and Crafts movement, where ideals departed from their integration into modern life. While the Arts and Crafts movement wanted a more egalitarian, democratic art, it also called for a return to individual craftsmanship. These two things were incompatible in the modern world. In order for these crafts to be affordable for the working class, they had to be machine-made. Similarly, in the Maker Movement, the ideals of democratic production veer away from the realities of the business world, where a truly successful product naturally goes into industrial production (even if it does not have mass appeal), and, so, the Maker Movement does not mark a return to DIY and doing things by hand (each individual producing their own custom goods) but rather a new economy where the market is flooded with a variety of niche "lifestyle" products like, for example, a foldable kayak. The Oru Kayak (as in, origami kayak) was designed by San Francisco resident Anton Willis, who was looking for a way to adapt his love of kayaking with urban living, and it was funded by Kickstarter. This project is held up in the Maker community as an example of a successfully launched lifestyle product, which has a very limited market appeal but nevertheless can be made in the Maker economy.[55] Do products like this folding kayak lead to a more open, democratic society? Probably not, but they will make it more convenient for urban residents to go kayaking. Likewise, the Arts and Crafts movement fell short of its political roots in that it did not produce the egalitarian labor environment it hoped to achieve but, instead, brought about a deluge of new decorative products for the home based on pastoral ideals.

The Arts and Crafts movement in the decorative arts that Ruskin and Morris cultivated in the 1850s and '60s was not named as such until 1887, when TJ Sanderson-Cobden coined the term ahead of the first of three annual shows by the Art

Workers' Guild. The guild had seen a need for public outreach to promote the "combined arts" they practiced and held the first of this series of exhibitions at the New Gallery in Regent Street in October 1888.[56] Continuing the tradition of exultant discourse on the potential of individual fulfillment through making, Sanderson-Cobden wrote, "… the soul of man, athwart all distraction, aspires to be at one, at one for the fruit of its energy in creation, at one for the control of its energy in rest, in rest interlocked, repose absolute."[57] By the early twentieth century, though, Arts and Crafts style had spread to America and become big business in both Britain and the States.

The manifestation of the Arts and Crafts movement in the United States was the closest historical analog to the present-day Maker Movement, where it married the "hand-made" aesthetic with capitalist enterprise. Although makers have laid claim to John Ruskin as the grandfather of their movement, Ruskin's aversion to industrial technology puts his philosophy, at its core, in opposition to the Maker Movement. Dean Brown, a maker and designer who was inspired by Ruskin, says, "The thing that makes him tragically outdated is that he was scared of – or against – the machine. If Ruskin was here now, I imagine he'd really like the grassroots attitude that is very much apparent in hackerspaces, but he'd get right wound up about 3D printing, basically."[58] While Ruskin may have been appalled by 3D printers, Gustav Stickley, a leader of the American Arts and Crafts movement, would have felt quite at home in the Maker Movement of today. Stickley built his company, Craftsman Workshops, into one of the most fashionable American furniture brands. Embodying a particularly American intellectual distance between ideology and commerce, Stickley used methods of mass-production and the latest industrial machines to produce his "craftsman" furniture (which was also popularized under the moniker "mission style").[59] Stickley started the magazine *The Craftsman* in 1901 to promote the ideas of the Arts and Crafts movement and his company United Crafts (changed in 1903 to the Craftsman Workshops). He was, at least at first, of the same mind as Ruskin and Morris on topics of industrial production, handicraft, and unity of the arts.

The first issue of *The Craftsman*, published in October of that year, dedicates the vast majority of its pages to Morris and his philosophy on art, praising his brand of socialism. The second issue, from November of that year, focuses primarily on the writings of Ruskin and is equally laudatory. The first sign of divergence from the reactionary perspective of Stickley's British counterparts came in July 1902 in an article titled, "An Old Art, Revived and Advanced by Modern Science," which describes advanced techniques for treating leather, pioneered by Stickley's company.[60] In 1903, Stickley introduced the "craftsman house" and distributed architectural plans to his subscribers through his Craftsman Home Builders Club, allowing his users to promote and implement these plans on their own.

Stickley also began publishing plans for his furniture in later issues of *The Craftsman*. The Arts and Crafts dream of returning to pre-industrial methods of labor may have fallen by the wayside at the turn of the century, but the dream of handicraft lived on in the DIY projects promoted and sold by *The Craftsman* and other magazines of the period (other titles included *Mission Furniture: How to Make It* and *Making Built-In Furniture*).[61] Like the Maker Movement, these handicraft projects were part of a new market for *leisure* craftwork. In no way did they provide an alternative to industrial production. *The Craftsman*, then, was very similar to *Make* magazine, couching its pragmatic, entrepreneurial aims in the soaring rhetoric of freedom and fulfillment. The magazines are also similar in structure and content, both featuring articles, reviews, and DIY projects for consumers. While the British Arts and Crafts movement also promoted DIY craft projects, Christian reformers focused their attentions on the working class, who they felt needed to fill their leisure time with crafts so that they would stay away from gambling and drinking.[62] For the American Arts and Crafts enthusiasts, DIY projects were a fun hobby and a new method of consumption for the middle classes.

Stickley's publication of his architectural plan was, in the lingo of the tech industry, an "open-source" approach to business. Many companies that associate themselves with the Maker Movement believe in a similar open-source model. OpenROV, a low-cost underwater robot, publishes its plans online so that makers can create their own (the company sells kits that consumers can assemble). Many of the maker creations are initially prototyped with Arduino boards, which run on an open-source platform, and allow users to easily program functionality into them. Once production is scaled up in successful gadgets, however, it is more cost effective to install ordinary circuit boards rather than Arduinos. The open-source movement is a key player in the ongoing battle over intellectual property happening in the tech industry. On first glance, it may seem rather generous to give away the plans for an invention for free, but ultimately it makes business sense, as it attracts more customers to the brand. In fact, even Apple's early products – the Apple I and Apple II computers – shipped with a wiring diagram and the monitor software source code. As 1960s counterculture figurehead Stewart Brand said in 1984, information wants to be free but it also wants to be expensive. The tech industry today (and its offshoot, the Maker Movement) developed out of government-funded computer research in the '40s and '50s. Tech industry leaders have, like Stickley, found a way to unite soaring rhetoric and extremely lucrative entrepreneurship. The paradox of open-source is no longer really a paradox at all – information can be both free and expensive in turn.

Chapter 3

Techno-Primitivism

In a 1995 issue of *TIME* magazine heralding the arrival of "cyberspace," Stewart Brand wrote a short essay titled, "We Owe It All to the Hippies," describing how the recent flowering of widespread Internet access and personal computing could be traced back to the philosophies of the countercultural in the 1960s and '70s. Brand says, "... hippie communalism and libertarian politics formed the roots of the modern cyberrevolution... The counterculture's scorn for centralized authority provided the philosophical foundations of not only the leaderless Internet but also the entire personal-computer revolution."[1] Brand himself was one of the key figures to bridge the divide between government-funded research labs and the acid-infused drop-out culture during this period. His *Whole Earth Catalog*, a compendium of tools and literature designed to aid these off-the-grid experiments, has at times been called the Google of the counterculture. The Maker Movement, as an outgrowth of Silicon Valley, also shares these libertarian roots, and, in many ways, marks a return to the core tenets of the counterculture, which revolved around the use of tools in building back-to-the-land, self-sufficient communities. While the communes of the 1960s and early '70s largely failed to create the ideal new societies they hoped to form, the autonomy, individualism, and do-it-yourself sufficiency they promoted were translated into Internet and hacker culture in the decades that followed. Today, these ideals live on in the Maker Movement and are embodied in hipster subculture. As detailed in Chapter 1, the hipster has undergone a number of stylistic transformations between 2000 and 2015 but has remained an essential part of contemporary culture through their embrace of Chris Anderson's "long tail" of consumption. Hipsterism is the end result of digital culture that facilitates niche, customizable, remixable excavation of new and existing fashions and consumer goods. Makers and hipsters both form identities around a constantly changing self-fashioning that is enabled by DIY software tools and the Internet.

The techno-utopianism of the counterculture stands apart from that of the early twentieth century in that it united Romanticist ideals of wholeness, individuality, and sharing, discussed in Chapter 2, with technological capitalism. The values and rhetoric developed during the counterculture was almost wholesale transferred to the tech industry, where it has changed very little over the last 50 years, even as the technologies themselves have evolved dramatically. For the counterculture, as for the Maker Movement, technology offers a way to build society anew. The failure of backwards-looking philosophies like those of Ruskin and Morris, which hoped to recreate the working methods and communities of the Middle Ages in the modern world, led to the full embrace of machine-like labor and techno-utopianism of the 1920s. Movements like the Bauhaus and Neue Sachlichkeit in Germany looked to the pragmatism of the United States for inspiration, where technological progress promised to foster democracy, egalitarianism, and individual freedom. It was not until the 1950s that the romantic conception of the individual remerged as a dominant cultural force for technological progressives.

The primary contradiction that arises from merging romantic philosophy and a progressive view of technology is that it simultaneously rejects the modern world while embracing the technology created by it. The counterculture rectified this contradiction by developing an outlook that can be described as techno-primitivism. They saw themselves as pioneers, creating society from scratch in the wilderness, off the grid. Like the first humans colonizing a new planet or the cowboys of the Old West, they would, naturally, need to take existing tools with them to settle the untamed wilderness. Although they drew heavily from and fetishized pre-modern modes of living and working, the counterculture very quickly saw the potential of the emerging computer industry to provide the tools to carry out their visions of communal living away from the administration and control of the State. They raided Romanticism for its rhetoric of individual experience and wholeness while largely discarding its reactionary anti-rationalist underpinnings and the belief in the socially transcendent power of aesthetic experience. The potential of networked culture and computing seemed to finally present a technological solution to the problem of alienated labor in industrial production. Many technophiles today still laud the Internet as a vehicle for democracy and social mobility – a viewpoint they owe to the counterculture. For the Maker Movement, then, Romanticism provides a convenient philosophical framework, combining the rhetoric of liberation with scientism. Sensuous experience and personal fulfillment – advertised within the Web 2.0 market by the likes of YouTube or Instagram that offer ways to "create" and "share" – are rationalized and quantified through their service in the production of commodities and circulation in capitalist systems of value.

The ideologies around the Maker Movement, like the Romantics, Arts and Crafts movement, and the counterculture, attempt to place the individual back at the center of an interconnected planet where human beings are increasingly plugged into mechanistic roles. The primal impulse of the Maker Movement, like the Arts and Crafts movement before it, looks back to the creative act of making as essential to human fulfillment. The wedding of this ideology with the individualistic rhetoric of neoliberal capitalism, however, betrays the utopian rhetoric on which it is founded.

Bureaucracy vs Free Will

The counterculture has traditionally been positioned against the bureaucratic and dehumanizing technocracy of the postwar military-industrial complex and the rise of computing. The popular history of the counterculture paints their rebellions with a broad brush. Those that were not involved in political activism were "dropping out" and forming communes off the grid as a reaction against the 1950s conformity of the Organization Man in the Cold War era.[2] Tracing the roots of cyberculture from government-funded research labs in the 1940s through the counterculture of the '60s, Fred Turner argues that, although the counterculture is commonly seen as a reaction to postwar technocracy and bureaucratic alienation, it was, in fact, part of a continuation of the ideas and modes of working initiated by the collaborative cybernetic research groups during World War II.[3] Turner argues that, although the New Left is often lumped together with the counterculture (which he calls the "New Communalists"), these two groups were politically divergent: the New Left involved itself in political action and protest in the hopes of effecting change through the existing structures of government in the US, while the New Communalists were essentially apolitical libertarians who rejected all of the existing systems of government and hoped to start their own new micro-societies off the grid.

The false opposition between the counterculture and cybernetics stems more from a misunderstanding of the nature of scientific and technological research in the postwar era than a shifting perception of the counterculture itself.[4] The ethos of both cybernetic research and the counterculture revolved around technophilic utopianism achieved through collaborative efforts. While both groups embraced collaborative problem solving and valued sharing, the younger generation in the counterculture emphasized on the importance of individuality and free will, as they were unwilling to see the individual subsumed in either

Communism or American bureaucratic corporations like IBM. This philosophical question underlying these two positions – the theories of control, prediction and statistical analysis of Norbert Wiener and the self-actualizing, individualistic motivations of the counterculture – traces its origins all the way back to the seventeenth and eighteenth centuries, when rationalist versus empiricist philosophers sparred over the question of free will and causality.

During World War II, cyberneticists Norbert Wiener and Julian Bigelow began to see pilots and anti-aircraft gunners as servomechanisms, devices that receive external information via sensors and correct their behavior based on negative feedback. Much like the algorithms that personalize data and product offerings or predict consumer desires online, cybernetics promised to accurately predict and map human behavior – a major boon for the war effort. On a deeper level, however, cybernetics seemed to reveal free will as a fantasy, at least in the realm of piloting fighter jets. The complexities of causality – too complex for the human mind – were finally within the reach of scientists with the aid of computers. Turner writes:

> By conceptualizing pilots and gunners as servomechanisms, Wiener and Bigelow also found a way to imagine the material world in terms of the computational metaphor. That metaphor in turn encoded two sometimes overlapping, and sometimes competing, socio-technical visions: the automaton and the self-regulating system.[5]

While this way of viewing the world proved extremely useful for the United States military, the lack of autonomy for the individual human was wholly unappealing to a generation of young people raised during the start of the Cold War, who were taught to fear the conformity and lack of individual rights imposed under Communist rule.

Like Communism, the "system" was a prison to be avoided at all costs. The idea that the world is made up of "systems" (political systems, social systems, systems of art making, etc.) shifted from a technical and engineering context into philosophy, the humanities, and the social sciences in the 1960s. Michael Corris writes:

> The concept of a "system," which became part of the *lingua franca* of the 1960s, was not destined to remain the exclusive property of a technologically-minded elite of engineers, scientists and mathematicians. In the hands of intellectuals, artists and political activists, it would become a key ideological component of the "cultural revolution."[6]

Under this model, human and machine are no longer separate categories that influence each other but rather two kinds of servomechanisms operating in global systems. These global systems threatened to dissolve individuality while at the same time uniting the whole world in one great anthropocene.[7] For the counterculture, marrying the ideals of Romanticism with techno-utopianism seemed to provide a way to save the individual lost in the system.

Technology vs Nature

Buckminster Fuller, designer/inventor, theorist and key figure for the counterculture, traveled around the United States in the 1960s giving speeches to young people, promoting his particular brand of technologically-enabled individualism. Having inherited a lineage of Unitarian and Transcendentalist philosophy from his family (his great-aunt Margaret Fuller was a key member of the movement), Fuller was a direct link between the counterculture and American Romantic philosophy, with its emphasis on individualism, self-reliance, primitivism, and communion with the natural world. Fuller "saw the material world as the reflection of an otherwise intangible system of rules. But unlike Emerson and the Transcendentalists, Fuller linked that system of rules not only to the natural world but also to the world of industry."[8] The embrace of the natural world, for the counterculture, translated into an interest in going back to the land, homesteading, or otherwise living in a Primitivist fantasy of the simple life, in communion with nature. At the same time, however, the counterculture fully embraced new technology, which seems to contradict their interest in returning to a simpler life living off the land. I would argue, however, that this world of industry, the technological world, replaced the concept of nature in the discourse of romanticism after World War II. Where once beauty was seen as the key to creating morally good individuals within a democratic society, now personal technology (or media/communications technology) has assumed this role.

As noted in Chapter 2, Friedrich Schiller saw beauty as the essential bridge between individual fulfillment and a harmonious society. For Schiller, beauty *is* the moral good: those who experience the beautiful are morally uplifted individuals. A society filled with beauty is, therefore, a liberated, democratic society, free from alienation. By the 1960s, the concept of beauty had been replaced by personal technology (including psychedelic pharmaceutical technology) as the bridge between individual wholeness and unity with the human race. Part of the Hacker Ethics outlined by Steven Levy states, "You can create art and beauty on the computer."[9] This may not seem like such a radical statement today, as computers are widely used for purposes other than number-crunching, but, at the time, the personal computer was still new and only a few groups of hackers had begun to explore the multimedia potential of computing.

For the counterculture, communications technology promised to be the force that would restore harmony between the individual and society. It would unite the globe and make man whole within himself and one with the world. The techno-centric vision of systems theory, with its predictable outcomes based on networks of complex variables, achieved the status of natural law for counterculturists. Personal technology, therefore, was connected with the good (just as beauty had been for Schiller) and offered an escape from the empiricist prison of the system (or the natural order). The moral dimension of personal technology remains with us today in the Maker Movement. Through the use of consumer-grade personal production technology, makers can find this sense of wholeness within themselves and create a more harmonious society in the process.

Once technological systems are seen as natural, the contradiction between the counterculture's techno-utopianism and primitivism is resolved. The romantic vision of the counterculture, like the Arts and Crafts movement, sought a way of living and working that harkened back to a pre-industrial time, while simultaneously maintaining a belief in the liberating potential of personal media and communications technology. Looking for a solution to the alienation of modern life, as countless moderns had done before them, the counterculture (and the Beats before them) turned to the cultures of non-western people for alternatives to Western philosophy. The counterculture, therefore, cultivated an odd techno-primitivism that melded media technology and tribal mysticism. The radio signals pulsating around the globe took on a mystical significance. Rituals included both technological aids – lights, sounds, music, psychedelic drugs – and ancient, communal incantations. Both mystical ritual and communications technology promised a way to expand individual minds while connected with the greater community.

Marshall McLuhan's theories on communication technology in *The Gutenberg Galaxy* (1962) and *Understanding Media* (1964) were instrumental in bridging the seeming contradiction between technological progress and this new primitivism.[10] McLuhan argued that communication technologies were breaking down the large-scale bureaucratic organizational structures that had organized society since the invention of movable type in favor of looser collections of individuals around the globe. The primitivist impulse in the counterculture was influenced by figures like DT Suzuki, who popularized Zen and other Eastern philosophies for the Western public in the postwar era, and Ananda Coomaraswamy, who was active in the Arts and Crafts movement, and introduced Indian culture and philosophy to the West. Coomaraswamy's influence continued within the counterculture and was popular with early communes like USCO in upstate New York. Fred Turner writes, "Coomaraswamy had asserted that artists in traditional societies were as anonymous as tradesmen. The members of USCO saw themselves returning to a more traditional mode of tribal living and collective craftsmanship."[11] While each individual craftsman finds fulfillment in executing an object from conception to completion, the object is part of the greater cultural or societal production. Like the Arts and Crafts movement, the counterculture viewed traditional craftwork with an idealized nostalgia. Practicing traditional craft in modern society had not historically been a tenable alternative to modern capitalism. For the Maker Movement, however, an updated version of "traditional" craft – with the aid of transcendent, society-shaping personal technology – has presented itself as a viable alternative mode of production *within* modern capitalism.

Techno-Primitivist Labor

The techno-primitivism of the counterculture lives on in the Maker Movement. The blog *Boing Boing* has been instrumental in promoting and publicizing the hacker-turned-maker culture of tinkering and invention. In science fiction, hacker culture has always had an eye towards the post-Apocalyptic. In 2009, Cory Doctorow, co-editor of *Boing Boing,* published his book *Makers,* a Randian work of fiction set in the techno-primitivist near future, which serves as an introduction to the ideology of the Maker Movement.[12] The book couches its philosophical outlook in two-dimensional characterizations and a thinly developed narrative structure set primarily in dead malls – disinvested and abandoned – around the US, as the Maker Movement stands poised to rescue a society on the brink of self-destruction. The central characters in the book are two hacker-tinkerers in an abandoned shopping center in Florida who are enlisted as part of an experimental new economy dubbed New Work. The New Work projects are sponsored by a corporate conglomerate of dying industrial titans Kodak and Duracell (now, Kodacell), which enlists teams of makers all over the United States to continue doing their hacks under the banner of this new corporate entity. While the book implies that Kodacell's maker groups exist around the globe, the narrative remains firmly focused on the United States. Kodacell teams these rogue makers up with "suits," who deal with the business end of the enterprise while the makers are left to create. The New Work teams are free to invent whatever whimsical hacks take their fancy: Elmo doll-robots hacked to drive cars, RFID room sorting systems, toaster robots, calculating machines run on G.I. Joe and Barbie heads that output M&Ms, a variety of souped-up hybrid vehicles, and all manner of 3D printed creations. Each invention goes quickly into production, hits market saturation and is replaced by another equally quirky new innovation. It is the essence of quick, disposable commodity. The model is reminiscent of the "fast fashion" strategy pioneered by down-market clothing retailers like Zara in the mid-'00s, where new clothing is stocked in stores every week or two rather than once a season.[13]

The revolution ushered in by the New Work economy quickly grows into a bubble. The business fails, not because the model of the company was flawed, but because the economic model of the world is flawed (which implies, perhaps, that the world is just not ready for the Maker economy). One of the "suits" describes the movement as a highpoint in American Exceptionalism, saying, "The average New Work collective shipped more inventions per year than Edison Labs at its peak. In a hundred years, when they remember the centuries that were America's, they'll count this one among them, because of what we made."[14] The Maker Movement (or New Works in this book) is positioned as the American Dream made real. After the bubble bursts for the New Works and Kodacell goes bust, the maker protagonists turn to other projects and eventually end up creating an amusement park ride that works on crowd-sourced input from its riders.

The ride consists of a constantly evolving pile of trash and old consumer goods, many of which were culled from the New Work projects, arranged in an evolving display by small robots. The ride draws an obsessive fan following and, soon, other cities around the country (and the world) make their own replica ("franchise") rides, creating a larger data set for the collection of consumer goods. As noted in Chapter 1, the Maker Movement often cites Edison as an example of the American Dream come true, so it is no surprise that a message broadcast at the beginning of the ride in *Makers* also cites him. The message states:

THERE WAS A TIME WHEN AMERICA HELD OUT THE PROMISE OF A NEW WAY OF LIVING AND WORKING. THE NEW WORK BOOM OF THE TEENS WAS A PERIOD OF UNPARALLELED INVENTION, A CAMBRIAN EXPLOSION OF CREATIVITY NOT SEEN SINCE THE TIME OF EDISON – AND UNLIKE EDISON, THE PEOPLE WHO INVENTED THE NEW WORK REVOLUTION WEREN'T RIP-OFF ARTISTS AND FRAUDS. THEIR MARVELOUS INVENTIONS EMERGED AT THE RATE OF FIVE OR SIX PER WEEK...[15]

Over time the ride begins to form around a collaborative crowd-sourced story that fans follow with religious zeal.

Although Doctorow describes the ride as a utopian creation ushering in a better, more democratic and creative world, it is difficult to see it as anything other than a rapacious consumerist ouroboros. The ride is a means of entertainment/leisure consumption to begin with, but, on top of this, the theme of the ride is consumerism itself: it involves riding through a random collection of other consumer objects and voting on which items should stay on display and which should be removed. It is as utopian as voting for an *American Idol* contestant (and would, if it actually existed, probably effect about as much economic/socio-political change). *Makers* is not always totally clear about what existing systems should be harnessed in building the Maker utopia or who exactly counts as a hero or a villain: it veers between rhapsodic descriptions of extreme individualism and an interest in community cooperation, and it contains diatribes against Disney and corporate "suits" while embracing other manifestations of corporate capitalism. There is no ambiguity, however, in Doctorow's core political position. His book is a full expression of the techno-utopian libertarianism that grew out of the counterculture and developed into the computer industry in Silicon Valley.

Makers is decidedly antigovernment, anti-regulation, and anti-authority. The characters inhabit a world that is semi-dystopian, where they are left to strike out on their own and use their innate creativity to effect change in the world. Their creativity, however, is always exercised in traditional capitalist contexts: buying and selling of commodities, corporate expansion, and distribution or outsourcing of labor. The protagonists of the book live in a world where deregulation and lack of authoritative oversight always lead to better products and more money made. A shantytown that develops around the dead mall where the makers work is described as a utopian model of DIY living. The residents open businesses, children play in the streets, and houses are built with 3D printed materials. The DIY infrastructure of the town even survives a hurricane because all the buildings, naturally, "met and exceeded county code."[16] The message is that any government intrusion into people's lives stymies innovation and entrepreneurship, and limits the abilities of people to express themselves. As is a common refrain in the libertarian paradise of Silicon Valley, if left to their own devices, people (and companies) would create much better products. This view disregards the deep debt the computer industry owes to government funding during the Cold War.

In California in the 1950s and 1960s, the nascent technology industry centered around two main Defense Department-funded research labs: the Stanford Research Institute (SRI) and the Stanford Artificial Intelligence Laboratory (SAIL). In the 1950s, computer scientists were philosophically divided over where computer technology was headed. The majority favored research in artificial intelligence, seeing the computer's (or robot's) role as one of replacement of human faculties, while the more rebellious researchers were interested in augmented intelligence, where the computer would simply amplify the power of the individual rather than replace her.[17] The most powerful computers of the era were massive, expensive machines that were shared between an entire (well-funded) research group, and the majority of computer scientists during the era believed that computers were essentially communal machines. They could not fathom a rationale for creating, at great expense, a computer that was not going to be shared between researchers, not only because of their enormous cost but also because computers were seen as specialist instruments that were designed to operate primarily as calculators. At the time, computer scientists wondered why anyone would need that kind of calculating power at home or in their office – it would be a tremendous waste of money.

A small group of researchers in the Santa Clara Valley (soon to be Silicon Valley), however, were obsessed with the idea that computers should be small, personal machines. These same scientists also saw the potential of computers to be media machines – musical instruments, graphics programs, gaming systems, etc. Doug Engelbart was one of the early proponents of augmentation in the '50s. He believed that the future of computers lay in enhancing or augmenting human intelligence, not replacing it, so he doggedly pursued this angle, even when it was unpopular, in his Augmentation Research Center at SRI. His team developed the first mouse, an early version of the Internet, hypertext, computer networking, and early graphical user interfaces (which, for a variety of reasons, would not be introduced to the public for another twenty-plus years). Unlike artificial intelligence, which sought to take humans out of the equation, Engelbart's work would keep "man in the loop." The results of the personal computer, according to John Markoff, an early chronicler of the tech industry, would be that "... organizations would be democratized, industries transformed, and a new wave of individual creativity would sweep across the world."[18] Given these goals for computing, it's unsurprising that the engineers of Santa Clara Valley were also simultaneously enmeshed in the counterculture and took part in some of the earliest experiments with mind-altering drugs like LSD.

The interest in LSD in the 1950s and '60s, in many ways, parallels the interest in computer augmentation. The Stanford area was already home to a bohemian community situated next to the Stanford Golf Course in a collection of cottages on Perry Lane in unincorporated Menlo Park. The community dated back to the beginnings of the university itself and the band of beatnik bohemians in the area became known as the Perry Lane Writers in the 1950s.[19] In 1959, while enrolled in a writing program at Stanford University and living on Perry Lane, a young Ken Kesey, countercultural figure and author of *One Flew Over the Cuckoo's Nest* (1960), was recruited by a fellow Stanford graduate student to participate in one of many CIA-funded experiments with psychedelic drugs at Menlo Park Veterans Administration

Hospital. At that point in time, the government was interested in psychedelics primarily as truth serums, but serious scientists soon believed that the drugs, particularly LSD, may have mind-expanding properties that would allow them to tap into a deep level of creativity.[20] In the early 1960s, future SRI researchers like Willis Harman and Jim Fadiman, affiliated with an organization called the International Federation for Advanced Study, were being paid hundreds of dollars by members of the counterculture, such as Stewart Brand, to take guided LSD trips in the name of scientific research.[21]

Researchers saw LSD as another tool, like computer augmentation, that could enhance and expand the human mind to new levels of creativity and invention. The impact of psychedelics in expanding the creative capacities of the human mind inspired Kesey to bring LSD to a wider community in the mid-1960s, outside the scientific establishment. Along with a group of countercultural writers and artists called the Merry Pranksters, Kesey organized huge communal raves, complete with music and light shows, called the Acid Tests. The Merry Pranksters saw both LSD and communication technology as means by which the wholeness and unity they sought could be achieved around the world. Fred Turner writes, "In the Pranksters' world, LSD and radio were harbingers of New Communalist possibilities. They were communication technologies through which humans could not only exchange information, but, at least imaginatively, merge with one another in a spiritually harmonious state."[22] Stewart Brand was also a member of The Merry Pranksters, and his *Whole Earth Catalog* would go on to inspire the engineering as well as the countercultural community of the Valley, forming the ethos of the tech industry that survives today in the Maker Movement.

The Whole Earth

As noted, the communalist movements within the counterculture were more interested in personal liberation than change within the existing political structure. Brand created *The Whole Earth Catalog* in 1968, which was a collection of tools and books that the communal movement could use to form their new societies in the wilderness. The catalog's name derives from Brand's crusade in 1966 to get NASA to release an image of the whole Earth. He even printed up buttons asking, "Why have we not seen a photograph of the whole Earth yet?" In 1967, Brand got his wish and used the photograph for the cover of the catalog, using the whole Earth as a metaphor for global unity. The likeness between the catalog and contemporary Internet culture is not just fanciful metaphor: Brand went on to play an instrumental role in the development of the tech industry in California. The philosophy of the *Whole Earth Catalog* revolved around empowering the individual in creative endeavors, providing a variety of tools for DIY living while promoting an ideology of global and philosophical oneness with all of humanity on "spaceship Earth." The catalog was marketed to and gained popularity in many of the short-lived communes that sprang up in the western United States in the early 1970s, and its listings grew substantially in size over the course of its four-year existence, from 1968–1972. The catalog was not a pure business endeavor by any means – readers could not order any of the items through the catalog itself. Rather, it served as a compendium of materials that *could* be bought elsewhere which might be useful to the new communards. It also served as a forum for readers to share their ideas or add items to the list of useful products. In this way, it became a kind of collaborative analogue database (hence, its connection to the search engines of the Internet era). The catalog directly influenced computing pioneers like Alan Kay at Xerox's PARC (Palo Alto Research Center), who fostered many of the innovations in computing and networking during the 1970s.[23]

The DIY spirit of the communes played heavily into American frontier mythology. If the Arts and Crafts movement saw themselves as medieval guilds of craftworkers, the counterculture saw themselves as cowboys and pioneers in the Old West. Turner writes:

> ... the *Catalog* emphasized that its products belonged to the do-it-yourself tradition of frontier elites: the cowboys and Indians of American myth, and now the commune keepers of the New Communalist movement. They were not simply tools to do a job; they were mechanisms that transformed their users into actors in the dramatic myths of American individualism. The readers of the *Catalog*, the nature of these items hinted, might be exceptional individuals, might be part of a vanguard, might in fact be able to merge consumption and technology with the dream of pre-industrial community.[24]

The "cowboys and Indians" rhetoric slipped easily into the Internet age, where hackers were either white hat or black hat (benign or destructive) and commerce operated in a free market.

The rhetoric of the counterculture and the *Whole Earth Catalog* is still very much alive in Silicon Valley and its offspring, the Maker Movement. Brand was a presence in the art scene as much as the tech scene in the Valley, which were quickly merging during the '60s. One of the nexus points of Brand's influence locally was his Whole Earth Truck Store, which sold a selected offering of goods from the catalog and was close to the SRI labs and frequented by many of the researchers who worked there.[25] According to Markoff:

> Brand saw himself not so much as an entrepreneur but as an artist who was exploring new media, and he was immediately struck by the possibilities of computers that were moving beyond being calculators. On the day he arrived at SRI, he walked into Dave Evans's office, found a large poster of rock singer Janis Joplin on the wall, and knew he was right at

home.[26]

But if, as Markoff argues, Brand did not identify as an entrepreneur at that point, he would soon develop a fierce entrepreneurial drive.

Organizing the Trips Festival, an amplification of the earlier Acid Tests, with Ken Kesey in 1966 marked Brand's emergence on the scene as a "countercultural entrepreneur."[27] This entrepreneurial drive would come to fruition in the *Whole Earth Catalog*, which served to capitalize on the needs of a growing communal movement among the counterculture around the Bay area. Despite the catalog's non-hierarchical structure and user-driven content, Brand, like a good tech industry CEO, remained at the center of the *Whole Earth* enterprise and exercised control over all of the output of his organization. In keeping with the ethos of the counterculture, Brand underemphasized his leadership role in the undertaking.[28]

After the demise of the back-to-the-land movement in the early 1970s, Brand remained ideologically close to the nascent computer industry in the Bay area, though he was not directly involved in computing. From 1974–1985, he produced a magazine called the *CoEvolution Quarterly*, which adapted the *Whole Earth* formula for counterculturists who no longer harbored illusions of off-the-grid utopia but rather wanted to cultivate counterculture ideas back in civilization. By 1980, Brand described himself as a small-business owner and an entrepreneur and was bitterly critical of the anarchic idealism that had driven the communal movements a decade earlier. Poking fun at the drug use of the era, Brand denounces his generation as "over-rewarded children" and indicates that they had all finally grown up and accepted the responsibilities of adulthood.[29]

The dictum "information wants to be free" has become the rallying cry of both hackers and advocates of open source technology. The quotation is usually attributed to Stewart

Brand, omitting the all-important caveat he presents in the full quotation: information is also expensive. Delivered during the Hackers' Conference of November 1984 and transcribed in the *Whole Earth Review*, a magazine that pre-figures *Wired* for the emerging tech industry of the mid-'80s, Brand says:

> It seems like there's a couple of interesting paradoxes that we're working with… On the one hand information wants to be expensive, because it's so valuable. The right information in the right place just changes your life. On the other hand, information wants to be free, because the cost of getting it out is getting lower and lower all the time. So you have these two fighting against each other.

Steve Wozniak, co-founder of Apple Computers, replies, "Information should be free but your time should not."[30] Brand and Wozniak's discussion carries on for a bit before Brand concludes, "One of the things I'd like to see shared here is the economics of how to be in business for yourself or in cahoots with other designers, and have the marketing guys working for you." At this point in the discussion, Terry Niksch, described in the transcript as a "homebrew hacker," interjects, "I think a hacker works to please himself first and to impress his peers, but as soon as you go for institutional approval, which includes the institution of the marketplace, I don't think you're hacking anymore."[31] The debate over the nature of information has continued from the 1980s onward in the open source, creative commons, and copyleft movements, but history has shown that the debate may, in fact, be moot: both the hacker ethic of open source and the conservative stance on intellectual property have facilitated, each in its turn, the growth and success of the computer industry. While it may seem like open source fights against business interest, it actually opens up new markets (which can later be closed into proprietary systems) and therefore benefits capitalist enterprise today.

The dream that the personal computer and the Internet would facilitate a more democratic, egalitarian, free and fair society has not been realized. While the Maker Movement, with the emergence of exciting new tools, again resurrects this dream, history has shown that networked tools do not, in fact, decrease inequality. As economist Thomas Piketty has thoroughly documented in *Capital in the Twenty-First Century*, inequality has steadily increased since the 1970s. After the economic stresses of World War II, government-funded reconstruction programs created an opportunity for social mobility and economic growth that would not have come about if not for the redistribution of wealth that the war facilitated.[32] The development of the Information Revolution was, indeed, akin to the Industrial Revolution of the nineteenth century in that it increased the wealth of a few at the expense of the many. Just as the Industrial Revolution created the astounding wealth of industrial capitalists in the Gilded Age, the Information Revolution has produced the Internet capitalists of the twenty-first century. How did the Information Age fall so far short of its promises for the dissolution of hierarchy and collectivism? Like the era of growth, immigration, and territorial expansion that gave rise, in the nineteenth century, to the American Dream myth, the Information Age has seen a similar rhetoric develop around the immaterial realm of the Internet.

Social and political re-codings often follow in the wake of new territorial expansion (whether virtual or physical). With the advent of the Internet, the countercultural hackers of the early computer era, who rejected the social and political codes of the old world and its existing power structures, suddenly found themselves in a position to define a new space. As new territories become old territories, the power structures again solidify and definitions become intractable. Philosophers Gilles Deleuze and Félix Guattari proposed, in the 1970s–80s, a system of socio-political organization that consists of interconnected nodes on a horizontal plane rather than a multileveled hierarchy called a "rhizome," after the plant structure of the same name. In the 1990s, Internet theorists latched on to Deleuze and Guattari's metaphor to describe the nature of the World Wide Web. In the art world, the term was used by '90s Internet artists in an e-mail list community called Rhizome, which was started by Mark Tribe in 1996 and is now part of the New Museum of New York. The rhizomatic model provided an alternative to the power of hierarchical systems and embodied the utopian promises of the Internet.

Deleuze and Guattari also developed an important theoretical structure to describe the global behaviors of capital, which they called deterritorializations and reterritorializations. Capital and economic growth operate in deterritorialized systems, which are stripped of context, borderless and free from former territorial restraints. These free and open systems provide the opportunity for capital to grow, a phenomenon we are very familiar with through its promotion in contemporary neoliberal doctrine. For Deleuze and Guattari, reterritorialization – the reinstatement of (often new) borders and creation of proprietary enclosures – goes hand in hand with deterritorialization. In *Anti-Oedipus*, they describe this process:

> ... there is the twofold movement of decoding or deterritorializing flows on the one hand, and their violent and artificial reterritorialization on the other. The more the capitalist machine deterritorializes, decoding, and axiomatizing flow in order to extract surplus value from them, the more its ancillary apparatuses, such as government bureaucracies and the forces of law and order, do their utmost to reterritorialize, absorbing in the process a larger and larger share of surplus value.[33]

Capitalism on the Internet followed the pattern outlined by Deleuze and Guattari: first it had to be deterritorialized from its ARPA-net beginnings in order to be reterritorialized within corporate capitalism.

In order to make business truly successful on the Internet, a certain amount of reterritorialization was necessary. Legitimation of online business through domain registration, secure monetary services, and the presence of established businesses offering their wares online helped to not only produce a climate where Internet consumption was acceptable and trustworthy but also regulated so that more money was funneled into creation of consolidated corporations. Most of those interested in the Internet during the 1990s were those which saw it with a commercially-oriented optimism. In their 1996 article, Richard Barbrook and Andy Cameron outlined an attitude toward technology, termed the "Californian Ideology," which:

> ... promiscuously combines the free-wheeling spirit of the hippies and the entrepreneurial zeal of the yuppies. This amalgamation of opposites has been achieved through a profound faith in the emancipatory potential of the new information technologies. In the digital utopia, everybody will be both hip and rich.[34]

At the advent of the Internet in the early 1990s, both those on the activist left and the libertarian right were quick to laud the new technology as the beacon of hope for building a new digital utopia. For the conservatives, the Internet provided an economic escape from the regulation of the government and an outlet for digital cowboys to stake out their territory and get rich through individualistic, entrepreneurial initiative.

Part II
Morgantown

Chapter 4

From Artist Neighborhoods to Maker Spaces

The same impetus that drove the counterculture to go "back to the land" and form communes in rural and remote regions of the United States has since driven similar populations of white middle-class young people several decades later to go "back to the city." Both the countercultural youth of the 1960s and the urban pioneers of the 1980s and '90s were escaping the rigid conformity of their suburban, middle-class upbringings by forming alternative communities in "untamed" geographies. Both of these groups built their own amusement parks of sorts, isolated from the political pressures of the larger world, engaging in a utopian desire to live as authentic individuals. The trappings of authenticity for both the counterculture communalists and the urban pioneers are expressed through their methods of consumption and the compromise they forged between individuality and community in a free market capitalist context.

Since the 1970s, scholars in a variety of disciplines have documented the transformation of the contemporary postindustrial city from a place of work to a place of leisure, entertainment, and tourism.[1] In New York City and other urban centers of Western Europe and the United States, this phenomenon is usually linked to deindustrialization that began after World War II and hit its peak in the 1970s. In popular culture, this transition to leisure and tourist economies has been dubbed the "Disneyfication" of cities. Various projects in New York City in the last twenty years have reinforced this trend: Times Square was made into a pedestrian plaza in 2009 to complete the transformation to a family friendly environment that had begun in the 1990s, the High Line was created on an old industrial railroad in the Meatpacking District and Chelsea, and numerous city parks, such as Bryant Park, were cleared of homeless residents to make way for a variety of middle-class family-friendly activities like yoga and ice skating. New York is not alone in its push toward leisure and tourism, London erected its giant London Eye Ferris wheel in 2000 across from Big Ben as a temporary millennial feature only to keep it active as a tourist attraction, and the bank of the Thames was redeveloped into a long pedestrian promenade, drawing visitors to the Tate Modern and the reconstructed Globe Theatre, among other attractions.

The link between deindustrialization in the second half of the twentieth century and the rise of leisure and tourism in the last twenty to thirty years is not as simple as the latter replacing the former. The displacement of production and labor by leisure and entertainment is merely an acceleration of an urban trend that has been ongoing since the development of the modern industrial city itself. In nineteenth-century Paris, the "capital of modernity", Baron Haussmann's sweeping overhaul of the city and its attendant changes to middle-class urban life ushered in an unprecedented growth of leisure activities and new modes of consumption.[2] Middle-class entertainment blossomed in Haussmannized Paris: department stores, lavish cafés, parks, spectacles, dance halls, and day-trips down the Seine became an integral part of middle-class city life. Leisure has always been a part of modernism and the modern city, but it has long since ceased to exist alongside large-scale industrial production in Western finance capitals. As traditional blue-collar labor all but disappears in New York City, or is transported out of sight in globalized capitalist markets, the service and information economies employ the vast majority of people across the spectrum of social class.

The distinction between labor and leisure is continually blurred. In *The Society of the Spectacle* (1967), Guy Debord famously pointed to the artificial separation of these two concepts, stating that, "what is referred to as 'liberation from work,' that is, increased leisure time, is a liberation neither within labor itself nor from the world labor has brought into being."[3] Production and consumption are, of course, reciprocal halves of an economic equation, so their associated acts of labor and leisure simultaneously oppose and overlap each other. For critics of capitalism like Debord, both labor and leisure are alienating activities divorced from authentic life and the "real."[4] Patterns of leisure consumption, particularly in the latter half of the twentieth century, have become important factors in self-definition. Communities are forged around leisure activities just as often if not more regularly than they are around labor and employment. A worker who is dissatisfied or alienated in his or her employment, particularly the classically alienated worker in a Taylorized system of production, can, following conventional wisdom, turn to hobby, leisure or craft in order to find fulfillment and express latent creativity.

The emergence of the Maker Movement reflects the growing popularity of DIY and craft practices in the postindustrial city. Members of this movement differ from previous generations of craft or DIY enthusiasts in their embrace of computer-enabled machines that translate ideas from digital data to physical products. Makers are attempting to bring hobbyist activities back into the realm of professional production. It is worth remembering that computers themselves, which facilitate so many varieties of makerism, were originally specialist professional machinery used only by scientists, researchers and military personnel. The advent of personal computers, the consumer-grade version of the professional apparatus, spawned an even larger array of consumer tools. PCs enabled consumers, via affordable and widely available software, to perform formerly difficult, specialized, professional techniques, such as photo and video editing, music production, desktop publishing, and 3D animation. Chris Anderson and other Maker Movement acolytes have called the movement the "New Industrial Revolution."[5] This moniker implies that craftwork has once again shifted between production and consumption. Where industrial mass-production transformed individuated craft into a leisure activity,

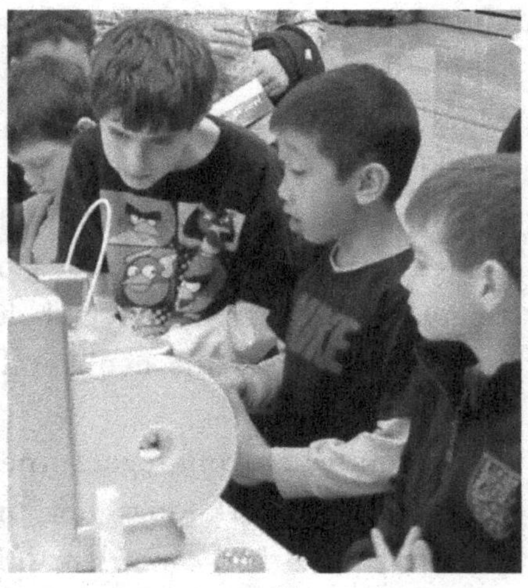

the Maker Movement claims to have brought craft practices back into the domain of production, hence the new *industrial revolution*.

While outward appearances support makers' claims that they are actively engaged in an individually empowered form of industrial production, I would argue that the Maker Movement, in fact, does the opposite of what they claim. In reality, the Maker Movement is a total conquest of the concept of production within the paradigm of consumption, subsuming labor within leisure. While media production has long been part of the consumer landscape, the last remaining and most stubborn realm of production – the creation of physical objects – has now, thanks to new technology, also been successfully domesticated within the space of consumption. Maker Movement products are not replacing mass-produced products from overseas factories, nor is that their goal. The motivation for makers is, rather, one that resonates with consumer culture: the expression of individual identity and creativity. Masquerading as the resurrection of long-lost industrial production, the Maker Movement has embraced consumer-grade computer-aided tools like laser cutters, 3D printers, and CNC machines. Professional tools become consumer goods for hobbyists and children alike.

Creativity and self-expression replace mechanized, alienated labor. Proponents of the Maker Movement regularly cite the Marxist adage that bourgeoisie power derives from control of the means of production.[6] They argue that makerism and the revolution in digital production technology finally allowed the proletariat to seize the means of production.[7] This continual reference to Marx, a cheerful declaration of the end of class conflict, disguises the neoliberal underpinnings of the Maker Movement.

Makers tend to congregate in neighborhoods like Morgantown, even if their work does not practically necessitate physical proximity to urban centers or other makers. The desire to live near concentrations of niche consumption and entertainment outweighs the economic advantages of living elsewhere. If leisure activities are the locus of self-identity and makers are the leaders of creative self-expression, it only makes sense that they would want to remain close to a variety of specialized consumer entertainment options. The makers of today are the artists and arts professionals of previous generations who moved into a succession of New York neighborhoods in the twentieth century, easing and/or abetting the transition of these neighborhoods to gentrified, middle-class, leisure-oriented locales. Gentrification tends to usher in this symbolic turn from labor to leisure, and the symbolism is particularly poignant in formerly industrial areas like SoHo. In this chapter, I will explore a trajectory of artist-led gentrification after World War II, beginning with SoHo, in order to build precedent for and point to the differences within the rapid gentrification of the Morgantown area of Brooklyn. The conversion of professional, industrial tools from implements of production to manifestations of consumption, as described on the preceding pages, begins with gentrifying industrial architecture. The industrial buildings of SoHo and Morgantown were tools designed for productive activity. In SoHo, the first manufacturing area of New York to be gentrified by artists, the combined powers of the city government, private real estate, and grassroots neighborhood activism brought about the conversion of loft buildings for residential use. This residential dwelling and the ensuing vogue for loft living facilitated the conversion of these structures into sites of consumption.[8]

In the 1980s and '90s, when Sharon Zukin published *Loft Living*, an ethnographic analysis of gentrification in SoHo, or when geographer Neil Smith published his work on gentrification of the Lower East Side, urban change was mostly affecting centrally located neighborhoods within the city.[9] In both these neighborhoods, gentrification has been explicitly linked to the influx of artists and arts organizations. Since that time, the process of artist-led gentrification has accelerated markedly. It would have been hard to predict that the interceding twenty years would see artist-led urban change extend to the far eastern border of northern Brooklyn and beyond into Ridgewood, Queens. The "frontier" of gentrification theorized by Smith continues to push further and further out along the L line on the subway.[10] The following analysis investigates the ways in which Morgantown mirrors the system of development proposed by these two scholars in SoHo and the Lower East Side as well as that of Richard Lloyd in the Wicker Park neighborhood of Chicago.[11] These scholars investigated their respective neighborhoods during the decades in which each was undergoing rapid gentrification and, while there are many similarities to the development of Morgantown in the first decade of the twenty-first century, the Maker Movement and its attendant implications on leisure consumption of production has facilitated a change in attitude for the young people moving into the area.

By the 1980s, artists hoping to live and work in the large-scale industrial spaces of SoHo found that the neighborhood was no longer affordable, and Williamsburg's industrial waterfront provided an enticing alternative. Only one stop across the river from the 1st Avenue L subway stop, Williamsburg was a convenient option for those that required larger working spaces. Industrial rentals were cheap and plentiful and the location was close enough to Manhattan via the subway that it became a convenient retreat from the modern city into a "land that time forgot."[12] Williamsburg's art scene was small and close-knit in the 1990s. Although the neighborhood was already gaining buzz by 1992, the artists living there were happy to be "protected by the river and the recession," claiming that Manhattanites were largely unaware of the burgeoning artistic community.[13] The subcultural aspect of the neighborhood in the '90s is encapsulated in *The Williamsburg Timeline* (2002), created by artist Ward Shelley. The timeline marks the years 1990–1995 as "The Golden Age" of the neighborhood and charts the rise and fall of art galleries and hangouts such as Four Walls, the Green Room, the Fly Trap, Teddy's, the Cat's Head, and Keep Refrigerated. By 2003, *The New York Times* was declaring that Williamsburg had "lost its cool" and residents were moving onto greener pastures (in some cases the same pastures abandoned by the avant-garde of gentrification ten years earlier: the East Village).[14]

After the turn of the millennium, remaining artists in the neighborhood saw a marked increase in interest in Williamsburg property. Those oblivious Manhattanites of ten years earlier had finally woken up to the appeal of the area. Unfortunately for any remaining bohemians looking for affordable live/work spaces, Mayor Michael Bloomberg and the city's real estate developers were eager to take advantage of Williamsburg's hip connotations lovingly cultivated by artists and hipsters in the 1990s. In 2005, Bloomberg sealed the neighborhood's fate in initiating the rezoning of the waterfront area, paving the way for the luxury condominium high-rises that now face Manhattan across the river.[15] The artistic community there faced similar problems to those experienced by their forebears in the Lower East Side and SoHo: evictions, rent increases, the insecurity of illegally occupying buildings, and, finally, the influx of young urban professionals.[16] With the knowledge of these neighborhoods fresh in their minds, artists who settled in Morgantown a short while later came with a different attitude toward building their environment. These early residents did not disillusion themselves with utopian idealism because they now knew exactly where the neighborhood would be heading with or without their help.

From Williamsburg in the late 1990s, the frontlines of gentrification marched down the L through East Williamsburg (and Morgantown) and down into Bushwick. The name "East Williamsburg," contrary to popular myth, predates gentrification of the area. There is, in fact, a widespread misconception that calling the area *East* Williamsburg is a developer's ploy to associate it with its fully "revitalized" neighbor, so most residents of Morgantown prefer to call their neighborhood Bushwick (although Flushing Avenue is traditionally Bushwick's northern border).[17] Since 2012, the development that follows the path of the L has picked up pace considerably, extending into the far reaches of Bushwick, past the DeKalb and Myrtle-Wyckoff stops and down to Halsey. Seeping over the edges into neighboring Ridgewood, the stream of young, mostly white, creatively inclined residents continues to overflow into each successive area down the line. By 2013 the frontline of gentrification reached the edges of the vast swath of real estate between Brooklyn and Queens occupied by the dead. The spread outward along the cemetery boundary is rapidly joining up with the slower but nevertheless persistent eastward spread of gentrification through Bedford-Stuyvesant. In November 2013, Houdini Kitchen Laboratory opened at 1563 Decatur Street in Ridgewood, named after the famous magician buried in the adjacent cemetery. Houdini's is about as far from the nearby neighborhood Little Caesars carryout counter as one could image. While Little Caesars offered five-dollar pre-frozen pizzas, Houdini's, located in a converted loft building, served upscale, artisanal brick oven pizza with obscure ingredients alongside pricey imported drinks in an area still largely isolated from other leisure and entertainment activities.

Seeking The Authentic and The Real: Artists As Gentrifiers

There are a number of broad generalizations and trends that emerge during the long and complicated history of artist spaces, residences, and galleries in urban environments: artists seek out large, cheap spaces; they often settle in areas that are racially, ethnically and economically different from their own upbringings or education levels; and artistic activity changes the nature of business in the neighborhoods in which they reside. While it is tempting to attribute these trends purely to economics, i.e. artists are financially constrained and so seek out inexpensive urban territory, there is a very strong symbolic element to artist colonization of city neighborhoods. Artists, like other gentrifiers, play into the frontier mythology described by Neil Smith in relation to SoHo and the East Village, where gentrifiers are recast as outlaws of the Wild West or pioneering adventurers, beating back the savage wilderness.[18] While artists may strongly object to this characterization, the sense of danger and otherness that artists embrace within poor and disinvested neighborhoods becomes part of the artists' rebellious self-identity and an expression of their adventurous, creative spirit.

The romanticized notion of the frontier for gentrifiers in urban areas had previously played out in the frontier mythology of countercultural communalists in the late 1960s and '70s. Fred Turner writes:

Married to the frontier rhetoric of "cowboys and Indians," systems theory offered *Whole Earth* readers a way to link their countercultural attempts to transform themselves and their communities to the trajectory of American myth. Like its New Communalist audience, the *Catalog* celebrated small-scale technologies – and again, itself – as ways for individuals to improve their lives. But it also offered up those tools – and itself – as prototypes of a new relationship between the individual, information, and technology.[19]

The *Whole Earth Catalog* was, thus, the nexus of an alternative consumerist identity for the communalists, who saw themselves as heroic individuals forging a new society. Similarly, urban pioneers from the 1980s to today have been building their own alternative consumerist activities in a series of disinvested neighborhoods in formerly industrial urban areas. The reactions of the existing residents – often ethnic minorities – in the rural areas where the counterculture's communes took root mirror those of the residents in gentrifying urban areas: they were furious at the rising property costs brought about by the presence of affluent white people playing out fantasies of alternative consumption.[20] Many of the values and desires of "hipsters" in neighborhoods like Morgantown are not so different from those of the counterculture, but they diverge from the counterculture in that they have developed a heightened sense of entrepreneurship, aided by the growth of social media, personalized computing technology, and new Maker Movement production tools.

Starting in the 1970s, David Ley saw the process of urban renewal as an outgrowth of hippie idealism that sought, unsuccessfully, to promote a socially progressive form of urban development in city centers.[21] Artists' attraction to poor, disinvested neighborhoods, according to Ley, lies in these neighborhoods' conceptual distance from the homogeneity of middle-class life and the "disciplined convention of the organisation man."[22] Richard Lloyd builds on the idea that artists seek out poor neighborhoods as a symbolic escape from conformity and homogeneity. In his study of the Wicker Park neighborhood in Chicago in the 1990s, Lloyd adds nuance to the long-standing truism that the existence of plentiful, cheap space was sufficient enough explanation for artistic activity in disinvested or poor neighborhoods, and charts the aesthetic appeal of the impoverished Wicker Park neighborhood that, in the 1980s and '90s, lacked the creeping corporate homogeneity found in other parts of the city and suburbs. He focuses on the symbolic significance of these neighborhoods and their incumbent grit and danger, saying, "Young artists frame elements of the local landscape that many would find alarming as instead being symbolic amenities."[23] These symbolic amenities include proximity to crime, disinvestment and urban decay.

Rosalyn Deutsch and Cara Gendel Ryan, who wrote one of the earliest critical assessments of the art world's role in gentrification of the East Village, describe a number of Lloyd's "symbolic amenities" in the art scene of the 1980s and the ways in which urban decay goes through a process of aestheticization in art production. One poignant example they provide is the homeless "bum" who becomes the unwitting subject of fine art photography. They state, "In the image of the bum, the problems of the homeless poor, existing on all sides of the East Village art scene, are mythologized, exploited, and finally ignored. Once the poor become aestheticized, poverty itself moves out of our field of vision."[24] Street art and graffiti likewise underwent a

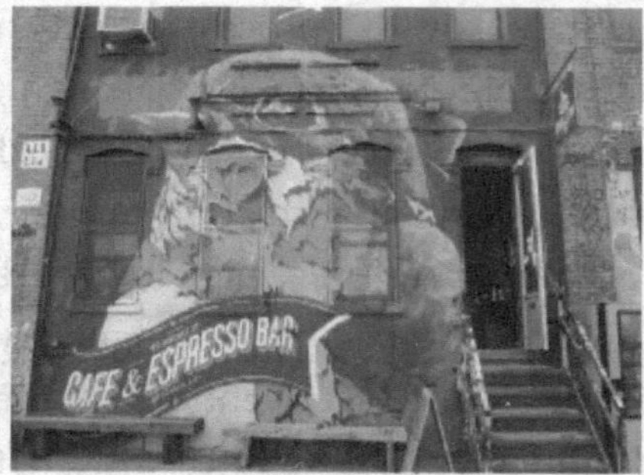

process of domestication by the commercial art world in the 1980s. What was once the marker of an antisocial and continually frustrated underclass suddenly became the aesthetic of a cool, rebellious new avant-garde.

The question of visibility between classes within gentrifying neighborhoods is complicated in a number of ways in Morgantown. In a movement that echoed the art world in the

1980s, the symbolic amenities of decay were not eradicated but rather domesticated. Graffiti and tags that arise out of spontaneous, illegal or unwelcomed intrusions onto private property disappear in favor of commissioned work on storefronts by hired local graffiti artists. There are numerous examples of this in both Morgantown and Bushwick, including the "professional" graffiti murals on the Swallow Café at 49 Bogart Street and the graffiti adorning the area around the Jefferson subway stop.

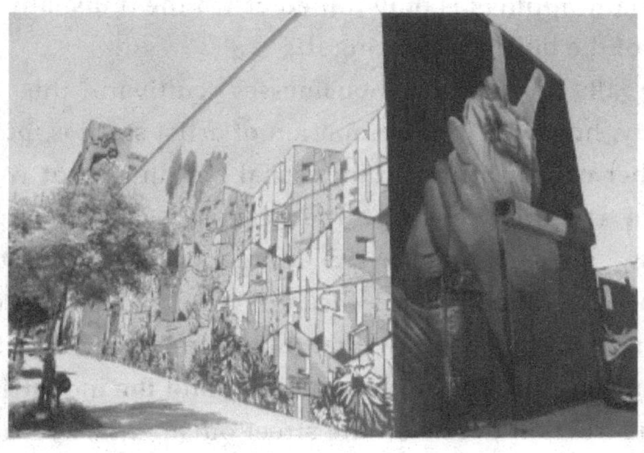

In the East Village, visibility between classes was curtailed during the gentrification process. A *Wall Street Journal* article that describes how, "Frosted glass windows protect diners from the sight of the burned out tenements across the street as they nibble their $18 loins of veal."[25] This chimes in many ways with the vogue for signage-free cafés and bars in Morgantown and Bushwick. Fair Weather Bushwick at 274 Wyckoff Ave. and the Owl Juice Pub at 48 Wyckoff Ave. both described their lack of signage as a way to cultivate a "cool" and "mysterious" allure to their establishments.[26] Many Morgantown establishments were similarly unadvertised: The Narrows at 1037 Flushing Ave. only added a vintage-style neon sign advertising "Cocktails" outside its anonymous black frontage several years after it first opened in 2010 and Roberta's at 261 Moore Street, despite the presence of a small sign, is notoriously difficult to happen upon, tucked around a corner in a unadorned, anonymous shed. The exclusivity and invisibility cultivated at these bars and restaurants follow the lead of commercial art galleries, which have long occupied spaces devoid of signage and are often accessible only via ringing a doorbell or making an appointment. Blue-chip Chelsea gallery Luhring Augustine's outpost in Morgantown is a noteworthy example in the neighborhood. The gallery behind its blank industrial trappings is only hinted at via the unusually pristine façade of the building housing it.

Not all Morgantown businesses cultivate this lack of visibility, however. The occupation of artist studios, businesses and other organizations in industrial buildings that were once daylight factories celebrate the aesthetics of the large glass window. Fitzcarraldo at 195 Morgan Ave., occupying the building that once housed the 3rd Ward maker space, has a large street-facing window that allows an integration between the luxurious interior of the restaurant and the industrial sheds and construction debris on the street outside. The occupants of these buildings can soak up the ambiance of the aestheticized industrial surroundings while in the comfort of the cozy restaurant. Similarly, Newtown café at 55 Waterbury Street has set up outdoor seating in front of its windowed exterior, where patrons can eat vegan and vegetarian food amidst the roughness of the working warehouses, potholes, and shattered glass on the streets. Unlike the aforementioned East Village establishment that tried to block out the roughness of its surroundings, some Morgantown locations have embraced the aesthetic attraction of the neighborhood.

Early residents of Morgantown, like those of Wicker Park, were attracted to the rawness and danger of the area, recalling these grittier elements with retrospective pride. Torben Giehler describes packs of feral dogs roaming the streets while a friend of his, Jeffrey Reed, speaks of its general emptiness and sense of abandonment, saying, "If you saw someone, you would start walking the other way. You just assumed there wasn't any reason that anyone would be there."[27] The sentiment sounds eerily similar to sentiments expressed by the first artists to inhabit SoHo in the late 1950s/early '60s, before a cohesive artist community had formed there. The minimalist artist Carl Andre spoke of: "SoHo being known as 'Hell's 100 Acres,' with those who lived there crossing the street to avoid contact with anyone who happened to be out and about, out of respect for the urban wilderness they had each sought out."[28] In 1959, SoHo did not yet have any of the trappings, the bars, restaurants, and nightlife it would later develop.[29] Leisure had not yet acquired a firm foothold in the neighborhood, and SoHo was still a rather inhospitable place for residential dwelling due to its remoteness from everyday amenities. The feeling that there was an anarchic lack of oversight in SoHo was mirrored in Morgantown forty years later. Early residents of Morgantown relate stories of a desolate area where they could set off fireworks from the rooftops without a single police officer or fireman taking note, where cars were regularly disposed of and set on fire in the streets, and where buildings were often inhabited only by crack addicts and drifters.

In the '90s, the death knell of Wicker Park's frontier status in Chicago was the arrival of a Starbucks coffee chain.[30] Urban change in Morgantown has not come in the shape of a Starbucks. In fact, chain stores no longer seem to be the ultimate harbingers of gentrification, as they were in the '90s. In two other fully gentrified areas of Brooklyn, Williamsburg's main shopping street, Bedford Avenue, and Park Slope's Fifth Avenue, the businesses are almost exclusively boutique stores and gourmet independent cafés and restaurants. It is only primarily in un-gentrified neighborhoods that one finds big corporate chains now. Morgantown's gentrification is embodied in high-end restaurants like Blanca (261 Moore St.) and Momo Sushi Shack (43 Bogart St.) and coffee shops like Swallow Café (49 Bogart St.). The introduction of Luhring Augustine (25 Knickerbocker Ave.) to the neighborhood in 2012 brought more than a few luxury vehicles with tinted windows into the area, whose presence was welcomed by increasingly upper class options for dining and shopping.[31]

The obsession with "the end" of gentrifying neighborhoods reflects residents' desire for a utopian bohemia.[32] Richard Lloyd suggests that this utopian bohemia may never have existed at all, even though residents often reference the "good old days" when things were better, cooler, and more edgy. Lloyd writes:

What is the source of this structural nostalgia? It is not reducible to the life course trajectories of participants, confusing lost youth with lost bohemia. Since it recurs incessantly, bohemia dying a thousand deaths, it cannot be only the product of some objective change, like the closing of Urbus Orbis [a neighborhood independent coffee shop in Wicker Park] or the opening of Starbucks. Rather, bohemia is always over because it always already falls short of its adherents' fantasies of social autonomy, expressed in the vaunted ideology of art pour l'art.[33]

While Morgantown residents have, to some extent, campaigned against the introduction of corporate chains into the fabric of the neighborhood, the anti-chain attitude is, in many ways, a leftover concern from a previous era. Evidence suggests that the process of gentrification still occurs in the wake of boutiques and smaller independent businesses. The concern over chains grows out of a larger desire for authenticity and the "real" that gentrifiers hoped to escape in other wealthier parts of the city or the suburbs.[34] Even though independently-run businesses contribute to gentrification, they are deemed acceptable (and even desirable) to residents of places like Morgantown because they maintain a semblance of authenticity and individuality without sacrificing middle-class consumer desires. The connection between autonomous living and autonomous art feeds into the larger ethos of self-fulfillment and creative expression found in gentrifying areas.

The fusion of neoliberalism and the art world came to fruition in the East Village in the 1980s, and Craig Owens was one of the first critical voices to address the complicity between developers and artists. He saw the development of the East Village art scene as "the surrender, by the East Village artist-entrepreneurs, to the means-end rationality of the marketplace."[35] The maker is the natural successor of these early "artist-entrepreneurs." Deutsch and Ryan realized that the art world had provided an aesthetic manifestation of the ideological shift towards neoliberalism with the Neo-Expressionist painting being made in the East Village in the 1980s.[36] The neoliberal overhaul of artistic practice in Morgantown has seemingly abolished the term "artist" entirely, conferring the hopes and dreams of personal self-fulfillment to the consumption patterns and start-up-driven practices of the Maker Movement.

Joining others in the art world concerned about the rapid gentrification of the East Village in the 1980s, artist Martha Rosler addressed the issue of homelessness in her work *If You Lived Here You'd Be Home* (1989). The work consisted of activist and archival materials and a community space in which to discuss the issues around housing, homelessness, and urban planning in New York City. She partnered with activists, the homeless themselves, and the art community, for the exhibition of this work at the Dia Art Foundation. With its community-based format, the piece reflected a Baby-Boomer-era idealism no longer in vogue in Neo-Expressionist-dominated galleries. It also foreshadowed, however, the subsequent "socially engaged" practices of a younger generation of artists in the 1990s/2000s. Rosler has written about and lectured on the subject of neoliberalism and gentrification in urban spaces in the intervening decades. She argues, often referencing Zukin, that cities are becoming more homogenous and losing local flavor, which she associates with working class neighborhoods, stating:

> As the vibrancy of interclass contention has been quelled by the damping off of working-class politics, a sanitized version of an industrial urban experience (or some image of one) can be marketed to the incoming middle class, who have the means and the willingness to pay for what was formerly a set of indigenous strategies of survival, of a *way of life*.[37]

The opposition of "indigenous" versus global is a problematic way of localizing and naturalizing the disappearing industrial working class within the fabric of the city. Echoes of the noble savage emerge: the implication is that the working class had such a *simple, pure* way of life. This simple life was certainly not a choice divorced from the flows of capital. The "indigenous," those rooted to a limited locale, are undervalued in global capitalism precisely because they lack mobility, or the ability to circulate.

Rosler also addresses the ludic nature of contemporary urban dwelling. She sees the ascendant leisure city as an assimilation of formerly suburban values, saying, "To point out the obvious, the stultifying, homogeneous experience of life in the suburbs, with its identical malls and fast-food joints, doesn't offer the would-be creative much in the way of identity formation; and insofar as the local exists today, it is found either in the city or in rural small towns, not in fenced-in suburbia."[38] For Rosler, the local, that which does not participate in a homogenized capitalist sphere, carries a mark of authenticity. It is, however, rather absurd that American artists who grew up in middle-class suburbs need to discover their identities in places that are completely unfamiliar to them. The popular youthful conviction that suburbia, with its strip malls and chain stores, produces a whole class of people without any kind of identity or individuality has become accepted doctrine among urban dwellers. While the ethnic or working class character of neighborhoods may appear unique and individuated, its appearance reflects the continuous flow of immigrant and migrant labor to the city over the course of modern history. The residents of these neighborhoods may have limited circulating abilities or choices due to their unfavorable economic position, but they nevertheless participate in a globalized economy, albeit one that seems alien to the American middle and upper classes. Identifying these areas as those with "local" and therefore authentic character only fetishizes the ways in which communities are segregated, for a variety of reasons, from the larger urban economy.

The media backlash against the millennial generation, who are seen as coddled, overgrown children unable to face adult realities, constantly searching for self-fulfillment rather than a decent job, acquires a modicum of veracity when the city is viewed as a ludic space. Like children playing house on a grand scale, first-wave gentrifiers (of multiple generations) chase an authentic existence through inhabiting the roles (and houses) of ethnic and working class people, whose separation/exclusion from mainstream middle-class consumption stems from reasons other than entertainment or fashion. These playful adult children – the poseurs and pretenders often derided as hipsters – are thus tragically locked in a vicious circle of ever-increasing levels of artifice and posturing as they chase a local-ness that constantly slips through their fingers. The role or pose that is most often celebrated by leftists and anti-globalist commentators is that of the manufacturing working class, which has been a nearly continuous source of nostalgia since the 1960s.

As a result of his study of SoHo published in 1987, James R. Hudson argues that artists were attracted to the area because of an identification with blue-collar workers. He writes:

> SoHo was not simply a place with cheap, large spaces that
> could be converted into artists' studios at minimal expense.
> SoHo was a blue-collar manufacturing area: an industrial
> section of the city where the streets were crowded daily with
> trucks and workers. This was a place where hard work was
> done and respected. Artistic production requires intensive
> labor, and there was a recognition by the blue-collar workers
> that artists did hard work, even if they worked odd hours.
> There was no distinctions made by those who worked in
> SoHo based upon social status or occupation – at least among
> those who "toiled."[39]

Hudson details the ways in which various manufacturing outfits such as print shops and welding companies in SoHo were utilized by artists who had branched out into nontraditional artistic materials during this period. Not only were artists utilizing these nontraditional materials, they were actively reimagining themselves as members of the industrial working class that was rapidly disappearing from American life. They were "playing" at being laborers, wearing their clothes, using their tools, and working in their former places of employment. Artist's identification with the worker became a major theme during this era, particularly in the work of Frank Stella in the late 1950s.[40]

By the early 2000s, however, both local manufacturers and artists were savvy about how the story of Morgantown's gentrification was likely to end. While maker culture proponents see themselves and define themselves in terms of their ability to do in-house DIY industrial production, the "culture" is *not* a blue-collar one. Instead, makers see themselves as extensions of the creative labor force described by Richard Florida in his book *The Rise of the Creative Class*, first published in 2000.

While writers like Florida seem to enjoy citing Karl Marx, they do so to assert that the working class is now irrelevant in the new maker economy. Florida writes, "Karl Marx had it more than partly right when he foresaw that workers would someday control the means of production... If workers control the means of production today that is because it is inside their own heads; they *are* the means of production."[41] Chris Anderson also cites Marx in his book on maker culture, saying, "If Karl Marx were here today, his jaw would be on the floor. Talk about 'controlling the tools of production': you (you!) can now set factories into motion with a mouse click."[42] The impulse to wish away the working class or, perhaps worse, to condescend to the economically disadvantaged by telling them that all they need to do is "tap into their creativity" is one of the most problematic facets of makerism. Similar to the old American Dream myth where hard work is rewarded by wealth and success, the new maker Creative American Dream promises wealth and success to anyone who can harness this latent creative potential and self-expression.

When asked about how he related to his manufacturing neighbors in Morgantown, Jason Goodman, maker-evangelist and founder of the now defunct co-working space 3rd Ward, related the following story in an interview:

> ... once there was a particular neighbor who really was freaked out, culturally. I didn't know who it was. Every single day the Fire Department was showing up – even when we were open for business during daytime... I finally figured out who it was and I confronted him. I said, "What's the problem?" He literally was like, "I don't want you in this neighborhood. This is for us to do manufacturing, and we don't want you coming here and changing it." [I said] "Well, you don't know what we do. We do manufacturing. We provide shop space for people who make things, and have on demand production

facilities." They were sort of getting it, and then they're like "Okay, cool. Sorry."[43]

The key to Goodman's story is his recognition that blue-collar manufacturing in the area was "culturally" different from his maker operation. Artists in SoHo sought kinship with a blue-collar manner of production and blue-collar workers seemed to, in turn, accept artists working in the area, even if the artists' attraction to working class aesthetics was somewhat fetishistic. Makers in Morgantown like Goodman, on the other hand, placed themselves on a level of sophistication above their neighbors. Even though they are quick to promote the idea that they are, in fact, doing manufacturing, it is always with the subtext that they are doing it *much better*.

The Blame Game

Commentary on gentrification usually pursues its underlying causes in order to assign blame and isolate the entities responsible for overthrowing the existing social construction of a neighborhood. Artists sit in an ambiguous position in this scheme, whereas real estate developers are seen as a universal evil. Sharon Zukin's critique of gentrification in SoHo blamed government funding of the arts, as well as government incentives and subsidies in real estate development, for the residential conversion of the neighborhood. She also lays a good deal of onus on an anti-blue collar and anti-industrial "patrician" class in New York who, she argues, had been plotting SoHo's demise for decades.[44] For Neil Smith, looking at the Lower East Side of New York, it was developers who disinvested and devalued land and property in order to poach it and pump it for value later on, working together with the full complicity of artists and arts organizations in the neighborhood.[45] Richard Lloyd pinpoints the twin forces of marketing and branding – the ad execs and digital design agencies as well as restaurateurs and talent scouts

– as driving forces in the gentrification of Wicker Park in Chicago in the 1990s.[46]

Looking at Morgantown, it seems that the creative residents themselves have seized the opportunity to gentrify the area in a manner they have some modicum of control over, not in fully dependent complicity with real estate developers but as somewhat autonomous agents. Zukin describes a catch-22 situation where residents in SoHo were stuck between wanting things to remain as they were in the neighborhood and wanting the right to live in their buildings residentially.[47] Certainly there have been outside forces that have set up shop in Morgantown, but, for the most part, the change and development came, rather unusually, from within. If it was not the young, middle-class creative types (hipsters) who set up the businesses in the neighborhood, then it was, surprisingly in the narrative of gentrification, previously marginalized ethnic groups that capitalized on development. Like artists, these marginalized groups were well acquainted with the narrative of gentrification in New York City. Members of conservative sects of Judaism, long self-segregated in isolated communities in South Williamsburg, Crown Heights, and other pockets of Brooklyn, own much of the building stock in the area and have been responsible for renovations aimed at attracting a wealthier rental base. Additionally, Latino residents of the area have participated in its gentrification by starting hipster-oriented businesses such as the aforementioned Owl Juice Pub and Arepera Guacuco at 44 Irving Ave. in the spillover gentrification throughout Bushwick.[48]

This would seem to paint a rather rosy picture of gentrification: suddenly everyone gets to share in the benefits and no one is unduly pushed out of the neighborhood, but this would be a vast overstatement. The fact remains that prices are rising and it is only the middle classes who are able to remain and who patronize the new businesses that are set up. Landlords, eager to charge market rates for apartment rentals, are still using questionable tactics to extract undesirable tenants from the homes they may have occupied for decades.[49] The future remains somewhat in doubt, but it is clear that the Maker Movement is more compatible with (or at least makes less of an effort to oppose) gentrification than the left-wing artistic avant-garde groups of the past.

In 1995 Richard Barbrook and Andy Cameron wrote their seminal essay "The Californian Ideology," announcing the end of the digital utopia on the Internet just as it began. As access to the World Wide Web grew steadily in the early '90s, many of the small, tightly-knit communities that developed online saw the potential for some sort of digital commune where sharing and horizontality (rather than hierarchy) were easily achieved. Twenty years later the meaning of the word "sharing" has been transformed into the "sharing economy," a corporate code word for an unregulated peer-to-peer service industry facilitated by smart phone apps. These services provide apartment sharing (Airbnb), ride/car sharing (Uber, Lyft, Zipcar), and the more longstanding sharing embodied in social media like Twitter, Facebook, Instagram, Vine, etc. Barbrook and Cameron realized, almost immediately, that the freedom facilitated by the Internet was not the freedom of equal or democratic participation but rather freedom of capitalist markets. Drawing a (now well-established) line between late-'60s counterculture values and the rise of the tech industry on the West Coast, they argue that, "With McLuhan as its patron saint, the Californian Ideology has emerged from an unexpected collision of right-wing neoliberalism, counterculture radicalism and technological determinism – a hybrid ideology with all its ambiguities and contradictions intact."[50]

The Maker Movement, an outgrowth of the same subcultures of hacking and technological experimentation that feed Silicon Valley tech companies, has been, from its inception, part of the Californian Ideology. Barbrook and Cameron pinpoint the tech magazine *Wired* as a powerful mouthpiece for neoliberal techno-evangelism.[51] It is no surprise, then, that Chris Anderson, who wrote one of the most celebratory books on the Maker Movement, was editor at *Wired* during Web 2.0's formative years between 2001 and 2012 before leaving to run a robotics start-up.[52] The Maker Movement sprang from within the tech industry, and the maker is the embodiment of the artist-entrepreneur. The language of the tech industry has, therefore, not only invaded the language of art practice but also the way art professionals address the urban environment they inhabit.

In early December 2014, Galapagos Art Space, which began in Williamsburg in 1995 before moving to DUMBO in 2007, announced it would be relocating to Detroit. Director Robert Elmes blamed their hasty departure on rising rents and encouraged others to join in the exodus, issuing the warning that "it's no longer a crisis, it's a conclusion."[53] With urban centers like New York City becoming increasingly expensive, the zeitgeist in the art world is firmly oriented toward bankrupted Detroit. Galapagos is just one of many national and international art world organizations interested in Detroit as an industrial relic ripe for bohemian colonization. Rosler sees the recent interest in Detroit as proportional to its former glory in industrial production, stating, " [...] most art-world projects centering on decaying places like Detroit are melancholic monuments to capital, in the sense of depicting both the devastation left in the absence but also the politics it provoked [...] mourning Detroit is a gesture that simultaneously evidences one's social conscience and testifies to its absolute impotence."[54] In another statement on Galapagos' decision to move, Elmes explains, "What it's gaining is artists, and what artists are finding in Detroit is opportunity, and other early adopters making community and working on their particular dream."[55] The term "early adopters" comes straight from the world of digital technology. Traditionally, early adopters were the beta testers who would pick up a new piece of technology before it had gained a critical mass of users. In a way, early adopters are the scouts or pioneers of technology. This terminology, transplanted to the urban environment, has exactly the same ethos as "urban settler" or "urban pioneer." Rather than the urban jungle or the Wild West, the city is yet another piece of technology to be "disrupted."[56]

Loft Living

Sharon Zukin's book *Loft Living* describes a fusion of bohemian and bourgeois culture that David Brooks would later label "bobo," a new manifestation of the middle class that arose in the latter half of the twentieth century where bohemian values are assimilated into capitalist consumption.[57] Like Barbrook and Cameron before him, Brooks' playful yet celebratory book, *Bobos in Paradise*, finds that the mixing of counterculture radicalism and neoliberal (or bourgeois) politics have produced a powerful social hybrid. Zukin's analysis of SoHo was truly groundbreaking in identifying and tracing the changing values of those most prone to gentrify neighborhoods. The book is, however, often heavily nostalgic for a past industrial order and urban working class, resulting in oversimplification of oppositional forces within the city. Zukin argues that there was a concerted effort and long-term plan to deindustrialize city centers, repeatedly implying that a unification of government forces and "patrician" elite of the city consciously conspired to eradicate industrial manufacturing throughout the twentieth century. No explanation is given as to why city elites may have wanted so desperately to remake the urban fabric. Other factors that may have come into play such as increasingly globalized markets with access to foreign labor, Cold War politics and the threat of nuclear attack after the Second World War, and urbanist rhetoric around light, air and open space (which denounced toxic industrial works in city centers or near residential dwellings) are left unaddressed. Nevertheless, Zukin makes a compelling case for the rebranding of artists as productive members of the workforce after their instrumentalization in the WPA projects of the 1930s. She states, "Far more significant was the regularization of their employment *as artists*, which enabled them for the first time in history to make a living off a totally self-defined art. The state played a crucial role in this transformation."[58] Zukin describes the ways in which "artist" is suddenly a viable middle-class career choice in the 1960s. As the market for contemporary art expands, artists become college-educated professionals with the potential to live off of their autonomous artistic creation.[59]

The main difference, then, between Zukin's assessment of SoHo and the urban change happening in Morgantown is the presence of government intervention. Zukin sees government intervention as instrumental in changing the nature of artists' work – from something that is about producing for a client or potential buyer to something that is essentially only about self-actualization and freedom of creation. Describing the sudden vogue for production-as-hobby, she states, "the arts-and-crafts movement of the 1970s also shows how deeply art has been incorporated into many middle-class patterns of consumption."[60] This emphasis on craft is an important precursor to the Maker Movement, and Zukin laments the fact that production is taken over by the middle class as hobby and lifestyle. One of the more telling examples she provides is how loft residents began to implement "professional" kitchen equipment into their residential space, solidifying this fusion of consumption of formerly productive domains.[61] This trend in professionalization of equipment for hobby or leisure purposes continued unabated since the time the book was published in 1982. As noted, we have seen increasing numbers of professional tools made into consumer products over the years, and the Maker Movement has introduced even more professional tools for consumers. It is almost as if the Arts and Crafts movement from the nineteenth century has come full circle, without the limitations that movement had due to its nostalgia for pre-modern methods of production. Makers claim the ability to work from home, control their production process, *and* compete in the open market.[62]

The transformation of SoHo from an industrial center to a residential area laid the legal groundwork in the city of New York for A.I.R. (artist in residence) spaces in Morgantown and protection by the Loft Law (Multiple Dwelling Law Article 7-C).[63] While at least one high profile site in the southern portion of Bushwick, the Rheingold Brewery, has attracted protesters, the vast majority of businesses in Morgantown are owned and operated by smaller independent entities and landlords remain in the background.[64] No one seems to have much interest in tearing down the old buildings. Zukin discusses, at length, the process by which older housing stock is aestheticized. A combination of modernist nostalgia and a phenomenon she calls AMP (Artistic Mode of Production) come together to save older buildings that would have previously been knocked down (and were perhaps less expensive for developers to tear down rather than renovate).[65] The crux of Zukin's AMP is focused on so-called "non-productive" activity (i.e. residential homes instead of light manufacturing).[66]

Zukin also addresses the role of artists in gentrifying neighborhoods, and has incurred the wrath of at least one former SoHo resident in her assessment of artist inhabitation of the area.[67] Foreshadowing Neil Smith, she argues that gentrifiers are positioned by bourgeois culture as urban outlaws who tame a wild, dangerous territory. Arguing against this characterization, she states:

> ... that is mythology, not urban history. It only makes sense to the urban ecologist or the arts constituency. An ecologist finds in it proof of an ineluctable competition over territory, particularly when one side in this competition can pay market rents. A member of the arts constituency finds it a satisfying

demonstration that though the artist seems to have achieved a new social status as hero, he or she is really still relegated to the position of society's victim. Neither version, however, can account for two apparent contradictions in the way the loft market was formed. On the one hand, loft living began as a "marginal" phenomenon, but in time it became chic. On the other hand, artists who moved into lofts were "powerless," yet they managed to win access to contested urban space.[68]

The "winning" of contested space was manifest in artist-formed co-ops. For example, Fluxus figurehead George Maciunas was one of the first to see the advantage of buying up cheap loft space in SoHo, starting a number of co-ops for artists in the neighborhood.[69] Zukin also describes how wealthy arts patrons like the Kaplan family supported artists by helping them found co-op spaces.[70] This utopian solution, however, did not help artists maintain their position in the neighborhood for long, and it remains to be seen if the alternative, more market-driven model in Morgantown will eventually force makers out of the area as well. A concerted effort to keep working spaces operating in Morgantown is underway, although the high profile closing of 3rd Ward certainly put a damper on the prospect of maintaining the maker culture of the neighborhood. Unlike SoHo, however, the downfall of 3rd Ward can be attributed primarily to overstretched entrepreneurship rather than outside forces of displacement intervening.

Building on Richard Lloyd's writing, the comparison between Wicker Park in Chicago and Morgantown provides many additional insights into the formation of the Maker Movement. Lloyd argues that the "end" of Wicker Park as a bohemian neighborhood is due to forces from outside the neighborhood capitalizing on the bohemian ethos cultivated by Wicker Park artists. He blames "industry scouts and digital designers" for changing the neighborhood, who were drawn to the aesthetic of the urban frontier.[71] Lloyd also blames the gentrification of Wicker Park on rising press publicity from newspaper journalists and an influx of music producers poaching artists of the area.[72] He notes that, "As I discovered during my years in Wicker Park, the contemporary bohemia constituted there was routinely mined for profit."[73] Lloyd identifies the rise of advertising and digital design agencies in the neighborhood as the driving forces of gentrification in the area. These advertising jobs produced jobs for artists or the artistically inclined and, in turn, fed the rise of the boutique design sector in Wicker Park.[74]

Nostalgia, as noted, figured prominently into the gentrification of SoHo and continues its symbolic importance in Morgantown. Zukin argues, "The changing appreciation of old loft buildings also reflects a deeper preoccupation with space and time. A sense that the great industrial age has ended creates melancholy over the machines and the factories of the past. Certainly such sentiments are aroused only at the end of an era, or with a loss of function."[75] Zukin argues that the mass production of a previous era seems like individuality to those who sought to preserve SoHo's iron clad factory architecture, implying that this identification of originality in SoHo was the product of *mistaking* industrial mass-production for originality. I would argue that this nostalgic impulse has nothing to do with the particular mode of construction, whether the buildings are more "handcrafted" or prefabricated. Rather, the authenticity or the individuality of these older buildings derives from obsolescence of building techniques and the visible connection they bridge to the activity of industrial production. Zukin describes the quest for authenticity in these structures in a way that is quite obvious to us now. She says, "In a sense, loft living is part of a larger modern quest for authenticity. Old buildings and old neighborhoods are 'authentic' in a way that new construction and new communities are not… loft living rejects functionalism, Le Corbusier, and the severe idealism of form that modern architecture represents. As a style, it is respectful of social context."[76] It's not the rejection of functionalism in general but rather the rejection of previous manifestations of functionality that breeds this nostalgia. The idea of authenticity is not only tied to the history of the structure itself and its continued existence over time in the space of the city, but the attendant symbolic meaning of the space in terms of previous ways of life for people utilizing the building.

For SoHo's early artistic residents, there was a direct and immediate connection to the blue-collar modes of production that still, at least in some form, operated out of this section of Manhattan. It was clear this way of life was waning in the postwar years and artists, whether consciously or unconsciously, began to harvest the detritus of industrial life and take up residence as blue-collar workers in a factory district. While a variety of blue-collar outfits continue to operate out of Morgantown, including cement factories and a variety of warehouses and food processing plants, most of the young, middle-class, college-educated residents who moved into Morgantown have no proximate experience of blue-collar life. The buildings and surroundings evoke the image of the blue-collar worker, but, rather than translating this into artistic production, makers have circled production back again toward white-collar business. The image of industrial production has been integrated with white-collar work. The maker does not want to mime the lifestyle or activity of the blue-collar worker but rather create nothing short of the aforementioned "New Industrial Revolution" with the help of consumer grade production equipment programmed via computers rather than run manually.

Labor and Gentrification

The nature of labor in Wicker Park serves as an interesting point of comparison to Morgantown. Lloyd classifies the artistic residents as middle-class kids who reject bureaucratized "corporate" jobs in favor of minimum wage jobs in the service industry such as bartending and food service. He states, "The contemporary bohemia likewise involves ostensible resistance to the terms of bureaucratized, 'corporate' labor-force participation. Ironically, such resistance now contributes to the ready acceptance by educated intellectuals of manual-labor jobs in the post-Fordist entertainment industry."[77] Zukin also discusses how the creative service industry operates in SoHo, stating, "A large arts proletariat, for example, pays for its proximity to art markets by waiting on tables and working 'off the books.'... this is a laudable example of 'symbiosis,' but it really represents how the new AMP work force is exploited in a labor market that has been restructured around the low end of the service sector."[78] Lloyd goes deeper in his analysis of this service sector work, describing how service industry jobs become "cool jobs" for artistic people in the neighborhood, ostensibly allowing artists freedom to pursue their work without the responsibility of corporate salaried positions. The disadvantage of these jobs is that they place artists in insecure contingent labor conditions and often end up being so physically draining or time-consuming that they eventually eat away any ambition toward creative pursuits.

In Morgantown, the new "cool jobs" are the freelance gigs in various digital design fields that do not require regular hours in an office environment. The legions of young creatives working in Wi-Fi enabled coffee shops in Morgantown and elsewhere point to a new manifestation of labor for the young people living in this neighborhood. The autonomy promised by service industry jobs has been partially replaced by the autonomy perceived in working freelance.[79] Although Lloyd focuses on the service industry, particularly bartending in Wicker Park, the trend toward utilizing young, educated creative professionals in freelance labor in the digital sector was already beginning in Wicker Park in the late 1990s and early '00s. Lloyd states, "The small firms in the expanding media-design sector use local artists as flexible labor and draw upon the local ambiance of creative energy."[80] Lloyd identifies the motivation for harnessing these youthful artists as partly due to the lower salary expectation among the young, as opposed to older professionals.[81]

Young Morgantown freelancers, when asked about their conditions of labor, will vehemently deny any innuendo that they are being exploited as a labor pool.[82] Most of these makers profess, like Lloyd's bartenders, that they have more freedom this way and they would not have it any other way. Like Lloyd's bartenders, however, young freelancers or bloggers are quickly pulled into a full-time hustle for gigs in the course of their working lives. The need to continuously produce commercial work seems to take over any kind of autonomous creative production for many in Morgantown.

If Morgantown residents are engaged in immaterial labor that can take place anywhere, what is the advantage of congregating in a specific neighborhood? Richard Lloyd writes, "while creative labor may resist the routinization of the factory floor, it still occurs in actual places. The practical interactions in these Wicker Park venues shed light on how this 'complex machine' operates in concrete locales. Art and the artist's lifestyle are organizing principles, giving coherence to the local scene, but the new bohemia generates value in a wide variety of ways."[83] Lloyd suggests that the lifestyle traditionally associated with artists or bohemias, independent and autonomous yet insecure and unprotected, is perfectly compatible with liberalized economics. He writes, "The traditional do-it-yourself ethos of bohemia fits in well with the entrepreneurial imperative of neoliberal capitalism."[84] In turn, the tech industry has made neoliberal values cool for the millennial generation. Airbnb and Uber dominated the news in 2014 with their battles against government regulators.[85] Any attempt to compel tech start-ups to offer some sort of consumer protection are denounced as backward and anti-progressive. Uber and Airbnb, like other large, heavily financed tech companies, paint themselves as tiny start-ups, little guys facing the goliath of evil government, hell-bent on stamping out "innovation." The long history of both labor and consumer rights have been eroded by the rebranding of large corporations as cool rebels, taking up the bobo posture of anti-authoritarian bohemians rather than old-fashioned men in suits.

How is it, then, that the bohemian lifestyle became an attractive prospect to a broader range of people, particularly those in the neoliberal tech industry? Sharon Zukin writes that, prior to World War II, no one wanted to live a lifestyle "like an artist."[86] Richard Lloyd claims that, "Both the accessibility and the appeal of bohemian lifestyles increase with the postmodern extension of an aesthetic economy."[87] While the avant-garde and bohemian segments of society have historically been associated with leftist politics, anarchism and communism, Lloyd argues that the left-wing and bohemia do not, in fact, mix very well, stating, "Generally speaking, though, bohemianism is a poor match with conventional left-wing politics."[88] Indeed, one would be hard-pressed to find these traditional left-wing political beliefs among the makers in Morgantown, although artists and creatives still generally hold quite liberal, progressive values.[89]

Lloyd details the way in which Gen Xers were seen as work-averse slackers, due to the recession of the 1990s and lack of employment for young people.[90] This finds an almost identical parallel to young people today. After the financial collapse of 2008, many young people fresh out of college found that there were few permanent, full-time jobs available. Inspired by the tech entrepreneur heroes of the day, makers in Morgantown were not content to settle in and wait for the market to pick back up. They turned to DIY business ideas, Kickstarters, and start-ups. Lloyd states, "Of course, by the later 1990s, Generation X 'slackers' would be renamed 'entrepreneurs' in the popular press, igniting the 'new economy' with their creative, iconoclastic approach to business."[91] Likewise, the millennial generation has been continually demonized in popular culture. Television shows like HBO's *Girls*, which parodied self-centered millennials in Brooklyn, help reinforce the characterization of this generation as grossly over-privileged and self-involved, eating away their Baby Boomer parents' retirement funds. Despite these depictions, millennials may soon be recognized for the new mode of neoliberal entrepreneurship they have embarked on in the context of the Maker Movement.

One of the key differences between Lloyd's description of Wicker Park and the state of Morgantown is the sense of community evident in each neighborhood and how third spaces constitute meeting points. While early residents can point to Starr Space, which is, at time of writing, on an indefinite sabbatical from programming, or other venues as places where a sense of community was created in Morgantown and Bushwick, the '90s cliché of bohemians dropping into their local coffee shop to hang out with a reliable cast of characters (most famously depicted in NBC's iconic TV show *Friends*) has largely disappeared in favor of solitary figures working alone on their laptops in coffee shops.[92] Lloyd describes the coffee shop in the center of Wicker Park, Urbus Orbis, as a kind of utopian meet-up place where artists could just hang out and loiter and strike up a conversation. While these places exist in Bushwick, most people are drawn in by free Wi-Fi and sit for hours solitarily working on freelance jobs. Maybe they are friendly with the bartender, and there are a few barflies drinking pints throughout the day, but the majority are working rather than making social connections with their peers.[93] This difference highlights the transition to a new economic model where workers are never at rest or away from their work. There is no social time as such because even hanging out in a coffee shop is an opportunity to get some work done. The spaces for simple socializing, before Internet connections became ubiquitous, are few and far between. No one is unconnected, and therefore, no one is unconnected to the possibility of squeezing in a few more hours of labor, regardless whether the workspace is a coffee shop or a bar.

The postwar history of gentrification in New York City has carried the seeds of the Maker Movement from SoHo to the East Village to Williamsburg and on to Morgantown. The key ingredients in the development of this movement were present from the time that artists took up residence in SoHo and continued to the present day in various forms. At every step, we can see the continual transformation of the productive industrial city to one of leisure and consumption, the nostalgia for craftwork and individual labor, and the simultaneous lionization and precarization of knowledge or creative work. Technology has finally caught up with some of the societal trends and changes that have been ongoing since the 1960s. Consumer tools enable makers to finally "consume" the manufacture of physical production, allowing these authenticity-chasers to seek ever-increasing levels of individualized self-fulfillment. The ludic model of the city allows residents to remain in a childlike state of play, while the new myth of the Creative American Dream promises that, if we are creative enough, we can do anything. For a generation fed on Richard Florida's brand of neoliberalism, success, wealth, and fame are within reach. We are promised that childlike imagination and creativity are all we need to succeed in the new economy. As we go out to play in the adult urban playground, we are allowed to dream of acting out various fantasies of production. We hardly recognize that all these fantasies, facilitated by consumer-grade tools, are merely shadows of the industrial past we are chasing.

Chapter 5

Pioneer Days in Morgantown

Although gentrification in Morgantown, the section of the East Williamsburg In-Place Industrial Park (EWIPIP) around the Morgan Avenue subway stop, has differed from that of older neighborhoods like SoHo, the East Village, and Williamsburg, this difference has very little to do with the physical construction of the space itself. The massive, windowed light-manufacturing buildings and single-storied sheds of the neighborhood are not so different from those of Williamsburg or even those of SoHo, and the aesthetic appeal and functional advantage of post-industrial building stock has only increased over the last fifty years. The industrial aesthetic is so appealing now that the mere presence of a few light-filled warehouse buildings nearby makes even the single-story, windowless garages and sheds in neighborhoods like Morgantown and Williamsburg attractive property, and newly-built luxury condominiums in Williamsburg are designed to look like the daylight factory buildings of the industrial era. The explanation for why Morgantown has become the center of the Maker Movement in New York is, therefore, based on something beyond the in-situ construction of the area: namely, its distance from Manhattan and the timing of its colonization during the Web 2.0 era. Around 1999–2000, the EWIPIP was one of the last massive tracts of industrial property remaining in New York City that had not been gentrified.

Industrial areas along the Brooklyn waterfront were the first to be transformed into residential lofts because of their proximity to Manhattan. Morgantown and neighboring Bushwick were a long way from Manhattan, with many affordable areas in between. The center of Morgantown is around four and a half miles from Midtown Manhattan, as the crow flies, and approximately twenty minutes to Union Square on the subway (given everything runs smoothly). It is too close to the city center to have developed into a suburb, but too far to have ever been a desirable location. Nineteenth-century activists worked hard to get dirty, heavily polluting factories out of Manhattan, and the most toxic industries – such as tanning and beer brewing – were reserved for far distant locales like East Williamsburg (now Morgantown), where canals extended the natural waterways in the area and facilitated the movement of industrial products. For most of its history, industrial Morgantown was surrounded by working class neighborhoods that were built up for the employees of the various factories there. As any regular rider of the L subway line knows, the one solitary local, two-track subway line that runs through north Brooklyn was not designed or prepared for the influx of residents along its pathway.

The L underwent regular upgrades and service closures between 2002 and 2012, as ridership along the entire length of line continues to increase.[1] Mobility has been a constant issue for L users, as they have few other transport options to get to Manhattan other than the subway. During these service closures or other disruptions, such as Hurricane Sandy in 2012, when the line was closed for ten days due to a flooded tunnel, it is either very difficult or impossible to travel into Manhattan. Although the MTA spent $443 million on a fleet of new subway cars in 2002, by 2006 they found that ridership had increased far more than projected and additional cars were necessary.[2] For most of Morgantown's industrial history, those that worked in the neighborhood also lived in the neighborhood and so would have had far less use for daily commuter lines, both express and local, the likes of which are found in other areas of Brooklyn. The poor transport links and remoteness of Morgantown from Manhattan had delayed artistic activity in the area, particularly while other areas closer to Manhattan were still cheap and available. By the time artists were looking to Bushwick in the late '90s, net culture and personal computing were growing in popularity. The neighborhood hit its peak in the mid-'00s, at the height of the Web 2.0 era, with its emphasis on self-expression, social sharing, and mobile technology, and the start of the Maker Movement, which continues the hipster remix culture of Web 2.0. Thus, Morgantown was annexed by a new bohemian generation of digital natives.

The history of the neighborhood was relatively quiet until the end of the nineteenth century, as most of the area remained farmland from the mid-seventeenth century until that time. North Brooklyn was settled primarily by Dutch farmers, and remained inhabited by the Dutch after the British gained control of the colony in April 1664.[3] The village of Bushwick was founded after tensions arose between settlers and indigenous people in the area around 1660. The residents were ordered by the governor to consolidate themselves in 1661 around the new town of Boswijk, meaning literally "forest district" in Dutch but indicating a "town" or "farm in the woods"; it was later Anglicized to Bushwick.[4] The village itself was located immediately to the northwest of present-day Morgantown between Conselyea Street and Skillman Avenue between present-day Humboldt Street (then Smith Street). All of North Brooklyn, now divided into the neighborhoods of Williamsburg, Greenpoint, East Williamsburg, and Bushwick, was once grouped together as Bushwick. In 1840, Williamsburgh broke away from Bushwick and became a separate town, and in 1854 both Williamsburgh and Bushwick were annexed by the city of Brooklyn and became its Eastern Districts.[5] For Brooklyn residents, the names of neighborhoods matter. While many places retain their historic names, real estate agents and property developers know that rebranding a neighborhood to associate it with a more attractive neighboring area can improve its desirability. Shortened names such as SoHo and TriBeCa in New York have become a cliché denoting gentrification. For residents of Bushwick (or Morgantown), the naming of the area is more than just legal boundaries or historic nomenclature.

The origin of the "Morgantown" moniker, however, is not clearly attributable to real estate developers.[6] In 2014, Bushwick entrepreneur Royal Chase attempted to rebrand the area of Bushwick directly south of Flushing, around the Jefferson L stop, as "Jefftown", which was picked up by city blog *Gothamist*, where it faced an onslaught of disdain. Chase shed some light on the Morgantown moniker in the process, saying, "That guy that helped create Morgantown, he told me that they made it up as a joke. That caught on, but it got a lot of negative feedback. It got hate from people that were there for 50 years. I get no hate from that community."[7] Despite Chase's claim to know "the guy" who coined "Morgantown," it appears to have caught on gradually among the residents of the area rather than emerging out of an entrepreneurial branding exercise.[8]

The use of the name Morgantown can be traced back to around 2007–2009, although *The New York Times* only first mentioned the area as Morgantown as late as 2013.[9] An early instance, dated January 13, 2007, comes from a list of favorite neighborhood bars and restaurants on ratings website Yelp. The user states:

> The East Williamsburg Industrial Area. What the hell is the real name of this 'hood, anyway? It seems like the Bedford Ave. types (and realtors) call it E. Williamsburg as if there were some similarities between it and its western cousin. The opposite types, likely in a move to distance themselves from the stigma of gentrification, call it Bushwick (though technically that would be farther south). Still others call it "Bushburg" or "Morgantown", reflecting the mixed identity and isolated nature of this small enclave.[10]

There are other indications that the name was up for debate at this time. A *Brooklyn Paper* article from June 2007 notes Bushburg as an early contender in the search for a new name. The notorious local property developers Bushburg Properties registered that name in 2000 and continue to have a strong presence in the neighborhood's real estate.[11]

The name Morgantown has a less visible connection to property developers. Morgantown Management LLC has been registered to the law firm Gottbetter and Partners since 2003, but there is no apparent neighborhood or web presence for this company.[12] In 2005, *The New York Times* reported that the neighborhood was as yet unnamed, quoting two local residents, who jokingly suggested the names "The Industrial Wasteland Border Territory Between East Williamsburg and Bushwick" and "MoJo" (after Morgan Avenue and Johnson Street).[13] Another early mention of the name Morgantown can be found in a comment, dated August 5, 2009, on a blog post from early 2008 detailing the changes the EWIPIP was undergoing at the time, titled "Bushwick Emerges as City's Next Artist Colony."[14] At least one early resident proposed the name MorganVille.[15] It seems that consensus toward Morgantown rather than Bushburg had solidified by 2009, although residents are still suspicious that any attempt at renaming or rebranding is nothing more than a real estate ploy.[16]

The Morgantown nickname represents the maker phase of the neighborhood. Not only does the name sector off the subsection of the EWIPIP where makers operate, but it demonstrates the maker/hipster desire for self-branding. While real estate developers often come up with new names for up-and-coming neighborhoods, in Morgantown, the residents themselves came up with their own brand.[17] Chase's attempt to single-handedly rebrand the subsection of Bushwick he calls Jefftown takes this process one step further, as Chase is hoping to personally profit off of the brand through merchandise and party promoting.

The main concentration of activity in Morgantown is near the second entrance to the Morgan Avenue L Stop, between McKibbin and Moore Streets. As recently as 1888, the eastern section of Morgantown between Stewart Avenue and Morgan Avenue from Flushing Ave. to Johnson Ave. was completely devoid of structures except for Powell's Chemical Works, a fertilizer plant at the corner of Varick and Ingraham Street, and three small wooden structures on the corner of Harrison Place and Varick. Just east of the boundary of Morgantown, on the corner of Gardner Avenue and Randolph Street was another heavily polluting industrial plant, Settle Bros. and Co. Tannery. Between Bushwick Avenue, on the western border of the neighborhood, and White Street, there was a good deal more infrastructure in place at the time, primarily dwellings for factory workers and the accompanying businesses such as bakeries, tailors, horse shoers, and wheelwrights. A few slaughterhouses lined Johnson Avenue from Bushwick to Bogart, and Binns' Chemical Works sat at the corner of Johnson and White Street.

On McKibbin Street, where the famous residential loft buildings now stand, a large rope manufacturer occupied the south side of the street and a number of glassworks sat on the north side. Just beyond the southwest corner of the neighborhood, from Flushing Avenue southward, along Bushwick Avenue, there were a number of beer breweries. Bushwick's history of beer brewing (and a hipster penchant for craft brews) has led to local entrepreneurs developing walking tours, which claim that, "Bushwick, Brooklyn was once the brewing center of America."[18] In the heart of contemporary Morgantown, along Bogart and Morgan, between Rock Street and Harrison Place, only a few wooden structures were extant in 1888, mostly dwellings, along with a few furriers and fur-dying works. It is clear that Morgantown of 1888, though sparsely developed at this point, was home to some of the most toxic and unpleasant of modern industries.

By 1907, many new dwellings and storage buildings had been erected in the Morgantown area, the majority of which were now brick lined rather than plain frame structures. The nature of the industry in the area, however, had not changed very much. The site where Gilbert Ramirez Park now stands, next to the McKibbin lofts, was FH Kalbfleisch Co. Chemical Work in 1907. A tannery and planing mill sat directly south of there between Seigel Street and Moore Street. A few newer food production factories had arrived in the neighborhood, such as Uneeda Ice Cream Factory at the corner of Morgan and Grattan Street, Star Baking Co. at the corner of Thames and Porter, and the sausage factory of Adolph Gobel, the "sausage king", at the corner of Rock Street and Morgan, which is still home to deli meat producer Boar's Head.[19] Morgantown is now a mixture of single story garage-type industrial buildings and 1920s or '30s-era four-story loft buildings which housed textile and print works after their construction (and still do in a few instances).[20] There were also still a number of food processing plants in the neighborhood between 2000 and 2015, when the neighborhood began to be used for artistic activity and residential loft dwelling.

The area's long history of toxic industry has undoubtedly left its mark. The English Kills waterway, a branch of the notoriously polluted Newtown Creek, still hosts a large waste management center at 123 Varick Street. The Newtown Creek Alliance, started in 2002 with the aim of cleaning up and revitalizing the waterway, states:

Up until the latter part of the 20th Century, industries along the creek had free reign over the disposal of unwanted byproducts... The legacy of this history today is a 17–30 million gallon underground oil spill caused by Standard Oil's progeny companies, copper contamination from the Phelps Dodge Superfund site, bubbling from the creek bed in the English Kill reach due to increases of hydrogen sulfide and a lack of dissolved oxygen, and creek beds coated with old tires, car frames, seats and loose paper. Nearly the entire creek had the sheen and smell of petroleum, with the bed and banks slicked black.

There is no natural freshwater flow into the creek as the historic tributaries were covered over. [...] The creek is mostly stagnant, meaning all the pollutants that have entered the creek over the past two centuries have never left. The creek is also home to a federal Superfund site, several State Superfund sites and numerous brownfields that have not yet secured the attention of regulators.[21]

Needless to say, the years of industrial waste in north Brooklyn have had a lasting impact on the local environment, but the damages to the area have had little effect on the desirability of the area.

A little toxic waste is no match for the booming real estate market in gentrified Bushwick/Ridgewood. Entrepreneurs and renters looking for cheaper real estate have chased low rents all the way down the L subway line to the Halsey stop near the Ridgewood cemeteries, where, in 2015, the opening of a new bar, Nowadays, demonstrated just how powerful the allure of the neighborhood is, toxic waste and all. Nowadays is an outdoor bar and BBQ restaurant located near the border of Bushwick and Ridgewood at 56-06 Cooper Avenue, which is directly adjacent to the former premises of the Wolff-Alport Chemical Company, a superfund site that *The New Yorker* called "the most radioactive place in New York City."[22] The owners, for their part, have tried to assure the public that there is no radioactivity on their site and that their establishment is safe.[23] Gothamist quotes a local real estate agent brushing off any suggestion that the presence of a superfund site would decrease the desirability of the property in the area, saying the pollution is simply "not a problem" for those that live in and frequent the area.[24] While, at one time, the foulest industries were pushed to the outer limits of the city, their remnants are now some of the most attractive properties to be had. In an expensive city like New York, some residents and business owners feel they have no choice but to try to ignore their proximity to the waste products of a neighborhood's industrial past.

Early residents of Morgantown overwhelmingly describe the neighborhood, from 1999–2005, as an empty and rather hostile environment. Eric, a 26-year-old Research Analyst who grew up in the neighborhood, described the area as "desolate and therefore dangerous." Eric's mother worked at a textile factory at 199 Cook Street and his father worked as an asbestos remover and did some factory work as a side job. Eric states, "After 5 or 6pm, the area would empty out since all the factory workers would go home. For this very same reason my parents would not let [me] play or hang around the area."[25] The first artists to arrive remember an un-policed atmosphere on the streets as well, where it was not uncommon to see packs of feral dogs roaming and cars burning.[26] Bill Driscoll, an artist who has lived in the area since around 2005, recalls, "It was empty. With mostly Hispanic families and such. Not many bars or restaurants. Just the occasional – and unwelcoming – bodega. I had a car then and my windows would get smashed out on a regular basis."[27] Stories of car break-ins were a common anecdote from early Morgantown residents. Eric, similarly, saw the arrival of bars and restaurants as a natural transition in the neighborhood, saying:

For the most part, I am fond of the businesses that have popped up in the neighborhood. A lot of the factories were on their way to shutting down in the early 2000s and the new business that opened up kept the area from getting worse than it was. Apart from the factories there was not really anything so these businesses definitely filled a void in the area – one that I did not understand until I became older.[28]

Those filling the void were mostly exiles from former artist-centric neighborhoods like the East Village and Williamsburg.

One of the first hipster-centric restaurants to move into Morgantown was Life Café in 2002, located at 983 Flushing Avenue. It was a branch of the famed bohemian East Village hangout of the same name, which was located at Avenue B and East 10th Street between 1981 and 2011, when it was forced to close down due to disputes with the landlord over repairs.[29] By 2012, owner Kathy Kirkpatrick also found herself closing down Life in Bushwick, apparently forced out by a landlord who would not renew her lease.[30] Shortly after Life closed, the space immediately became another very similar café called 983-Bushwick's Living Room. Kirkpatrick wrote on the café's blog that the landlord had originally been the one to invite her to open a café:

At the time, Bushwick looked like a post-apocalyptic industrial wasteland, with nowhere for existing and incoming artists and loft dwellers to eat or drink. He told me the incoming residents desperately needed a watering hole. He said having a café close to his buildings would attract the kind of tenants he wanted. It was the East Village story all over again and I saw it. Except profit wasn't my motive. Rather, it was another chance to do what I seem to be naturally compelled to do: create a sense of home and connect the neighborhood folks together, offer a safe haven with comforting food and good drink at reasonable prices.[31]

Kirkpatrick had been part of an older generation of arts-led urban change, and her idealism has not been matched in the neighborhood since. Unfortunately, stories of landlord disputes are all too common in New York, as real estate markets like Bushwick explode in value almost overnight. The younger generation of business owners in Morgantown are, for the most part, more realistic than their bohemian forebears in the East

Village. They are not only looking to make a profit but also looking to widen the net of customers beyond a close-knit local community and invite the rest of New York (and, even, tourists) to Morgantown. The pizza restaurant Roberta's was one such business.

Shortly after Life opened in Morgantown, Rob Herschenfeld, a furniture designer and early local resident, opened Brooklyn's Natural, a small grocery store at 49 Bogart Street, now the nexus of the neighborhood.[32] Other businesses like the Archive Café, now closed, and the bar King's County, still in operation, cropped up around the same time as Life and Brooklyn's Natural. Herschenfeld, for his part, has gone on to a variety of entrepreneurial projects subsequently, including property development, contracting work, and investing as a partner in hip coffee brand Brooklyn Roasting Company.[33]

As stated in the Introduction, some of the early neighborhood pioneers were OfficeOps, the McKibbin Lofts, Brooklyn Fire Proof, Roberta's, and 3rd Ward. Generally speaking, the gentrification of Bushwick below Flushing happened later than the initial settlements around the Morgan Avenue L stop, although there are a couple of factory buildings south of Morgantown that had similar histories to those further north and there were a few early-arriving bars or restaurants like Northeast Kingdom, which opened in 2005 near the Jefferson L stop and offered sustainable, foraged, and locally-sourced food until it closed in 2016.[34]

The McKibbin Lofts

The McKibbin Lofts, at 248 and 255 McKibbin Street, are two four-story industrial lofts (five-stories if the basement level is included) facing each other on either end of McKibbin Street, built in 1942 and 1936 respectively.[35] Long swaths of paned-glass windows cover the façades of the buildings, which face off against each other across the narrow street. Unlike some other live/work loft spaces in the area, 248 McKibbin was officially sanctioned as a legal residency (J-2 Residential) in 2003, although numerous building code violations have piled up over the years.[36] 255 McKibbin has remained listed as an L9 Loft (classed as COM or D-1 Industrial) but residence in the building has been protected under the Loft Law since around 2012.[37] Conversion of these buildings into dwellings for young artists began around 1999 and they remain relatively unchanged today, both in terms of demographic and infrastructure.[38] While some external graffiti has been removed subsequently from the façade of 248 and other minor repairs have taken place, the buildings have not been polished up to meet the professional standard of converted lofts like the Loom Building at 1087 Flushing Avenue, developed by Bushburg Properties.[39] More often than not, the residents themselves have illegally built up lofted rooms in the units, in flagrant violation of building code.

The McKibbin lofts were frequently described as "dorms" due to the young, college-aged or recently-graduated residents who occupy them and their reputation for anarchic, unkempt dwellings and wild parties. *The New York Times* reported in 2008, "There are no known children living in the McKibbin," and one would have been hard-pressed to find any there in 2015 either.[40] The article goes on to claim that the McKibbin lofts, "could have been Greenwich Village 60 years ago, or SoHo 30 years ago, or the East Village in the 1990s."[41] The notable difference between the McKibbin lofts and these previous artist enclaves is that the McKibbins were converted into residences after similar development trajectories had already been successfully fulfilled in places like Williamsburg and SoHo. In these places, live-work spaces gradually evolved into live-only spaces.

According to early Morgantown resident Bill Driscoll, the lofts of the neighborhood have gradually shifted from providing adequate space for artists and builders to providing space to squeeze large groups of residents into. Driscoll states:

I didn't know the neighborhood very well in the beginning. I mostly stayed within the confines of the loft building. Only venturing out to buy groceries or go to the train. Any feelings of community were limited to the other tenants that lived on my floor; there were a lot of artists and builder types who were there for the affordable space so that they could get work done. That evolved into mostly people just out of college who began to cram as many people as they could into their loft spaces.[42]

Although many who move into the McKibbins are still seeking workspace, the buildings' use in this capacity has declined as cost and desirability have increased. The landlords of the McKibbin lofts must have realized early on that residents would buy into the romance of being the next generation of urban pioneers. They, therefore, kept rents relatively high while relying on the tenants to build up the space. By 2003, *The New York Times*, never quite at the forefront of trends, had finally declared the Williamsburg art scene dead. Artists at the time were keen to make sure they were on the ground floor of development in the next area.[43]

Both the writer of the 2008 *Times* article and the residents of McKibbin wistfully cite various predecessors to the area, all of which were difficult places to inhabit for artists of previous generations but at least sustained low price tags for much of their development period. In 2008, the *Times* reports that rooms in the McKibbin lofts rented for between $530 and $800 per month. These tiny cubical spaces in shared lofts often stretch the definition of "room" to the extreme. They typically consist of thin board or plywood walls, no doors or very minimal closure, and no windows or just simple cutouts in the top of thin walls. In many cases these rooms are far too small to fit a bed and will have claustrophobic lofted areas for beds above the tiny space below. Still other rooms have no lower level access at all and are more like treehouses or cubbyholes that can only be accessed via ladder.

The ramshackle construction of the rooms provides minimal personal space, so communal space, which is often light-filled and airy thanks to large paned glass windows and high ceilings, is seen as one of the charms of living in the McKibbin lofts. It is no surprise, given the number of people living in each loft and the lack of private space, that these buildings are known more for partying and socializing at all hours than artistic activity. The hedonistic lifestyle and youthful disorder of the McKibbin's residents also gave the buildings an unfortunate reputation for bedbugs around 2007, when a renaissance in infestations was building in New York City.[44] One resident of 248 McKibbin posted a complaint in April of 2007 on the Bed Bug Registry site, stating, "I have noticed bedbugs over several months. We have constantly fought with the landlord, and they say they will send an exterminator, but they often lie and don't. If you move here, you will get bedbugs, because the management doesn't care, as all the tenants are young and have no money to fight them."[45] Many similar complaints on the registry detail the management's refusal to deal with the bed bug infestation in the buildings over the course of several years, sometimes even trying to bully tenants into paying for exterminators or trying to convince them that their infestations are merely mosquitos.

In early 2013, the management of the lofts banned parties on the premises, claiming that residents were continually damaging units being brought up to code under Loft Law provisions. David Colon, a former resident, blogged about the ban, saying:

> I'm skeptical of the idea that it's getting too expensive to put up with the parties. When I was moving out, brokers showing my apartment kept talking about how they were turning my four-bedroom into a five-bedroom, and jacking the rent from $2500/month to $4000. Which is a goddamn ridiculous amount to pay to live in bedrooms with no windows, even

before you get a policy that says having a few people over has to be cleared by building security.[46]

The shoddy living conditions and the high prices are a constant source of complaint among former tenants of the McKibbin Lofts, and the prices of the units seem to be increasing steadily without much change in the interior infrastructure.

In May 2014, the rooms in McKibbin listed on Craigslist were being offered for between $800 and $1200 per month (in apartments that are typically shared with 2–5 other people). Brokers were listing units in 248 McKibbin for $4500 (for four "bedrooms" which were still, based on the images, tiny lofted spaces) and $5000 (for five bedrooms) in May of 2015, advertising the rentals as "penthouse" apartments. Rooms in the lofts were offered on Craigslist in October 2015 for $1100 per month (in apartments shared between 4 people) and $2100 (shared with only one other person). In Fall of 2015, Zumck Realty, responsible for 255 McKibbin, had accumulated over $50,000 worth of fines for construction violations which were still unresolved.[47] The stories of absentee landlords, constant Department of Buildings and Fire Department inspections, and tenants living in substandard conditions while paying exorbitant rent are common among the loft buildings in Morgantown. While previous generations of loft pioneers in SoHo or Williamsburg dealt with similarly dicey living conditions, they did so with far less interference from city authorities and at extremely low rental costs.

For a brief period of time, however, between the late 1990s and 2003, the McKibbin lofts were not on the radar for city officials. The rate of development, which finds its equivalent in the slow formalization of SoHo from the mid-1950s to the early '80s, occurred with astonishing speed, between approximately 1999 and 2003 in McKibbin. Dan Nuxoll, who was one of the first to move into the lofts in 1997, moved out in 2003, claiming the community spirit of the building was not what it used to be.[48] During Nuxoll's tenure in McKibbin, a small group of young men were able to establish studios and arts activities on the premises. In 1997, Mark Elijah Rosenberg founded Rooftop Films, an organization that, as the name suggests, began showing films for local residents from loft rooftops. Rooftop Films had its start at McKibbin in 1998, using Nuxoll's loft and rooftop. Access to the roof of 248 McKibbin was first prohibited when management installed an alarm system in 2012 and then totally banned in August 2015, but, back in the late '90s no one was policing the tenants' use of the space.[49]

In 2003, Rooftop Films also moved out of the McKibbin lofts and into OfficeOps, another loft building in the neighborhood. The year 2003 seems to have been an important year in terms of formalizing neighborhood institutions and transitioning McKibbin from a place where a ragtag group of guys squatted to a more desirable and hip place for students and other young people to live. The evolution of Rooftop Films embodies the entrepreneurial spirit that set Morgantown residents apart from earlier bohemians. Rosenberg and his associates were all involved in the arts in various ways and Rosenberg, a filmmaker, began his screenings as an "innovative way to get people together."[50] Not content to keep his screenings as an underground small-scale operation, Rosenberg was immediately thinking bigger. Registered as a nonprofit, Rooftop Films has expanded to cities around the country. One of the key qualities that Morgantown artists have always exhibited is a desire to go bigger and expand their organizations.

OfficeOps

Kevin Lindamood was also involved in the early renovations of the McKibbin lofts starting around 1999. A native of western Virginia and a photographer, Lindamood moved to the area because he saw an opportunity to create an artist community and a space for his photography while profiting off of property development in the area. With the help of some of his relatives, he started OfficeOps in 2002 in space rented in a 1925 factory building at 57 Thames Street, which is still zoned as an F-9 Factory/Industrial building even though there are live/work units in the building.[51] OfficeOps provides a combination of studio space, apartments, and rental spaces for weddings and events. While this loft building has less of a reputation for residential difficulties than some of the other live/work lofts in the neighborhood, there have been, nevertheless, several complaints filed with the Department of Buildings in 2005 and 2009 against owner Shimrit Associates, Inc., reporting that there were Class A apartments on the third and fourth floors, the building had no residential certificate of occupancy, and was being used to throw parties on the rooftop and ground floor and cater weddings and events (all functions clearly advertised on the OfficeOps website).[52]

In many ways, Lindamood epitomizes the artist-entrepreneur of Morgantown, having started his organization around a model typical of more formalized workspaces in Williamsburg and SoHo. OfficeOps eases the transition of industrial space to artist workspace, cutting out the more difficult steps that artists have to go through to make industrial space habitable, which often involve a great deal of grass roots organization and DIY. In the case of OfficeOps, Lindamood and his company have done the difficult part of molding the space, leaving it fresh and ready for young artists and renters to move in. Although Lindamood, unlike other makers in the area, never had aspirations of expanding his business to other venues and neighborhoods, he entered into the venture with the same business mindset as his contemporaries. Like most of the artist-entrepreneurs in the area, Lindamood saw his start-up as an asset to the neighborhood and a way to cohesively form some sense of community amongst Morgantowners who were interested in "making."[53]

In the *Journal of Aesthetics & Protest* from June 2004, Lindamood wrote a piece detailing how OfficeOps was "innovating its role as property managers." He writes:

> ... our foray into arts administration proved more of an education than we had anticipated... This work resulted in much lower returns... We were trying to sell an idea that most people bought when they moved here. Artists and young professionals weren't paying any less to live this far outside of Manhattan; they were just getting more space... We would like to organize content producers beneath an umbrella of individual ownership and licensing. All non-profits and non-governmental organizations share in the battle against commercial and consumption-based messaging. Those same organizations must turn to indifferent commercial producers for services, be it housing, production facilities or event venues. The disparity between our operational overhead and that of organizations akin to ours provides an incentive for content producers to invest in supporting OfficeOps.[54]

Lindamood is, essentially, promoting his company as an ethical and community-serving developer that is interested in sustainability as well as profit. While he nods vaguely to left-wing concerns such as "consumption-based messaging," he is approaching these issues from a market-driven point of view. The artist-entrepreneur of Morgantown is positioned as a figure of community empowerment, blocking the "indifferent" commercial producers in favor of more community-connected businesses.

Dance Spaces, Business Opportunities

In addition to those looking to create live/work spaces at McKibbin and OfficeOps, some of the first artists moving into Morgantown were dancers looking for large practice spaces. OfficeOps would regularly rent out their space for dance and avant-garde theater events in the mid-'00s. On June 6th, 2003, Curious Noise Theater performed *Travelogue: An Illustrated Motion Picture of Memory*, in which dancers performed using parachutes and roller skates, a detail that was perhaps inspired by the well-known Rock 'n' Roller Skate parties hosted at OfficeOps at the time.[55] On June 4th and 5th, 2004, Project Fuse performed *The Sunset Clause* on the rooftop, a "reflection of contemporary urban life."[56] OfficeOps often collaborated with other early arts organizations of the neighborhood, including Chez Bushwick, the pioneering Morgantown dance troupe that *The New York Times* labeled "one of the hippest places to see dance in New York City today."[57]

The four-story loft building at 304 Boerum Street, built in 1929, housed some of the earliest residents of the neighborhood and noted artist-entrepreneurs.[58] Rob Herschenfeld bought the building in 1996 and began renting out space to artists (as soon as he could clear the building of drug addicts).[59] In 2003, Jonah Bokaer, formerly a dancer with the Merce Cunningham Dance Company, started Chez Bushwick at 304 Boerum, which serves as a meeting point for dancers and offers rentable practice and event space. Bokaer's primary motivation for the enterprise was to provide cheap rentals, which cost five dollars per hour in 2006, and, nearly a decade later in 2015, still only cost eight dollars an hour. Bokaer was also interested in promoting more experimental programming to combat a perceived conservatism in the New York dance scene. Like other Morgantown makers, Bokaer had plans to expand to a second space in 2006 and held multiple benefits and fundraisers with the goal of raising $25,000.[60]

In 2009, Bokaer and John Jasperse of Thin Man Dance founded the Center for Performance Research (CPR) in Williamsburg, to the northwest of Morgantown, which provides practice space, residencies, and performance programming.[61] CPR, which is housed in a LEED (Leadership in Energy and Environmental Design)-certified green building, came together thanks to a unique entrepreneurial partnership between the artists and property developer Derek Denckla that was initiated in 2007. Bokaer and Jasperse were able to pay only $650,000, less than half of market value, for the space because Denckla, who was keen to incorporate the arts in his development, was able to make up the losses through selling condominiums in the building, a one-bedroom for $715,616 and a two-bedroom for $920,150.[62] It is clear that the days of artists inhabiting a bohemian demi-monde outside the confines of bourgeois culture are long gone.

Artists of Morgantown are practically-minded and have no qualms about partnering with developers or even becoming developers themselves. While it would be easy for outsiders or older generations to label the makers of Morgantown makers as sellouts, the entrepreneurial drive comes from a place of pure necessity. In 1975, bohemians were able to survive and thrive in artist enclaves like St. Mark's Place on the Lower East Side of Manhattan, where Bob Constant, quoted by Ada Calhoun in her book on the neighborhood, recalls earning $2.50 per hour and living in a four-room apartment for $125 per month.[63] Between 2000 and 2015, artists working minimum wage jobs made too little and rents are too high to sustain a pure bohemian lifestyle. Today's hipsters and makers simply cannot afford to inhabit urban space without participating in entrepreneurial projects and the powerful property development market.

Tom Le, a dancer turned real estate broker, was featured in a 2006 *New York Times* write-up on Bushwick. He is yet another example of an artist-entrepreneur who was eyeing Morgantown in the mid-'00s with a maker's mindset. Unabashedly pragmatic, Le wanted to see other artists turn entrepreneurial as well. The *Times* states, "He dreams of helping artists invest in real estate, of opening an artists' studio in Bushwick himself, with an upstate affiliate perhaps." He is quoted as saying, "The machine keeps going, and it's not the developers, it's not the Realtors. It's the demand that keeps the machine going, and you have to invest so that you are ready when the next transformation occurs. We can ride the wave or get kicked out."[64] Le's attitude is an optimistic kind of jadedness.

Artists have learned that, in order to avoid being priced out of a neighborhood, they have to sit in the driver's seat of development rather than allow themselves to be run over by the voracious "machine." These makers were not only thinking about the limited confines of their new neighborhood, but also continuously dreaming of expansion. Like Bokaer of Chez Bushwick and Rosenberg of Rooftop Films, Le was thinking about the market beyond the neighborhood. He claims to not only want to start an artist space in the Morgantown area but also to expand to another branch upstate once that project is off the ground. It seems that Le never found his way back to dance and choreography, though he claims to have applied the lessons learned from his time in the arts to his real estate careers, saying, "Being an artist – juggling work, manage expectation, being flexible with life's persistent challenges and personal time – was a perfect training ground to becoming a real estate broker. [...] the passion, the love and the creativity in solving problems."[65] For Le and others of his generation, arts and entrepreneurship can be equally rewarding and even go hand-in-hand together in hyper-developing neighborhoods like Williamsburg and Bushwick.

Another early Morgantown institution, Brooklyn Fire Proof, is currently headquartered at 119 Ingraham Street in a building that was built in 1921.[66] Like many of the other organizations that were early on the scene, BFP expanded beyond their original premises to another space at 56 Bogart, built in 1932.[67] Thomas Burr Dodd, who describes himself as an "artist/jack of all trade" started Brooklyn Fire Proof Inc. in 1999, and his girlfriend (later wife), Pearl Son Dodd, a fashion designer, joined him in 2001. BFP started as a commercial gallery and studio space in Williamsburg and moved shortly afterwards to its current location in Morgantown. Burr Dodd describes his decision to move to the area as a choice between Chelsea or Bushwick. The former was deemed "too snobby" and the latter a more "friendly environment."[68]

Brooklyn Fire Proof has been criticized for its inaccessibly expensive studio space. In 2015, listings for space in the building advertised $525 for 200 square feet of space in a shared studio, $550 to share a 325 square foot space, and $1200 for a 600 square foot space (shared between four people).[69] As noted, William Powhida once described Brooklyn Fire Proof's spaces as "criminally overpriced," a comment which particularly stung for Burr Dodd, who sees himself as providing a much-needed service in the neighborhood, which contributes positively to the artistic community.[70] He recalls that, in the early days, when artists began flooding out of Williamsburg and into Morgantown, as property developers took over the waterfront, the atmosphere was uncertain. Burr Dodd took a great many risks and sacrificed time working on his own artwork to start up BFP, though he does not claim to regret that decision. He attributes the elevated rates for rental spaces in BFP to increasing costs of maintaining the buildings and losses due to delinquent tenants who do not pay their rent. He also describes BFP's rather rapid expansion into music, television, and film spaces as well as opening a bar and gallery and managing property as strains on the organization's finances. This expansion went, perhaps, a bit too far, as Brooklyn Fire Proof Café was forced to close in November 2014.[71]

Like many of the artist-entrepreneurs in Morgantown, Burr Dodd's ethos is quintessentially Maker Movement. He describes wanting to build "green systems" and "science projects" and wanting to find solutions to a variety of social problems in the realm of environmentalism and education. He says that BFP strives for "art as lifestyle." While he certainly has good intentions for this declaration, it is difficult not to read this as a stripping down of artist practices to an aesthetic product.

These older institutions in the neighborhood, in many ways, short-circuited the development of the area. Some of the early residents, like Bill Driscoll, have managed to lay low and continue to live in the way they always have in the neighborhood. Driscoll explains:

> I am an artist. I spend a lot of time in my studio. I'm not that involved with any sort of localized scene beyond participating informally with the Bushwick Open Studios once a year when I open my loft for walk-throughs. The rest of the hood is always pulsating on some level indefinable to me, but there seems to be an emphasis on performance, music shows, and studio showings. I've noticed over the last few years that big production rave-parties have been rearing their ugly heads.[72]

Many of the more plugged-in artist-entrepreneurs of the neighborhood, however, have facilitated the rapid gentrification of Morgantown by establishing broad-thinking, entrepreneurial, arts-oriented businesses right from the start.

Rather than allowing arts events or institutions to evolve gradually from insular communities or groups of friends who performed for each other (as those in SoHo and 1990s Williamsburg claimed they did), the Morgantown generation skipped straight to the point where they were founding legitimate and professional incorporated businesses and nonprofit organizations. The accelerated development may be due, at least in part, to the bleed-over of artists from Williamsburg. The EWIPIP is, essentially, a continuation of the industrial development along Newtown Creek and Morgantown that could be classified as part of Williamsburg. Taking what they learned from past experiences in urban space, notably Williamsburg, the Morgantown settlers described in this chapter developed their arts organizations with an instinctive maker-like outlook. The organizations that came to the scene later, like 3rd Ward and Roberta's, however, were more explicitly plugged into the larger cultural phenomenon of the Maker Movement and helped further accelerate the rapid development of the area.

Chapter 6

The Makers of Morgantown

*It may have peaked. But one person's peak is another person's new
beginning.*
– Bill Driscoll, 2015[1]

In 2009, entrepreneur Bre Pettis, an active player in the Maker
Movement, along with Adam Mayer and Zach Smith, founded
MakerBot to bring a cheaper consumer 3D printer to the masses.
The Brooklyn-based company was acquired by Stratasys in 2013
and opened, in 2015, a new 170,000 square foot factory in Industry
City in Sunset Park, Brooklyn. By October 2015, the company had
already gone through two rounds of firings that year (each of
which took down twenty percent of its workforce) and the future
of the company remains unclear.[2] The ribbon cutting ceremony
for the new factory was presided over by Brooklyn Borough
President Eric Adams, who lauded the new jobs that the factory
would bring into the borough. According to the company's press
release in July, 2015, at the opening of the Industry City facility,
"[…] the new factory, which streamlines production, doubles
production capacity compared to MakerBot's old Industry City
facility, and follows principles of lean manufacturing."[3] Their
choice of the word "lean," one would assume, was not evoked to
foreshadow more cuts to the company's workforce, but, rather,
as a tech-industry buzzword signifying efficient business. Given
the 2015 bankruptcy filings of made-in-the-USA hipster clothing
brand American Apparel, however, uncertainty remains over the
viability of re-introducing manufacturing to the United States.[4]

Whether or not manufacturing can effectively be brought back
to the US is, to some extent, beside the point. For a company like
MakerBot, a Brooklyn location has heady symbolic resonance

and plays into the libertarian ethos of the Maker Movement. MakerBot cultivates its own do-it-yourself, bootstraps origin story, despite the founders' tech industry pedigrees and, as of 2011, large amounts of venture capitalist funding from Foundry Group and others.[5] When MakerBot started, it was, like other Maker companies, kit-based and open source. Founder Zach Smith was forced out of the company in 2012 over disagreements with the other founders over MakerBot's continued open source availability.[6] The company is, therefore, a perfect example of how, like Apple and countless other tech companies before them, the lofty ideals of the industry are eroded when the scale of the undertaking grows. Diana Pincus, MakerBot's Vice President of Operations, joined the company in 2012, "when the factory was in a Gowanus garage and her desk was a plank on two sawhorses" (and also after they had received millions of dollars in VC capital, but never mind that). By 2015, she was celebrating the opening of the new Industry City factory. At the time of the opening, Pincus said, "I consider myself very lucky to have built a factory not only in the United States, but in Brooklyn, my home."[7]

In 2015, Voodoo Manufacturing opened up in the heart of Morgantown at 361 Stagg Street, in the same building that once housed Morgantown's pioneering maker space 3rd Ward. Founded by former MakerBot product manager Max Friefeld, whose 3D printing software gained him admission to famed Silicon Valley incubator Y Combinator in 2013, and three other former MakerBot employees, Voodoo offered 3D print-on-demand services from their fleet of 127 MakerBot Replicator 2Xs. Not surprisingly, given that Morgantown has become mecca for makers, Friefeld and his cohorts based their operations in the neighborhood, "because it's where they live, because it's cheaper than Manhattan and for the creative people here."[8] Some of Voodoo's first clients were large companies such as Viacom and start-ups like BioLite.

Voodoo joins another tech company, Livestream, in the former 3rd Ward premises. Like Wicker Park, Chicago before it, Morgantown is now being touted as the next "Silicon Alley" tech hub in New York City. Developers have snapped up a number of former industrial properties in the area, including a former coffee-roasting warehouse at Jefferson Street and Cypress Avenue, a former bottling plant at Evergreen Avenue and George Street and an industrial tract on Johnson Street for new office, restaurant and retail developments, the latter of which has plans for an "artisanal food" space.[9] The Maker Movement in Morgantown has blossomed but it remains to be seen whether the artistic activities of the neighborhood will continue alongside it.

3rd Ward

The ghost of 3rd Ward haunts these second-generation maker spaces taking up residence in its former premises. While the other nascent arts organizations in the neighborhood did not deviate too much from the ways in which industrial loft buildings had been organized and used in previous generations, 3rd Ward radically overhauled the concept of artist space in Morgantown. More than any other organization in the area, 3rd Ward paved the way for the transition of the creative professional from artist to maker. Opening its doors in May 2005 as a complex of studios and workshops designed to meet the needs of every type of maker imaginable, 3rd Ward enjoyed an incredible eight years of growth and expansion before closing suddenly in October 2013. *New York Magazine* praised 3rd Ward in an article from 2008 under the headline "Business Plan? What Business Plan?" which, looking back at the events leading up to its demise, reads eerily like an omen.[10]

3rd Ward was located in a loft building at 195 Morgan Avenue that was built in 1926.[11] The organization was co-founded by Jason Goodman and Jeremy Lovitt who were students together at the School of the Museum of Fine Arts in Boston. Goodman seems to have been the leader of the venture, energetically and enthusiastically promoting 3rd Ward for the length of its existence.[12] He describes how he first proposed his idea for a new kind of artist workspace to Alan Messner, a property developer, who initially rejected Goodman's idea only to come back to him six months later offering to rent out the ground floor of a building he had just bought at 195 Morgan Avenue to Goodman for the project.[13] While Goodman and Lovitt did not have a clear idea of where they were heading, their ambition was endless.

They employed the same rhetoric as the Maker Movement and became the definitive maker mecca in the area. Initially holding dance parties and club nights and providing studio space, 3rd Ward was quick to branch out into other ventures. A key factor in the transformation to makerism was the creation of a so-called "co-working space," a flexible workspace or facility with a membership fee (a dedicated desk space could be purchased at a premium rate). Metal and wood workshops were also available for members, and classes in everything from web design to woodworking to sewing were offered.

3rd Ward was already on the radar of trend spotters in 2006, when it was mentioned in an article in the *Village Voice* about DJs, artists and promoters who were forming their own dance clubs throughout the city. The article declares that the club nights 3rd Ward hosted in their space fit in with a trend of "putting the emphasis on art over commerce, but not at the total expense of the latter." Jason Goodman is quoted in this article, saying, "We're all doing it because we love it. Not because there's some big payoff at the end."[14] Within seven years, people would be calling Goodman, "a selfish, duplicitous crook disguised as a pioneering leader of the Brooklyn arts/hipster community."[15] Thinking like a maker and not an artist, Goodman tried to reach a larger and larger audience in an increasingly diverse set of ventures.

One of the earliest projects Goodman embarked on in 2007 was a straightforward web start-up venture, demonstrating the intimate entanglement between the Maker Movement, Morgantown artistic activity, and the world of tech entrepreneurialism. Working with William Etundi, a party-promoter operating under the name "Danger," he came up with the idea for a website called ArtistsWanted.org where artists could pay a fee to submit their work online in the hopes of garnering enough votes for a gallery show in Manhattan.[16] One hopeful participant described the pitfalls of this fee-based system in a lengthy blog entry, concluding, "I guess my point is that while on the surface this may have been a noble effort to support the arts, it turned out to be a combination of a clusterfuck and a scam."[17] The project was rebranded as See.Me, merging social network and marketplace, a Facebook meets Etsy for art professionals.[18] Goodman also expanded the real estate holdings of 3rd Ward into Williamsburg in a loft building at 573 Metropolitan Avenue and opened a food truck across from it called Goods. The building was shut down due to occupancy violations on October 15, 2010 and Goods was apparently in financial trouble as well, reportedly paying their employees in IOUs and closing shortly after 573 Metropolitan shuttered.[19] 3rd Ward, however, continued to expand in the next few years, with Goodman opening a second space in Philadelphia in April 2013 (which also closed in October of that year along with the rest of 3rd Ward's holdings) and a culinary "incubator" in Brooklyn.[20]

In a 2010 *New York Times* article published before 3rd Ward began to show evidence of cracks along the seams, Jason Goodman explains the transition from artist- to maker-focused space. He is quoted by the *Times*, saying:

We've changed a lot. When we opened, because we came from art backgrounds, we were thinking, like, artist, artist, artist, but really it's like designer, designer, designer, artist. We have way more inventors, furniture makers, cabinet makers, commercial photographers, hackers, than we do what you would originally conceive of like an artist.[21]

Despite Goodman's impressive self-promotion, he was essentially a DIY businessperson. His business was a cobbled together affair that was mired by disorder and unprofessional handling of staff and funds throughout its existence. It is clear that Goodman really did want to start a community of sorts: not an insular collection of friends and neighborhood locals nor an old-school artist co-op or communal space but a community more akin to online social networks where the room for expansion was potentially global and the user market included everyone.

Goodman, in true maker spirit, was creating a product (or series of products) and a brand that he marketed and promoted tirelessly, just as many of his co-workers created niche products in his facilities with the aspiration of growing bigger. As Chris Anderson enthusiastically outlines in his book, maker culture is essentially a continuation of the tech entrepreneurship from the immaterial world of bits to the real world of things.[22] In a 2012 interview, Goodman stated, "At the end of the day we're still running a business, so we want to expand and make money, but really we feel like we're participating in something that's so much bigger – this maker culture movement. People are craving this tactile, self-efficient practice and we give them a place to do that, a place to learn and connect with other creatives."[23] Maker culture, like tech entrepreneurship, is infused with a neoliberal ethos and celebrates extreme individuality and self-reliance. The proponents of maker culture sing its utopian promises with an evangelical zeal, but, like many Maker Movement DIY projects, 3rd Ward was built with a lot of enthusiasm, very little thought and planning, and a heavy dose of megalomania.

In an interview in March 2013, Jason Goodman discussed the opening of 3rd Ward's Philadelphia branch and his plans to open a restaurant on the ground floor of the new complex, saying, "We want this building to be a hub for the community. You can't really have that without food and drink."[24] True to hipster stereotypes, any old anonymous coffee shop or Starbucks would not be sufficient to satisfy the highly-personalized tastes of makers. Food and drink are just as much a part of the Maker Movement as design and craft. Hard-to-find ingredients and unusual vegetables as well as specialist meats and cheeses like sopressata, guanciale, burrata and caciocavallo are accompanied by qualifiers like "artisanal," "foraged," "small batch," "farm to table," and "locavore."

Food

Like 3rd Ward, pizza restaurant Roberta's was started in an unplanned, chaotic way and has had a quick ascent and wild successes, expanding into frozen food, various pop-up ventures, and, most notably, gaining two Michelin stars for its high-end chef's table restaurant Blanca. As the money and acclaim has come flowing in, however, the DIY, improvised approach to business has become a problem for Roberta's, as it did for 3rd Ward. In 2015, *The New York Times* reports that tensions between the founders of the restaurants were heating up, with calls to the police, restraining orders being issued, and major disagreements over the seemingly exponential expansion plans of the business.[25] Roberta's is by far the quintessential example of Maker Movement foodie-ism and has, more than any other

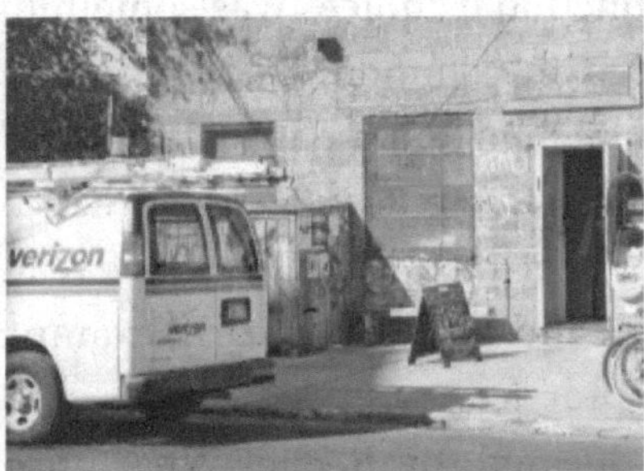
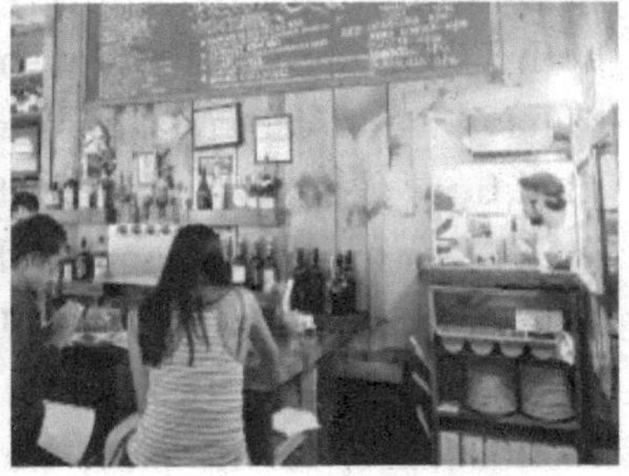

business in the neighborhood, put Morgantown on the map. Located at 261 Moore Street, tucked around the corner of the main stretch of shops on Bogart Street, it is situated in an unassuming single-story former industrial garage.[26] Started by Chris Parachini, who named it after his mother and who has been seen as the figurehead of the venture, Brandon Hoy, and Carlo Mirarchi, it is an anchor point of the neighborhood and a pilgrimage site for foodies from across the city, offering gourmet pizzas with twee names and unusual ingredients.

There is an important historical precedent for the artist-turned-restaurateur. FOOD in SoHo, a culinary experiment started by Gordon Matta-Clark, Carol Goodden, and Tina Girouard in 1971 at 127 Prince Street, had, on the surface, a DIY spirit similar to Parachini's at Roberta's. Like Morgantown in the 2000s, SoHo in the 1970s was an industrial area that initially lacked basic amenities. When artists first took up residence in its former sweatshops and light industrial manufactories there were no grocery stores, restaurants, and laundromats to accommodate the new residential community. The tight-knit community in SoHo during this time regularly staged elaborate dinner parties at each other's loft spaces, and FOOD was a natural extension of this communal activity.

The interest of FOOD's founders in locally and ethically sourced ingredients, interesting and inventive flavor combinations and fresh rather than pre-frozen or processed ingredients was way ahead of its time in the 1970s. Even the desire to make aesthetic over purely functional choices was something both FOOD and Roberta's shared in common. Goodden chose to have wood cabinets, an open kitchen and a particular type of tiled floor despite the fact that these elements were less practical than other materials she may have selected.[27] FOOD can be read, at least in the years between 1971 and 1973, as an early example of relational aesthetics or social practice.

Roberta's, for its part, was deemed, by Rachel Wharton of

Edible Brooklyn as "... like a conceptual art happening, though one where the mismatched chairs at the mismatched tables look like the crap even your aesthetically challenged younger brother passes up at garage sales."[28] Roberta's atmosphere and décor seems to have an unusual ability to elicit these kind of wide-eyed descriptions. Jeff Gordinier, in *The New York Times*, likens Roberta's (and its founders) to a garage band, saying, "The place has always styled itself as being about much more than food. Equipped with picnic tables and a tented tiki bar and an on-site radio station, Roberta's can feel like a slacker version of Studio 54 as staged by *Portlandia* extras in an abandoned abattoir."[29] Lizzie Widdicombe of *The New Yorker* writes, "[...] the décor – Christmas lights, pogo sticks – seems genuinely amateurish and unstudied. It's the kind of operation you probably once dreamed of building in your parents' garage."[30] Underneath the shared visual signifiers of "conceptual art" or artistic food experiment, however, Roberta's was founded on a wholly different philosophy than the one on which FOOD was founded. FOOD's ideological underpinning was rooted in the social movements of the late 1960s/early '70s while Roberta's subscribes to the present-day Maker Movement.

Matta-Clark, Goodden and Girouard had an inward looking, communal and non-business-oriented outlook. They wanted to create something that was for *their* community, to create a mini-utopia in SoHo. They never intended to grow their business beyond its service to their friends and associates in the neighborhood and they certainly were not looking to turn a tremendous profit. In fact, they left the project just as it was turning into an actual business.[31] Lori Waxman argues that their DIY attitude was an expression and natural extension of the social movements of the time, including the women's movement, black power, and gay liberation, that attempted to put political rhetoric into direct action. It was a commune of sorts where they actively sought to employ other artists rather than, for example, use dishwashers or other convenience tools to do the jobs that could be filled by people in need of income. They also had relaxed scheduling where artists could work as much or as little as they wanted, despite labor laws that made this flexible arrangement disadvantageous from a business perspective.[32] Roberta's, in contrast, has more in common with the tech start-up than the commune. As a maker business, Parachini and his associates aim to grow and expand so that their business can reach as wide an audience as possible. It has been reported that they were looking at ventures in all corners of New York City, as well as the West Coast and even Asia.[33] The disagreement between the three original partners has seen Hoy and Mirarchi attempt to buy out and, ultimately, oust Parachini from the venture. After years of legal battles, Parachini settled in early 2017, though Roberta's was still embroiled in ongoing ownership disputes.[34] Roberta's faced other legal troubles in July 2015 when an employee sued the restaurant for unpaid overtime after being told he was not entitled to any because he was paid off the books.[35] In August of that year, it emerged that Roberta's owed approximately $480,000 in unpaid taxes, putting the business on an eerily similar trajectory to 3rd Ward, where rapid expansion led to a quick succession of employee pay complaints and financial difficulties.[36]

In what has now become the familiar narrative of Morgantown makers, Chris Parachini, described by *New York Magazine* as a "musician/bartender/conceptual artist," moved to the area around 2004 in search of space for his hybrid creative activities.[37] Another refugee from rapid development and gentrification of the Williamsburg waterfront, Parachini came up with the idea for Roberta's in late 2006 and, together with his friend and fellow musician Brandon Hoy who contributed $13,000 in start-up funds, he began building the space in March 2007. Joined by Carlo Mirarchi, who contributed $30,000 and signed up to be head chef, Roberta's finally opened in January 2008, named after

Parachini's mother.[38] The opening of Roberta's marked a turning point for the neighborhood and its entrepreneurs. Again, the restaurant is not just a restaurant, but, like 3rd Ward, it is an "incubator." *Food & Wine* named Parachini and Hoy as "locavore leaders" and calls Roberta's, "an incubator for other locavore projects."[39]

Following expansionist business tactic much like Jason Goodman of 3rd Ward, Parachini infused Roberta's with a DIY spirit and the incumbent chaos of hosting many projects at once: publishing cookbooks, starting local farming operations, opening a high-end restaurant Blanca, operating an artisanal bread bakery, opening a take-away business, and running booths in food markets and festivals. Parachini, echoing the maker mantra of creativity above all, is quoted in 2009, saying, "We are most interested in the creative process. We have a really hard time saying no to anything. It's a pretty chaotic thing over here. We don't have any hard-and-fast rules."[40] While Parachini's product has had more success than Goodman's over the course of its existence, they both demonstrated a boundless enthusiasm for expansion and presence beyond the artistic community in Morgantown.

The year Roberta's opened, 2008, ushered in a period of consolidation and formalization of the Morgantown area into a neighborhood rather than an industrial park. While Brooklyn's Natural, the small supermarket a few doors down from Roberta's, had been in the area since 2002, one of the key facets missing in Morgantown, as noted, was the infrastructure needed to conduct daily life: grocery stores, shops, restaurants, etc.[41] With the arrival of Roberta's, Morgantown was no longer an uninhabitable wasteland but had become a desirable and amenable place to live and work. While FOOD in SoHo filled a need for the locals, Roberta's made Morgantown a destination.

Foodies

The food movement and the Maker Movement have been flirting with one another for years without making their relationship explicit. In 2015, more makers were experimenting with food and more foodies were joining the Maker Movement. An article from the foodie section of hipster publication *Vice* states that there is "[...] a new generation of chefs and home cooks who are embracing the principles of maker culture and applying them in the kitchen. The same thing is also happening on the flip side: Techies are making the move from computers to kitchens."[42] Much like the larger Maker Movement, foodie-makers are aiming to deregulate the kitchen environment, armed with the belief that everyone is capable of producing quality food and inventing new kitchen equipment. While traditional DIY inspires hobbyists to craft their own foods at home, the Maker Movement urges them to turn their kitchen experiments into a viable product with a business to back it up.

The food movement, which was initiated by the same countercultural forces of the 1960s that started the tech industry, has been gaining momentum in the last fifteen years. While New York's current obsession with artisanal food may be partially attributable to the environmentalism initiated by Rachel Carson's *Silent Spring* and the hippies of Haight-Ashbury, it is also, in an oblique way, attributable to the tech industry that grew out of the do-it-yourself, individuality-obsessed counterculture. The particular interest in food in recent times has been part of the larger phenomenon of hipster culture. Chris Anderson's "long tail" of Internet content applies, not only to music, video, and other digital content, but also to food. Along with fashion and music tastes, hipsters look for ways to individuate themselves from their peers, if even for an ephemeral moment until others "catch up" and the fickle hipster is forced to move on to a new fad. Craft brewed beer, the resurgence of traditional cocktails, Brooklyn's many small distilleries, artisanal breads, pickles, and condiments, restaurants with foraged or self-grown ingredients from rooftop gardens, etc., are all part of the expanded universe of consumption, enabled by the Internet, that have fueled hipster culture in the twenty-first century.

One of the oft-repeated sentiments in the Maker Movement is that existing manufacturing does not have "exactly what you're looking for" – a niche product with an equally niche market, such as the underwater open-source ROV or foldable kayak discussed in Chapter 2. The same sentiment can easily be applied to food. Empire Mayonnaise in Prospect Heights, Brooklyn, which is now closed, produced Nori, Yuzu Chili, Bacon, and White Truffle flavored artisanal mayonnaises for around eight dollars per jar.[43] An episode of *Saturday Night Live*, which aired on January 17, 2015, parodied the arrival of an "artisanal mayo" producer in Bushwick, much like Empire Mayonnaise, poking fun at how maker businesses are gentrifying formerly tough Brooklyn neighborhoods. Questioned about the role of her business in gentrification after the episode aired, co-owner Elizabeth Valleau responded cheerfully to accusations that Empire is a force of gentrification, claiming that they *wanted* to be "a little provocative" – not unlike the rhetoric of the tech entrepreneur who is aiming to "disrupt" the market. Valleau says, "People are trying to politicize us, but ultimately we're just a couple folks from the neighborhood who have a condiment business and we're making it in the neighborhood instead of in a big warehouse out in New Jersey or something like that. Which we're proud of."[44] Valleau's fairytale story is a classic narrative for maker-foodies that has been repeated many times over: just a few local folks who took their passion for making things and started selling them to help the community.

Many of the Brooklyn-born or Brooklyn-made products are first launched or marketed at Brooklyn Flea, a hipster craft market where vendors sell handmade products and secondhand goods, located in Fort Greene on Saturdays and Williamsburg on Sundays. Founded in 2008 by Jonathan Butler, who created the Brooklyn real estate blog Brownstoner.com, and Eric Denby, a former communications director and political speech writer, the market has not only become a testing ground for a variety of niche food items but a tourist attraction in its own right.[45] Smorgasburg, a spin-off from Brooklyn Flea that focuses only on food, was launched in 2011 and is located in Williamsburg and Prospect Park on Saturdays and Sundays, respectively.[46]

One Brooklyn-Flea incubated company, Maiden Preserves, was started by Alison Roman and Eva Scofield after their employer, dessert shop Momofuku Milk Bar, offered to let employees sell their wares from Milk Bar's booth. Roman and Scofield decided to purchase more expensive Weck jars for their products and combined luxurious and unusual flavors like blood orange-Campari, grapefruit-hibiscus, and orange-bourbon. They found a good deal of success both at the market and at shops around the New York area, but, ultimately, like 3rd Ward and Roberta's, financial difficulties arose due to the high cost of production and unanticipated overheads. This caused a rift between the two partners, who disagreed whether/how to scale up their business.[47] It seems that, in order to succeed in the maker business, a large portion of artisanal idealism must be sacrificed.

It is striking how similar the stories of artist-entrepreneurs in Brooklyn are. A long line of former "somethings" (often creative occupations like artist, designer, dancer, etc.) launch artisanal businesses with little prior knowledge of either the product or running a business. One such company, sold at Brooklyn Flea, is Brooklyn Sesame, which makes artisanal halva spreads. The company was started by former professional dancer Shahar Shamir, whose "Story" states that, "Since sugar-heavy commercial halva was not an option, he combined the passion of a dancer and the know-how of a cook to experiment with sesame, pure honey and raw almonds until he found the perfect balance of ingredients."[48] Brooklyn Soda Works, another Brooklyn Flea vendor, created "artisanal, handmade sodas" with fresh fruit and flavors like Red Current & Shiso and Watermelon & Tarragon. The company was started by an installation artist, Caroline Mak, and her partner, chemist Antonio Ramos, in Brooklyn and financed by Kickstarter.[49] Mak explains, like many other maker-foodies, how the skills she acquired in her art practice feed into her food business, saying, "As an installation artist, I am used to working on large-scale projects with short deadlines. These skills prove useful as a small food business entrepreneur. Both of our professional lives have and continue to involve figuring out how to make things; working in a huge commercial kitchen is not a huge leap."[50] Brooklyn Soda Works also struggled with the issue of scale and whether their artisanal, fresh ingredients would suffer in the process, apparently opting to remain closer to home for the sake of their product.[51]

One artisanal Brooklyn company that has survived the process of scaling up their production is organic ice cream maker Blue Marble, which was co-founded by former actress Jennie Dundas. In an interview, which focuses on her transition from actress to ice cream maker, Dundas says, "When we first opened in 2007, we had a little sign on the register that said, 'Please be patient with us as we learn how to run an ice cream shop.' That really said it all. I would say 2010 to 2012 were really hard learning years for us because we knew nothing about business. I had never opened Excel in my life."[52] Dundas also explains, like Mak and Shamir, that acting and being in the creative professions has been an asset to her business, as it taught her an "unwillingness to give up" and the ability to "bounce back and think positively."[53] Another pair of artisanal entrepreneurs, Chris Poeschl and Tony Lanuza, were also both pursuing acting when they decided to embark on a bakery business called The Brooklyn Baking Barons, despite not having any experience in professional baking. Like many Brooklyn foodie-makers, their website tells their fairytale story, saying, "It all started with a dinner party on a cold Brooklyn night – great friends, good wine, and of course, a killer menu. It was flawless; our friends were quite impressed. It wasn't long before someone mentioned: 'You know, you should sell this stuff. Or have a blog. Something!'"[54] Although their story is a classic Brooklyn maker-hipster business story, Poeschl makes a point to assert he and his partner are *not* hipsters. They merely wanted to celebrate Brooklyn in the name of their business.[55]

Even though artisanal condiments, baked goods, and obscure world foods have become a cliché many times over by now, the flow of new products has not let up. Perhaps one of the most honest and transparent, though no more self-aware, "our story" write-ups comes from Sunny Bang Private Label Probiotic Hot Sauce, a company which certainly packs as many niche/luxury adjectives as possible into one name. After reading *New York Magazine*'s feature on artisanal food, "The Twee Party," which looks critically at the artisanal food movement, Sunny Bang's (and his wife's) take-away from the article was that hot sauce was one of the few untapped market openings in the artisanal scene. Bang boasts, "Raw, additive and preservative-free, gluten-free and vegan with a fruit-forward complex flavor, heat and health benefits... what more could you want from your hot sauce? Besides, how cool is it that the vinegar in the hot sauce is made by a Benedictine monk?!?"[56] Not only do niche products appeal to their makers, who feel that they are creating something unique and personalized, they also fill a need for consumers to constantly upgrade or change their product consumption to continue to feel unique in their consumption habits. This should not be good news for artisanal food entrepreneurs. If they survive the learning curve of starting a business, they may not remain popular for long. Bang, for instance, had a lot of competition. Heatonist, a hot sauce "tasting room" and shop, complete with "hot sauce sommelier," opened in Greenpoint in May 2015 after raising almost $27,000 on Kickstarter, and offers a range of artisanal brands of hot sauce.[57] With the Brooklyn brand seemingly saturated, a new brand of hot sauce was launched from the Bronx in July 2015, The Bronx Hot Sauce, with a community-focused agenda.[58]

The make-or-break, risk-it-all model of the tech industry has been translated across the board to all types of business, starting primarily with small-scale artisanal "start-ups." Like the tech industry, these companies are looking to the donations of Kickstarter users for small business loans rather than traditional channels. While the Maker Movement may be literally bringing the Internet into the world of real things, the Internet and the libertarian ideology of the tech industry have already saturated the business landscape and colonized "creativity."

Maker Movement proponents like Chris Anderson, Cory Doctorow, and Dale Dougherty view the movement as an emerging phenomenon, which will eventually revolutionize the world. Much of the technology being developed under the umbrella of the Maker Movement will change our lives in profound ways. Perhaps the educational initiatives will create a new generation of more capable and creative individuals, but the directions new technologies will take us are not as problem-free as makers lead us to believe. For example, the constant surveillance promised by various life-logging products – those that record every moment of one's life from vital signs to imagery – is not without its pitfalls. Given the sudden ubiquity of selfie sticks in public places, it is not too difficult to imagine makers developing selfie drones to follow us around day and night, recording our life events. In fact, several cameras already exist for this purpose, including the Narrative clip camera developed by Swedish company Memoto in 2012 and funded by – no surprise here – Kickstarter. The Narrative automatically takes two pictures every minute, ensuring that no moment goes undocumented. The company advertises the product as a way for busy parents to capture every moment of their child growing up, without disrupting whatever activity they're engaged in. It is equally easy to imagine corporations or governments using this data for their own purposes.

The Maker Movement, however, seems to be simply an effect rather than a cause of the change we are seeing, and the term "maker" is no more than a branding exercise. This change was already beginning to blossom around 1999 or 2000 with the advent of hipster culture and its Internet-enabled insatiability for personalized, individualized *everything*, including things in the real world. While these tendencies have existed since the counterculture of the 1960s, the rise of neoliberal political ideology in the '80s and the advent of the mass market Internet in the '90s fueled a cultural push toward extreme individualism. The non-robotic branch of the Maker Movement, which did not grow out of hackerspaces and incubators and was not pioneered by people who know programming languages, has developed almost in tandem with the more traditionally techy side of the movement and was easily assimilated into the fold. These non-robotics makers are the ones turning to knitting, homemade pickling, or craft brewed beer. The transformation of society that makers are hoping to achieve with the Maker Movement has, essentially, already occurred in hipster culture, where a turn back to DIY in every aspect of life was the end result of Internet-enabled individualism.

Luddites and tech acolytes fervently discuss the advent of the so-called "Internet of Things," a networked version of our world where everything is connected to the Internet, exchanging and collecting data from every object we own – from the refrigerator in the kitchen at home to the clothing racks at the local department store. The term was first coined in 1999 by British tech entrepreneur Kevin Ashton while he was working on RFID (radio-frequency ID) tagging technology, which he saw had the potential to network the physical world. The Internet of Things promises "smarter" environments that can react in real time to changing conditions and that can be controlled remotely.

One early product to the market in this arena is Nest, a smart home thermostat that allows the user to monitor energy usage and control the temperature from afar. It was founded by Tony Fadell, a former Apple designer who is considered the "father" of the iPod, and was acquired by Google in 2014 for $3.2 billion. In 2012, Fadell, breaking with the conventional wisdom of Silicon Valley, issued a warning against using Kickstarter to fund hardware projects, saying, "When you see a lot of these Kickstarter and Indiegogo projects, there are passionate people behind them, but they don't always necessarily understand what they're getting themselves into. Well, you can build one of anything. To manufacture something and make 100,000 is a whole other scale of problems you have to face."[59] Fadell, unlike many Maker Movement proponents, is looking realistically at manufacturing and can see that the Maker Movement and its New Industrial Revolution is still no substitute for industrial production. Nevertheless, many makers are interested in not only inventing objects that communicate with each other and collect data, thereby participating in the Internet of Things, but also objects that can be replicated solely through data, such as the Autodesk designs that a 3D printer can quickly replicate. The Internet of Things, therefore, has come to encompass both networked devices and objects stored as data on the network.

While these networked devices and objects are only in the beginning stages of development, we have, via the Internet, already created a network of things. Even though they are not *themselves* communicating with digital networks, they are part of our networked world in the form of pictures and text, moved around by websites like eBay, Etsy, and Amazon. Almost everything that has ever been produced is catalogued and documented, and most of the objects that are still extant are available for sale somewhere online. We have access to not only the consumer goods of our time but those of previous generations.

Where once the secondhand shop or flea market was the only place to find old clothes or household items, now countless websites and vendors sell vintage clothes and retro consumer goods online. In their quest to keep the curation of their lives continually fresh, unique, and individual, hipsters mine both the past and the present. While vintage clothing boutiques have been around since the 1960s, the rise in popularity of vintage clothing and secondhand shops among young people in the last twenty years tracks with the hipster need to curate individuality.

Foodie culture, as part of the larger hipster movement toward personalized, curated self-identity, seeks out authenticity through raw, organic, natural, or local ingredients. Like vintage clothing shopping, old methods of production are sometimes valued above newer ones due to their authenticity and originality. The Maker Movement, as an extension of this, favors the handmade or homemade, but, like other aspects of hipster culture, these techniques are always aided by networked technology. Even the most rudimentary craft activities are facilitated by online how-to videos and shared/published on social media once the task is complete. The self-promotion or "sharing" that goes along with handmade or homemade products is essential to the project. As Mark Hatch, CEO of TechShop says, "You cannot make and not share."[60]

Artists In Morgantown

How artists make and share their work is changing in Morgantown. Many artists, both by choice and out of necessity, no longer identify solely or primarily as artists. According to a 2008 report from the National Endowment of the Arts (NEA), the number of fine artists in the United States (grouped together with art directors and animators) declined between 1990 and 2005 while the number of designers increased. The report explains, "Some of this shift probably can be attributed to the change in occupation definitions [...]."[61] According to the statistic gathered from the National Center for Education Statistics, approximately 15,000 bachelor's and 2,100 master's degrees were granted in Fine Art in 1991–92 (excluding non-visual art disciplines such as Music, Dance, and other performing arts, as well as Art History and Arts Management).[62] By 2011–12, universities were awarding approximately 57,000 BA and 6,500 MA degrees.[63] Looking at these statistics, it is clear that the number of Fine Art graduates has increased.

These art students are specifically studying disciplines like painting, sculpture, and intermedia arts that place them squarely in a fine art tradition and context. As the NEA has noted, arts occupations and their definitions are shifting. Even those who graduated in fine art are, perhaps, now finding themselves in more commercial disciplines like design. Some have probably given up on traditional art practice, seeking creative outlet in maker businesses like the artisan food ones described above. Although New York City has long been a haven for arts graduates and a hub of arts activities, artists are finding it harder and harder to carve out workspaces. The rough early days of Morgantown were condensed between 1999 and 2003 and, in the future, other gentrifying neighborhoods will perhaps move ever quicker.

One organization in Morgantown, The Active Space at 566 Johnson Avenue, has been providing studios to artists since 2011, when a freshly minted art graduate from the Rhode Island School of Design (RISD), Ashley Zelinskie, teamed up with property developer David Welner of Welner Associates to transform the former feather factory into studio and gallery space. Zelinskie is the quintessential maker/artist-entrepreneur, producing sculptures funded by Kickstarter and printed with a MakerBot 3D printer. Zelinskie, in line with her young peers entering the neighborhood, is filled with optimism and enthusiasm for remaking the urban industrial fabric of Morgantown and harnessing the self-promotional tools of the Internet. Her 2011 Kickstarter, for a project titled "Reverse Abstraction," raised

$3,020. Reiterating the tenets of the Maker Movement, her fundraising page states, "Reverse Abstraction stemmed from my obsession with computers and the Internet. I had such a passion for the democratizing qualities that this technology provided, that, I knew I had to make it work with my art."[64] Zelinskie also attempts to tie the use of Kickstarter in with the work itself, as a statement of the "positive" effects of technology. She writes:

> I chose to use Kickstarter to raise the money for the work because I am replicating a system of how things are accomplished on the Internet. Groups, forums, and underground online communities use community and charity based systems in order to accomplish goals they deem worthy. The most reported on use of this system is probably the negative use of it such as hacker groups taking down media or government websites. However, this system is also used everyday to accomplish positive goals but is seldom recognized by the general public. Kickstarter is one of the more popular positive uses of the system so I wanted that to become a part of the work.[65]

The integration of platforms such as Kickstarter into artists' work can be seen within the broader trend of "Post-Internet" art, which was coined by Marisa Olson in 2008 to describe the way that the Internet infuses all aspects of life and so it cannot be separated from "new media" art practices.[66]

Since the mid-90s, the art world has been splintered between more institutional practices and so-called new media art. The hacker, DIY or Maker attitude pervades new media art and was often sneered at by powerful art world commentators throughout the early '00s.[67] This may be partly due to the ways in which new media art turns away from post-structuralism and leftist critical theory and often embodies a techno-utopian optimism and an un-tempered enthusiasm for new gadgets and software tools that mirrors the rhetoric of tech start-ups. As Claire Bishop writes, "New media feels like a dated category because today everyone is 'postinternet,' a confusing term that indicates not the chronological end of the Internet but simply its prevalence and banality."[68] Post-Internet is not only the banality and pervasiveness of the Internet – which seems far too vague of a definition – but it is, in effect, what I have been describing as maker or hipster culture. The sharing economy has compelled a generation of people to curate their own unique and totally individualized tastes, styles, music, films, images, and interests, which are all easily accessible online and make up Chris Anderson's long tail of consumption. It might be useful to think about Post-Internet art as maker or hipster art instead (although the term hipster is probably too negatively loaded) because the term Post-Internet describes the same quest for uniqueness and individuality that Web 2.0 and the Maker Movement have enabled. Post-Internet art takes this solitary, individualistic existence in the maker economy as a point of departure. The Internet is not just pervasive; it has atomized a generation and set them off on a quest to formulate themselves through totally unique forms of consumption.

The desperate unpopularity of new media art has been replaced by growing excitement for Post-Internet art in art markets and at international exhibitions and biennials. Artists and art groups associated with the Post-Internet moment include *DIS Magazine*, Camille Henrot, Jon Rafman, Cory Arcangel, Marisa Olson, Artie Vierkant and Cécile B. Evans among many others.[69] The popularity of Post-Internet has risen along with the Maker Movement and, indeed, many of these artists are excited about the same tools as self-described makers. The art market took very little interest in digital art in the past, but, as Post-Internet brings Internet logic to the realm of physical objects, the lives of the digital natives are suddenly in the spotlight. The transition from artist to maker seen in Morgantown is, thus, also transforming the art world.

The use of "post" in Post-Internet has come to mean "after the advent of the Internet," not "after the *end* of the Internet," unlike "postmodernism" which theorized the end of modernism. But what if Post-Internet means the end of the artist in favor of the maker? What if the term "artist" no longer has meaning outside of narrowly defined professionals within the global contemporary art market? Maybe the term "artist" does not even adequately describe what these art-world-types do today and how they relate to one another; maybe they are also acting in the hybrid roles of artist-entrepreneur/maker. "Creativity" is more popular than ever in business, urban planning, and academia, but we should perhaps pause to take note of the way the rhetoric of creativity is mobilized to change the urban fabric in places like Morgantown and the way we consume it in this hyper-individualized age. The new Creative American Dream has promised to bring jobs back to industrial cities and foster a new age of autonomy and fulfilment for those that tap into it. But the truth is that we are *not* all makers, as Dale Dougherty says. At least not yet, anyway.

Endnotes

Introduction

1. Hrag Vartanian, "Is Ridgewood Breaking Away from the Bushwick Scene?" *Hyperallergic*, May 8, 2012, http://hyperallergic.com/51210/actually-its-ridgewood/.

2. Paddy Johnson and Whitney Kimball, "Jules de Balincourt Issues Call to Arms Against Bushwick Gentrification," *Art F City*, June 9, 2013, http://artfcity.com/2013/06/09/jules-de-balincourt-issues-call-to-arms-against-bushwick-gentrification-on-facebook/.

3. Starr Space is located at 108-110 Starr Street. See, Jillian Steinhauer, "Bushwick Artists Ponder Ways to Fight Gentrification," *Hyperallergic*, June 21, 2013, http://hyperallergic.com/73855/bushwick-artists-ponder-ways-to-fight-gentrification/.

4. The Rheingold Brewery site is located roughly between Flushing Avenue and Melrose Street to the north and south and Evergreen and Bushwick Avenues to the east and west.

5. Meredith Hoffman, "Controversial Bushwick Rezoning to Add High Rises, Streets and Retail," *DNAinfo New York*, June 20, 2013, http://www.dnainfo.com/new-york/20130620/bushwick/controversial-bushwick-rezoning-add-high-rises-streets-retail/.

6. William Powhida, "The Yellow Building," May 15, 2014, https://docs.google.com/document/d/1dLl0V_7AejNr2eSPgZyZ5Vd3IrSZPgvROMlEW5Jd-EI/.

7. Steinhauer, "Bushwick Artists Ponder Ways to Fight Gentrification."

8. Morgantown is often referred to as Bushwick although Bushwick's northern boundary is technically Flushing Avenue, just to the south of Morgantown.

9. William Powhida, "Bushwick Don't Worry," May 15, 2014,

http://williampowhida.com/wordpress/archives/476.

10. Thomas Burr Dodd, conversation with the author, May 3, 2014.

11. Both published books on the subject: Cory Doctorow, *Makers* (New York: Tor, 2009); Chris Anderson, *Makers: The New Industrial Revolution* (New York: Crown Business, 2012).

12. Richard L. Florida, *The Rise of the Creative Class, Revisited* (New York: Basic Books, 2012).

13. Neil Smith, "New City, New Frontier: The Lower East Side as Wild, Wild West," in *Variations on a Theme Park: The New American City and the End of Public Space*, ed. Michael Sorkin (New York: Macmillan, 1992); Neil Smith, *The New Urban Frontier: Gentrification and the Revanchist City* (London; New York: Routledge, 1996).

14. Another name for the area, Alphabet City pays homage to its alphabetic rather than numerical avenue names and was coined by the artistic community in the late 1970s and early 1980s. Puerto Rican residents had previously used the Spanglish name Loisaida. See: Christopher Mele, *Selling the Lower East Side: Culture, Real Estate, and Resistance in New York City* (University of Minnesota Press, 2000), xi, 287.

15. Emily Nonko, "How Bloomberg Changed New York Real Estate," *NewYork.com*, August 29, 2013, http://www.newyork .com/articles/real-estate/how-bloomberg-changed-new-york-real-estate-99465/.

16. Ann Fensterstock, *Art on the Block: Tracking the New York Art World from SoHo to the Bowery, Bushwick and Beyond* (Macmillan, 2013), 169.

17. Deborah Brown, "Luhring Augustine Arrives on The Scene," *Bushwick Daily*, February 20, 2012, http://bushwickdaily. com/2012/02/luhring-augustine-arrives-on-the-scene/.

18. Norman Mailer, Jean Malaquais, and Ned Polsky, *The White Negro* (San Francisco: City Lights Books, 1957).

19. Christina Dunbar-Hester, "Radical Inclusion? Locating

Accountability in Technical DIY," in *DIY Citizenship: Critical Making and Social Media*, eds. Matt Ratto and Megan Boler (Cambridge, MA: MIT Press, 2014), 84.

20. Jen Jack Gieseking, "Queering the Meaning of 'Neighbourhood': Reinterpreting the Lesbian-Queer Experience of Park Slope, Brooklyn, 1983–2008," in *Queer Presences and Absences*, ed. Yvette Taylor (New York: Palgrave Macmillan, 2013), 178–200.

21. STEM is used in education circles and stands for science, technology, engineering, and mathematics.

22. Andrew Dugan, "Americans Most Likely to Say They Belong to the Middle Class," *Gallup*, accessed May 29, 2016, http://www.gallup.com/poll/159029/americans-likely-saybelong-middle-class.aspx; Atkinson, Anthony B. and Andrea Brandolini, "On the Identification of the Middle Class," *Income Inequality: Economic Disparities and the Middle Class in Affluent Countries* (2013): 77–100; Peter Moore, "YouGov | Poll Results: Middle Class," YouGov: What the World Thinks, May 28, 2015, https://today.yougov.com /news/20 15/05/28/poll-results-middle-class/; Jay Livingston, "Why Rich People Think They're Middle Class," *Sociological Images*, April 22, 2015, https://thesocietypages.org/socim ages/2015/04/22/is-chris-christie-middle-class-class-and-selfperception/. More recent data has shown that the number of Americans identifying as middle class is decreasing. See "The American Middle Class Is Losing Ground," *Pew Research Center's Social & Demographic Trends Project*, December 9, 2015, http://www.pewsocialtrends.org/2015 /12/09/the-american-middle-class-is-losing-ground/; Frank Newport, "Fewer Americans Identify as Middle Class in Recent Years," *Gallup*, April 28, 2015, http://www.gall up.com/poll/182918/fewer-americans-identify-middle-class-recent-years.aspx.

23. Kazys Varnelis, "The Rise of Network Culture," May 15,

2014, http://varnelis.net/the_rise_of_network_culture.

24. OfficeOps, accessed May 15, 2014, http://www.officeops.org.

25. Occupancy records for 119 Ingraham: "Property Profile Overview: 119 INGRAHAM STREET," NYC *Department of Buildings*, May 15, 2014, http://a810-bisweb.nyc.gov/bisw eb/PropertyProfileOverviewServlet?boro=3&houseno=119&s treet=ingraham&go2=+GO+&requestid=0.

26. The Loft Law was a piece of legislation from 1982 in New York State, also known as Article 7-C of the New York Multiple Dwelling Law. In brief, the law provides basic protection against eviction for people living in non-residentially zoned buildings and its provision compels landlords to bring the buildings up to code and forbids them from charging tenants for these upgrades. Many tenants and building owners alike would rather not have their properties classified under the Loft Law and, as was the case with my building, it's often used as a last-ditch method of preserving residences in industrial buildings. See, *NYC Loft Tenants*, accessed May 16, 2016, http://nyclofttenants.org/loft-law-101/.

27. Rebecca Baird-Remba, "Permits Filed: Hotel And Medical Offices at 25 Stewart Avenue, Bushwick," *New York YIMBY*, May 20, 2015, http://newyorkyimby.com/2015/05/permits-filed-hotel-and-medical-offices-at-25-stewart-avenue-bushwick.html.

28. "NYAB Venue – The Active Space," *NY Art Beat*, accessed October 24, 2015, http://www.nyartbeat.com/venue/00E 394AC.

29. At time of editing this book, the Trump administration has proposed this final, drastic cut to dissolve the NEA.

Chapter 1

1. "Dale Dougherty – O'Reilly Radar," March 16, 2015, http:// radar.oreilly.com/dale.

2. Chris Anderson, "20 Years of Wired: Maker Movement," *Wired UK*, February 5, 2013, http://www.wired.co.uk/mag azine/archive/2013/06/feature-20-years-of-wired/maker-movement.

3. Guy Debord, *The Society of the Spectacle* (New York: Zone Books, 1994). See also, Tiziana Terranova, "Free Labor: Producing Culture for the Digital Economy," *Social Text* 18, no. 2 (Summer 2000): 33–58.

4. See the cases of Rob Klingberg, Mike Hord, and Andrew Huang in John Baichtal, ed., *Maker Pro* (Sebastopol, CA: Maker Media, 2015), 51, 81, 127.

5. Mu-Ming Tsai, *Maker*, documentary (2014).

6. Mark Hatch, *The Maker Movement Manifesto: Rules for Innovation in the New World of Crafters, Hackers, and Tinkerers* (New York: McGraw-Hill Education, 2014), 65.

7. Baichtal, *Maker Pro*, 127.

8. Anderson, *Makers*, 82–84.

9. *Ibid.*, 13.

10. Chris Anderson, *The Long Tail: Why the Future of Business Is Selling Less of More* (New York: Hyperion, 2006).

11. *Ibid.*

12. A sampling of the myriad articles published on millennial selfishness include: Andrew Snavely, "Is the Millennial Generation Really Lazy, Entitled, and Selfish? A CNN Comic Strip by Matt Bors," accessed May 16, 2014, http://www .primermagazine.com/2013/live/is-the-millennial-gener-ation-really-lazy-entitled-and-selfish-a-cnn-comic-strip-by-matt-bors; Joanna Chau, "Millennials Are More 'Generation Me' Than 'Generation We,' Study Finds," *The Chronicle of Higher Education*, March 15, 2012, http://chronicle.com/ar ticle/Millennials-Are-More/131175/; "Millennial Generation Money-Obsessed And Less Concerned With Giving Back, Study Finds," *Huffington Post*, March 16, 2012, http:// www.huffingtonpost.com/2012/03/16/millennial-generation-

study-fame-money_n_1354028.html.

13. Kelly, Kevin, "1,000 True Fans," *The Technium*, March 4, 2008, http://kk.org/thetechnium/1000-true-fans/.

14. Jeff Howe, "The Rise of Crowdsourcing," *Wired*, June 2006, 1 September 2010. http://www.wired.com/wired/archive/14.06/crowds.html?pg=1&topic=crowds&topic_set.

15. Jeff Howe, "Is Crowdsourcing Evil? The Design Community Weighs In," *Wired*, 10 March 2009, 1 September 2010. http://www.wired.com/epicenter/2009/03/is-crowdsourcin/comment-page-2/; Amanda Wasielewski, "Grains of Gold in All This Shit," *Hz Journal* 16 (March 2011), http://www.hz-journal.org/n16/wasielewski.html. See also, Andrew Keen, *The Cult of the Amateur: How Today's Internet is Killing Our Culture* (New York: Doubleday/Currency, 2007).

16. Daniela Castrataro, "A social history of crowdfunding," *Social Media Week*, December 12, 2011, http://socialmediaweek.org/blog/2011/12/a-social-history-of-crowdfunding/.

17. Hatch, *The Maker Movement Manifesto*, 94.

18. Tsai, *Maker*.

19. Hatch, *The Maker Movement Manifesto*, 95.

20. The ideas described derive from the classic text of Adam Smith, *An Inquiry into the Nature and Causes of the Wealth of Nations* (London: W. Strahan and T. Cadell, 1776).

21. Jason Schreier, "*Unsung Story* Is A $660,000 Kickstarter Disaster," *Kotaku*, September 22, 2015, http://kotaku.com/unsung-story-is-a-660-000-kickstarter-disaster-1732312002.

22. Casey Johnston, "Between Kickstarter's frauds and phenoms live long-delayed projects," *Ars Technica*, June 26, 2015, http://arstechnica.com/information-technology/2015/06/worth-the-wait-inside-kickstarters-world-of-delays/.

23. Qtd. in Kyle Orland, "On Kickstarter, everyone is Peter Molyneux," *Ars Technica*, February 13, 2015, http://arstechnica.com/gaming/2015/02/on-kickstarter-everyone-is-peter-molyneux/.

24. Matt Ratto and Megan Boler, eds., *DIY Citizenship: Critical Making and Social Media* (Cambridge, MA: MIT Press, 2014).

25. Matt Ratto and Stephen Hockema, "FLWR PWR: Tending the Walled Garden," *Walled Garden,* 2009, 52. See also, Matt Ratto, "Critical Making: Conceptual and Material Studies in Technology and Social Life," *The Information Society* 27, no. 4 (2011): 252–260; Matt Ratto, "Critical Making," in *Open Design Now: Why Design Cannot Remain Exclusive* (Amsterdam: BIS Publishers, 2011), 202–9, http://opendesignnow.org; Matt Ratto, "Textual Doppelgangers: Critical Issues in the Study of Technology," in *DIY Citizenship: Critical Making and Social Media*, eds. Matt Ratto and Megan Boler (Cambridge, MA: MIT Press, 2014), 227–36.

26. Ratto, "Textual Doppelgangers: Critical Issues in the Study of Technology."

27. David Peters Corbett, "Visual culture and the history of art," in *Dealing with the Visual: Art History, Aesthetics and Visual Culture*, eds. Caroline van Eck and Edward Winters (Farnham, Surrey: Ashgate Publishing, 2005), 17–36.

28. Ratto, "Textual Doppelgangers: Critical Issues in the Study of Technology," 229.

29. Bruno Latour, *Reassembling the Social: An Introduction to Actor-Network-Theory* (Oxford; New York: Oxford University Press, 2005); Levi R. Bryant, Nick Srnicek, and Graham Harman, eds., *The Speculative Turn: Continental Materialism and Realism* (Melbourne: Re.press, 2011); Graham Harman, *The Quadruple Object* (Washington DC: Zero Books, 2011); Jane Bennett, *Vibrant Matter: A Political Ecology of Things* (Durham: Duke University Press, 2010).

30. Richard Barbrook and Andy Cameron, "The Californian Ideology," in *Proud To Be Flesh: A Mute Magazine Anthology of Cultural Politics after the Net*, eds. Josephine Berry Slater and Pauline Van Mourik Broekman (London; Brooklyn, NY: Mute Pub. in association with Autonomedia, 2009), 27–34.

31. Patricia Falguières, "A Questionnaire on Materialisms," *October* no. 155 (Winter 2016): 40.

32. Armen Avanessian, "A Questionnaire on Materialisms," *October* no. 155 (Winter 2016): 9.

33. D. Graham Burnett, "A Questionnaire on Materialisms," *October* no. 155 (Winter 2016): 20.

34. "DARPA Mentor Award to Bring Making to Education," *Make: DIY Projects and Ideas for Makers*, January 19, 2012, http://makezine.com/2012/01/19/darpa-mentor-award-to-bring-making-to-education/.

35. Mitch Altman, "Mitch Altman – It's official. I'm greatly saddened that I won't be..." *Facebook*, April 3, 2012, https://www.facebook.com/photo.php?fbid=10150649823645918&set=a.92403175917.100186.540310917&type=1&theater.

36. Tim O'Reilly, "Mitch Altman – It's official. I'm greatly saddened that I won't be..." *Facebook*, April 3, 2012, https://www.facebook.com/photo.php?fbid=10150649823645918&set=a.92403175917.100186.540310917&type=1&theater.

37. Garnet Hertz, "Making Critical Making," in *Critical Making: Introduction*, ed. Garnet Hertz (Hollywood, CA: Telharmonium Press, 2012), 2, http://conceptlab.com/critical-making/.

38. Ratto and Boler, *DIY Citizenship*.

39. The "gig economy" is a term for the increasingly common practice among companies to hire temporary workers on a per-task basis. Without having to maintain any employees, start-ups are able to save a significant amount of resources. These companies are connected to their employees online through custom-built platforms that link up workers with customers. Examples of the gig economy model are: Amazon Mechanical Turk, TaskRabbit, Uber, Airbnb, Elance, Etsy, and others.

40. Mailer, Malaquais, and Polsky, *The White Negro*.

41. Mark Greif, Kathleen Ross, and Dayna Tortorici, *What Was

the Hipster?: A Sociological Investigation (New York: N+1 Foundation, 2010), 141.

42. Jonathan Krisel, "Farm," *Portlandia* (IFC, January 21, 2011).

43. Jonathan Krisel, "Cops Redesign," *Portlandia* (IFC, February 3, 2012).

44. Sharon Zukin, *Naked City: The Death and Life of Authentic Urban Places* (Oxford; New York: Oxford University Press, 2010), 101.

45. Fensterstock, *Art on the Block*, 169.

46. Dayna Tortorici, "You Know It When You See It," in *What Was the Hipster?: A Sociological Investigation*, eds. Mark Greif, Kathleen Ross, and Dayna Tortorici (New York: N+1 Foundation, 2010), 122–35.

47. Greif, Ross, and Tortorici, *What Was the Hipster?*

48. Rob Horning, "The Death of the Hipster," in *What Was the Hipster?: A Sociological Investigation*, eds. Mark Greif, Kathleen Ross, and Dayna Tortorici (New York: N+1 Foundation, 2010), 82.

49. Sophy Bot, *The Hipster Effect: How the Rising Tide of Individuality Is Changing Everything We Know about Life, Work and the Pursuit of Happiness* (Sophy Bot, 2012), 135.

50. Michelle Higgins, "Priced Out of Brooklyn? Try Manhattan," *The New York Times*, May 8, 2015, http://www.nytimes.com /2015/05/10/realestate/priced-out-of-brooklyn-try-manhattan.html; "No, Brooklyn is not more expensive than Manhattan – but it's getting closer," *Brick Underground*, October 8, 2015, http://www.brickunderground.com/blog /2015/10/brooklyn_market_reports; Jessica Dailey, "It's More Expensive to Rent In Brooklyn Than Ever Before," *Curbed NY*, September 17, 2015, http://ny.curbed.com/2015/9/ 17/9920468/its-more-expensive-to-rent-in-brooklyn-than-ever-before; Daniel Goldstein, "Brooklyn Now Even Hotter than Manhattan When It Comes to Rentals," *MarketWatch*, September 28, 2015, http://www.marketwatch.com/story

/brooklyn-now-even-hotter-than-manhattan-when-it-comes-to-rentals-2015-09-28.

51. Richard Florida, *The Rise of the Creative Class: And How It's Transforming Work, Leisure, Community and Everyday Life* (New York: Basic Books, 2002).

52. Richard Florida, *The Rise of the Creative Class, Revisited* (New York: Basic Books, 2012), 38–44.

53. *Ibid.*, xi.

54. Landry claims credit for the term, but a competing claim has also been made by David Yencken in "The Creative City," *Meanjin* 47, no. 4 (Summer 1988): 597.

55. Charles Landry and Franco Bianchini, *The Creative City* (London: Demos, 1995); Charles Landry, *The Creative City: A Toolkit for Urban Innovators* (London: Earthscan, 2000); Charles Landry, *The Art of City Making* (London: Earthscan, 2006).

56. John Howkins, *The Creative Economy: How People Make Money from Ideas* (London: Penguin, 2002). See also, Richard Florida, *Cities and the Creative Class* (New York: Routledge, 2005); Richard Florida, *Who's Your City?: How the Creative Economy Is Making Where to Live the Most Important Decision of Your Life* (New York: Basic Books, 2008); Maurizio Carta, *Creative City: Dynamics, Innovations, Actions* (Actar Coac Assn Of Catalan Arc, 2007); James E. Doyle and Biljana Mickov, eds., *The Creative City: Vision and Execution* (London: Routledge, 2016). Authors who have provided concurrent critiques of the role of arts/culture in city planning include: Graeme Evans, *Cultural Planning: An Urban Renaissance?* (London: Routledge, 2001); Beatriz García, "Urban Regeneration, Arts Programming and Major Events," *International Journal of Cultural Policy* 10, no. 1 (March 2004): 103–18; Beatriz García, "Cultural Policy and Urban Regeneration in Western European Cities: Lessons from Experience, Prospects for the Future," *Local Economy* 19, no. 4 (November 1, 2004): 312–26;

David Ley, "Artists, Aestheticisation and the Field of Gentrification," *Urban Studies* 40, no. 12 (November 1, 2003): 2527–44; Malcolm Miles, "Interruptions: Testing the Rhetoric of Culturally Led Urban Development," *Urban Studies* 42, no. 5–6 (May 1, 2005): 889–911.

57. Hatch, *The Maker Movement Manifesto*, 22.

58. Chief among those declaring the end of the struggle is *Wired* techno-evangelist Chris Anderson. See, Anderson, *Makers*.

59. Hatch, *The Maker Movement Manifesto*, 52–54.

60. *Ibid.*, 52–3.

61. Henri Lefebvre, *Critique de la vie quotidienne* (Paris: Éditions Bernard Grasset, 1947); Guy Debord, *La Société du spectacle* (Paris: Buchet/Chastel, 1967); Jonathan Crary, *24/7: Late Capitalism and the Ends of Sleep* (London: New York: Verso, 2013).

62. Tsai, *Maker*.

Chapter 2

1. TED (Technology, Education, Design) is a global network of conferences that started in 1984. TED talks have become an important vehicle for capitalist start-ups and cultural figures to promote their ideas. These talks are organized by the Sapling Foundation, an independent nonprofit started by Chris Anderson of *Wired* magazine, and they have direct links to both the counterculture and the early computer industry. http://www.ted.com/talks/dale_dougherty_we_are_makers?language=en.

2. Joseph Beuys, "Introduction," in *Joseph Beuys*, by Caroline Tisdall (New York: Solomon R. Guggenheim Museum, 1979), 7.

3. Many other art critics and theorists were dealing with this question in other ways. Beuys' position can be juxtaposed with that of Rosalind Krauss, "Sculpture in the Expanded Field," October 8 (April 1, 1979): 31–44. See also, Irene V.

Small, "Site and Sociality: Joseph Beuys and the Relics of Modernist Sculpture," *Yale University Art Gallery Bulletin*, January 1, 2009, 86–88.

4. Thierry de Duve, "Joseph Beuys, or The Last of the Proletarians," *October* 45 (July 1, 1988): 55–56, doi:10. 2307/779043.

5. A selection of rankings include: Avakian, Talia, "American's most expensive cities for renters," *Business Insider*, August 25, 2015, http://www.businessinsider.com/americas-20-most-expensive-cities-for-renters-2015-8; Angelina Fomina, "The Cost of Living in the Top 25 Startup Cities," September 18, 2015, https://tech.co/cost-living-top-25-startup-cities-2015-09; Madeline Stone, "San Francisco Is More Expensive Than New York City," September 17, 2014, http://www.businessinsider.com/san-francisco-is-more-expensive-than-new-york-city-2014-9.

6. Florida, *The Rise of the Creative Class, Revisited*.

7. *Ibid.*, xi.

8. Hatch, *The Maker Movement Manifesto*, 1.

9. Friedrich Schiller, *On the Aesthetic Education of Man*, trans. Reginald Snell (Mineola, NY: Dover Publ., 2004), 39.

10. *Ibid.*, 86.

11. Baichtal, *Maker Pro*, 93.

12. Hatch, *The Maker Movement Manifesto*, 124.

13. Ray Oldenburg, *The Great Good Place: Cafés, Coffee Shops, Community Centers, Beauty Parlors, General Stores, Bars, Hangouts and How They Get You Through the Day* (New York: Paragon House, 1989).

14. Hatch, *The Maker Movement Manifesto*, 53.

15. "Revenge porn" is a term to describe the posting of nude pictures of women without their permission (usually given to websites by a scorned boyfriend or admirer) and posted to the wider Internet, resulting in embarrassment, harassment, and loss of livelihood for its victims. "Doxxing" or "doxing"

describes the activity of researching and broadcasting personal details and information on a person to provide Internet bullies with fodder to harass the victim. "Swatting" refers to prank calling in fake 911 calls serious enough to get a SWAT team to harass someone. Anonymous is a hacker/activist offshoot of the 4chan message board (an online forum where users are anonymous and postings are automatically deleted rather than saved). It is made up of a mob of anonymous users who are called to action by one of the members of Anonymous on a variety of moral crusades.

16. Schiller, *On the Aesthetic Education of Man*, 124.

17. Novalis and Margaret Mahony Stoljar, *Philosophical Writings* (Albany, NY: State University of New York Press, 1997), 72.

18. Veronica Freeman, *The Poetization of Metaphors in the Work of Novalis* (New York: Peter Lang, 2006), 58–59, http://catalog .hathitrust.org/api/volumes/oclc/58546089.html.

19. Jennifer Jenson, Negin Dahya, and Stephanie Fisher, "Power Struggles: Knowledge Production in a DIY News Club," in *DIY Citizenship: Critical Making and Social Media*, eds. Matt Ratto and Megan Boler (Cambridge, MA: MIT Press, 2014), 169. See also, Dunbar-Hester, "Radical Inclusion? Locating Accountability in Technical DIY."

20. Alexandra Bal, Jason Nolan, and Yukari Seko, "Mélange of Making: Bringing Children's Informal Learning Cultures to the Classroom," in *DIY Citizenship: Critical Making and Social Media*, eds. Matt Ratto and Megan Boler (Cambridge, MA: MIT Press, 2014), 158.

21. Hatch, *The Maker Movement Manifesto*, 1.

22. *Ibid.*

23. *Ibid.*, 20.

24. Tim Ingold, *Making: Anthropology, Archaeology, Art and Architecture*, Routledge, 2013, 11.

25. Daniela K. Rosner and Miki Foster, "Woven Futures: Inscribed Material Ecologies of Critical Making," in *DIY*

Citizenship: Critical Making and Social Media, eds. Matt Ratto and Megan Boler (Cambridge, MA: MIT Press, 2014), 190, 195; Owen Chapman and Kim Sawchuk, "Creation-as-Research: Critical Making in Complex Environments," *RACAR: Revue D'art Canadienne/Canadian Art Review* 40, no. 1 (2015): 50; Garnet Hertz, "Interview with Matt Ratto," in *Critical Making: Conversations*, ed. Garnet Hertz (Hollywood, CA: Telharmonium Press, 2012), 5, http://conceptlab.com /criticalmaking/.

26. Ingold, *Making*, 7.

27. *Ibid.*, 1.

28. Bal, Nolan, and Seko, "Mélange of Making: Bringing Children's Informal Learning Cultures to the Classroom," 160.

29. *Ibid.*, 164.

30. Ingold, *Making*, 5.

31. Hatch, *The Maker Movement Manifesto*, 35.

32. Ratto, "Textual Doppelgangers: Critical Issues in the Study of Technology," 230.

33. Arthur C. Clarke, *Profiles of the Future; an Inquiry into the Limits of the Possible* (New York: Harper & Row, 1962).

34. Marc J. Seifer, *Wizard: The Life and Times of Nikola Tesla: Biography of a Genius* (New York: Citadel Press, 1998), 32, 34.

35. Roger Malina, "Informant No 11: 100 Years of Scientific Making in Celebration of Frank Malina," in *Critical Making: History*, ed. Garnet Hertz (Hollywood, CA: Telharmonium Press, 2012), 3, http://conceptlab.com/criticalmaking/.

36. Steven Levy, *Hackers: Heroes of the Computer Revolution* (Garden City, NY: Anchor Press/Doubleday, 1984), 111. See also original use of terms in Stewart Brand, "Spacewar: Fanatic Life and Symbolic Death Among the Computer Bums," *Rolling Stone* 7 (1972): 50–57.

37. Schiller, *On the Aesthetic Education of Man*, 94.

38. Baichtal, *Maker Pro*, ix.

39. See Benjamin, Baudrillard, etc.

40. Plato and CDC Reeve, *Republic* (Indianapolis: Hackett Pub. Co., 2004), 300.

41. Philip Sidney and Ben Jonson, *Sir Philip Sydney's Defense Of Poetry: And Observations On Poetry And Eloquence Of Ben Jonson* (Kessinger Publishing, LLC, 2009).

42. Percy Bysshe Shelley, Zachary Leader, and Michael O'Neill, *Percy Bysshe Shelley: The Major Works* (Oxford: Oxford University Press, 2009), 677.

43. Thomas Love Peacock et al., *Four Ages of Poetry, Shelley's Defense of Poetry, Browning's Essay on Shelley* (Boston: Houghton Mifflin, 1921), 16.

44. Ingold, *Making*, 5.

45. Andrew Sleigh, "John Ruskin: Grandfather of the Maker Movement? The Lamp of Life, The Lamp of Truth, 7 Lamps in the Hackerspace," *Medium*, October 12, 2015, https://medium.com/@andrewsleigh/john-ruskin-grandfather-of-the-maker-movement-853706eb2bd; "The art and craft of business," *The Economist*, January 4, 2014, http://www.economist.com/news/business/21592656-etsy-starting-show-how-maker-movement-can-make-money-art-and-craft-business; "The Prehistory of Maker Culture: the arts and crafts movement," accessed June 30, 2016, https://wiki.p2pfoundation.net/Maker_Movement#The_Prehistory_of_Maker_Culture:_the_arts_and_crafts_movement.

46. Baichtal, *Maker Pro*, 119–20.

47. John Ruskin, *Modern Painters*, vol. 2 (New York: CE Merrill, 1891), xiii.

48. John Ruskin, *The Stones of Venice*, vol. 2 (New York: J. Wiley, 1867), 182.

49. *Ibid.*, 2:178.

50. John Ruskin, *Sesame & Lilies; The Two Paths & The King of the Golden River* (London: Dent; New York: Dutton, 1907), 137.

51. William Morris, *Hopes and Fears for Art* (New York:

Longmans, Green, and Co., 1901), 53–54.

52. *Ibid.*, 34.

53. *Ibid.*, 55.

54. *Ibid.*, 58, 64.

55. Tsai, *Maker*.

56. Elizabeth Cumming and Wendy Kaplan, *The Arts and Crafts Movement* (New York, NY: Thames and Hudson, 1991), 26.

57. TJ Cobden-Sanderson, *The Arts and Crafts Movement* (Hammersmith, England: Hammersmith Pub. Society, 1905), 34–35.

58. Sleigh, "John Ruskin."

59. Cumming and Kaplan, *The Arts and Crafts Movement*, 141.

60. "An Old Art Revived and Advanced by Modern Science," *The Craftsman* II, no. 4 (July 1902), 205.

61. Cumming and Kaplan, *The Arts and Crafts Movement*, 168.

62. *Ibid.*, 21–22.

Chapter 3

1. Stewart Brand, "We Owe It All to the Hippies," *Time*, March 1, 1995, http://content.time.com/time/magazine/article/0,917 1,982602,00.html.

2. William H. Whyte, *The Organization Man* (New York: Simon and Schuster, 1956).

3. Fred Turner, *From Counterculture to Cyberculture: Stewart Brand, the Whole Earth Network, and the Rise of Digital Utopianism* (Chicago: University of Chicago Press, 2006).

4. *Ibid.*, 33–34.

5. *Ibid.*, 21.

6. Michael Corris, "Systems Upgrade," in *Proud To Be Flesh: A Mute Magazine Anthology of Cultural Politics after the Net*, eds. Josephine Berry Slater and Pauline Van Mourik Broekman (London; Brooklyn, NY: Mute Pub. in association with Autonomedia, 2009): 108.

7. The "Anthropocene" has been defined as the geological era

in which human activity on Earth has impacted the planet's geology and ecosystems. See Simon L. Lewis and Mark A. Maslin, "Defining the Anthropocene," *Nature* 519, no. 7542 (March 12, 2015): 171–80; Rosa M. Albert, "Anthropocene and early human behavior," *The Holocene* 25, no. 10 (October 1, 2015): 1542–52; Biermann, Frank, *Earth System Governance: World Politics in the Anthropocene* (MIT Press, 2014); PJ Crutzen and W. Steffen, "How long have we been in the anthropocene era?" *Climatic Change* 61, no. 3 (2003): 251–57; Jason W. Moore, *Capitalism in the Web of Life: Ecology and the Accumulation of Capital* (New York: Verso, 2015); Jedediah Purdy, *After Nature: A Politics for the Anthropocene* (Harvard, 2015); Jan Zalasiewicz, Mark Williams, Alan Haywood, and Michael Ellis, "The Anthropocene: a new epoch of geological time?" *Philosophical Transactions of the Royal Society A: Mathematical, Physical and Engineering Sciences* 369, no. 1938 (March 13, 2011): 835–41; Christophe Bonneuil and Jean-Baptiste Fressoz, *The Shock of the Anthropocene: The Earth, History, and Us* (New York: Verso, 2016).

8. Turner, *From Counterculture to Cyberculture*, 56.

9. Levy, *Hackers*, 35.

10. Marshall McLuhan, *The Gutenberg Galaxy: The Making of Typographic Man* (Toronto: University of Toronto Press, 1962); Marshall McLuhan, *Understanding Media: The Extensions of Man* (New York: McGraw-Hill, 1964).

11. Turner, *From Counterculture to Cyberculture*, 49.

12. Doctorow, *Makers*.

13. Donald Sull and Stefano Turconi, "Fast Fashion Lessons," *Business Strategy Review*, Summer 2008; Suzy Hansen, "How Zara Grew Into the World's Largest Fashion Retailer," *The New York Times*, November 9, 2012, http://www.nytimes.com/2012/11/11/magazine/how-zara-grew-into-the-worlds-largest-fashion-retailer.html; Ashley Lutz, "Zara Has Fundamentally Changed Fashion And There's No Going

Back," *Business Insider*, November 10, 2012, http://www
.businessinsider.com/how-zara-is-changing-fashion-forever-
2012-11.

14. Doctorow, *Makers*, 96.

15. *Ibid.*, 82.

16. *Ibid.*, 224.

17. John Markoff, *What the Dormouse Said: How the Sixties
Counterculture Shaped the Personal Computer Industry* (New
York: Viking, 2005), 46.

18. *Ibid.*, 150. See also Turner, *From Counterculture to Cyberculture*,
106–9.

19. Markoff, *What the Dormouse Said–*, 29.

20. *Ibid.*, 65–67.

21. Turner, *From Counterculture to Cyberculture*, 61.

22. *Ibid.*, 63.

23. *Ibid.*, 112.

24. *Ibid.*, 93.

25. Markoff, *What the Dormouse Said–*, 68.

26. *Ibid.*, 156.

27. Turner, *From Counterculture to Cyberculture*, 67.

28. *Ibid.*, 90.

29. *Ibid.*, 128–9.

30. "Discussion from the Hackers' Conference, November 1984,"
Whole Earth Review, May 1985, 49.

31. *Ibid.*, 51.

32. Thomas Piketty, *Capital in the Twenty-First Century*, trans.
Arthur Goldhammer (Cambridge, MA: Belknap Press of
Harvard University Press, 2014), 118.

33. Gilles Deleuze and Félix Guattari, *Anti-Oedipus: Capitalism
and Schizophrenia* (London: Althone Press Ltd., 1984), 34–35.

34. Richard Barbrook and Andy Cameron, "The Californian
Ideology," *Science as Culture*, 6:1 (no. 26, 1996), 44–72.

Chapter 4

1. Dean MacCannell, *The Tourist: A New Theory of the Leisure Class* (New York: Schocken Books, 1976); Costas Spirou, *Urban Tourism and Urban Change: Cities in a Global Economy* (New York: Routledge, 2010); Steven Miles, *Spaces for Consumption*, 1st edition (Thousand Oaks, CA: SAGE Publications Ltd, 2010); Volkan Aytar and Jan Rath, *Selling Ethnic Neighborhoods: The Rise of Neighborhoods as Places of Leisure and Consumption* (New York, NY: Routledge, 2012); Michael L. Silk and David L. Andrews, *Sport and Neoliberalism: Politics, Consumption, and Culture* (Philadelphia: Temple University Press, 2012); Mark Jayne, *Cities and Consumption* (London; New York: Routledge, 2006).

2. David Harvey, *Paris, Capital of Modernity* (New York: Routledge, 2003), 204–18.

3. Debord, *The Society of the Spectacle*, 22.

4. *Ibid.*, 14, 126.

5. Anderson, *Makers*.

6. Karl Marx and Frederick Engels, *Manifesto of the Communist Party*, PDF (Marxists Internet Archive, 2014), 17, https://www.marxists.org/archive/marx/works/1848/communist-manifesto/.

7. A selection of quotations regarding Marx and the Maker Movement come from the following sources: Anderson, *Makers*, 25; Florida, *The Rise of the Creative Class, Revisited*, 26; Evgeny Morozov, "Making It," *The New Yorker*, January 6, 2014, http://www.newyorker.com/magazine/2014/01/13/making-it-2; Ted Curran, "'Own the Means of Production': What Karl Marx Knew about Opportunity in the Digital Economy," *Ted Curran.net*, accessed December 7, 2014, http://tedcurran.net/2013/04/09/own-the-means-of-production-what-karl-marx-knew-about-opportunity-in-the-digital-economy/.

8. See Sharon Zukin, *Loft Living: Culture and Capital in Urban Change* (Baltimore: Johns Hopkins University Press, 1982).

9.   *Ibid.*; Smith, "New City, New Frontier: The Lower East Side as Wild, Wild West"; Smith, *The New Urban Frontier*.

10. Smith, "New City, New Frontier: The Lower East Side as Wild, Wild West"; Smith, *The New Urban Frontier*.

11. Richard Lloyd, *Neo-Bohemia: Art and Commerce in the Postindustrial City* (Routledge, 2010).

12. Brad Gooch, "The New Bohemia," *New York*, June 22, 1992, 28.

13. *Ibid.*

14. Denny Lee, "Has Billburg Lost Its Cool?" *The New York Times*, July 27, 2003, sec. 14; Column 2; The City Weekly Desk.

15. Nonko, "How Bloomberg Changed New York Real Estate."

16. Fensterstock, *Art on the Block*, 169.

17. Julie Strickland, "The Neighborhood Name Police: East Williamsburg," *Brooklyn Based*, July 14, 2012, http://brooklyn-based.com/blog/2012/07/24/the-neighborhood-name-police-east-williamsburg/.

18. Smith, *The New Urban Frontier*.

19. Turner, *From Counterculture to Cyberculture*, 79.

20. *Ibid.*, 77.

21. David Ley, "Liberal Ideology and the Postindustrial City," *Annals of the Association of American Geographers* 70, no. 2 (1980): 238–58; David Ley, *The New Middle Class and the Remaking of the Central City* (Oxford; New York: Oxford University Press, 1996).

22. Ley, "Artists, Aestheticisation and the Field of Gentrification," 2530.

23. Lloyd, *Neo-Bohemia*, 78.

24. Rosalyn Deutsche and Cara Gendel Ryan, "The Fine Art of Gentrification," *October* 31 (December 1, 1984): 110–11.

25. Qtd. Smith, *The New Urban Frontier*, 18.

26. Serena Dai, "Bushwick Coffee Shops Skip Names for Mysterious Vibe," *DNAinfo New York*, accessed December 7, 2014, http://www.dnainfo.com/new-york/20140728/bushw

ick/bushwick-coffee-shops-skip-names-for-mysterious-vibe/.

27. Robert Sullivan, "Psst... Have You Heard About Bushwick?" *The New York Times*, March 19, 2006, sec. Section 6; Column 3; Magazine.

28. Caroline A. Jones, *Machine in the Studio: Constructing the Postwar American Artist* (Chicago: University of Chicago Press, 1996), 151.

29. *Ibid.*, 152.

30. Lloyd, *Neo-Bohemia*, 251.

31. Brown, "Luhring Augustine Arrives on The Scene."

32. Andrew Russeth, "'Williamsburg Is Over,' Says Art Writer James Kalm," *New York Observer*, accessed December 7, 2014, http://observer.com/2011/09/williamsburg-is-over-says-art-writer-james-kalm/; Foster Kamer, "The Apocalypse and End of Williamsburg's 'Cool' Factor Has Arrived (Video)," *Runnin' Scared*, accessed December 7, 2014, http://blogs.villagevoice.com/runninscared/2010/10/the_apocalypse.php; Tara Palmeri, "New hipsters fight old hipsters in Bushwick," *New York Post*, December 2, 2013, http://nypost.com/2013/12/02/new-hipsters-fight-old-hipsters-over-luxury-bushwick-digs/; Powhida, "Bushwick Don't Worry"; Andy Cush, "The Campaign to Keep Chains Out of Bushwick," *Animal New York*, accessed December 7, 2014, http://animalnewyork.com/2012/the-campaign-to-keep-chains-out-of-bushwick/.

33. Lloyd, *Neo-Bohemia*, 242.

34. Cush, "The Campaign to Keep Chains Out of Bushwick."

35. Craig Owens, "Commentary: The Problem with Puerilism," *Art in America* 72, no. 6 (1984): 162–63.

36. Deutsche and Ryan, "The Fine Art of Gentrification," 105–6.

37. Martha Rosler, *Culture Class* (Berlin: Sternberg Press, 2013), 148.

38. *Ibid.*, 203.

39. James R. Hudson, *The Unanticipated City: Loft Conversions in*

Lower Manhattan (University of Massachusetts Press, 1987), 49.

40. Jones, *Machine in the Studio*, 151–53.

41. Florida, *The Rise of the Creative Class, Revisited*, 25.

42. Anderson, *Makers*, 26.

43. Pauline Pechin, "Jason Goodman Relates Failure to Progress," *All That We've Met*, March 17, 2011, http://www.allthatwevemet.org/2011/03/jason-goodman-relates-failure-to.html. [Offline]

44. Zukin, *Loft Living*.

45. Smith, *The New Urban Frontier*.

46. Lloyd, *Neo-Bohemia*.

47. Zukin, *Loft Living*, 51.

48. One example of a "native" Bushwick Latino-owned business, The Coffee Shop at 44 Wilson Ave., which opened in the summer of 2014, was the center of early scandal after its owner went on an anti-Semitic tirade on Instagram against Jewish real estate developers who visited the premises. It was originally heralded as a neighborhood success story. See Erin Wicks, "The Coffee Shop: Bushwick's Newest and Most Aptly Named Spot for a Cup O' Joe," *Bushwick Daily*, July 7, 2014, http://bushwickdaily.com/2014/07/the-coffee-shop-bushwicks-newest-and-most-adeptly-named-spot-for-a-cup-o-joe/; Doyle Murphy and Philip Caulfield, "'Greedy Infiltrators': Bushwick coffee shop bashed after anti-Semitic rant," *NY Daily News*, December 7, 2014, http://www.nydailynews.com/new-york/brooklyn/greedy-infiltrators-bushwick-coffee-shop-bashed-anti-semitic-online-rant-article-1.1961070.

49. Danielle Furfaro, "Bushwick residents rally against gentrification," *The Brooklyn Paper*, October 16, 2014, http://www.brooklynpaper.com/stories/37/43/dtg-rent-stabilization-law-anti-gentrification-rally-2014-10-24-bk_37_43.html.

50. Barbrook and Cameron, "The Californian Ideology," 29.

51. *Ibid.*

52. "Wired Editor-in-Chief Chris Anderson Steps Down to Run Robotics Startup," *Wired*, November 2, 2012, http://www.wired.com/2012/11/wired-editor-in-chief-chris-anderson-steps-down/. See also: Anderson, *Makers*.

53. Colin Moynihan, "Galapagos Art Space Will Make Detroit Its Home," *The New York Times*, December 7, 2014, http://www.nytimes.com/2014/12/08/arts/galapagos-art-space-will-make-detroit-its-home.html.

54. Rosler, *Culture Class*, 164.

55. Jen Carlson, "Galapagos's Robert Elmes Discusses Move From Brooklyn To Detroit," *Gothamist*, December 9, 2014, http://gothamist.com/2014/12/09/robert_elmes_galapagos.php.

56. The terms "disruption" and "breaking" are often used in tech circles to describe new start-ups or business that overturn the marketplace and introduce new technologies and networked tools. The term "disrupt" is most famously associated with the TechCrunch Disrupt contest where hopeful start-ups face off against one another for prize money.

57. David Brooks, *Bobos in Paradise: The New Upper Class and How They Got There* (New York: Simon & Schuster, 2000).

58. Zukin, *Loft Living*, 96.

59. *Ibid.*, 88.

60. *Ibid.*, 98.

61. *Ibid.*, 71–72.

62. See Morozov, "Making It."

63. Many residents of illegal loft buildings in Morgantown still reject implementation of the Loft Law because it mandates buildings be brought up to fire code – something that landlords and tenants are loath to do when large portions of their square footage are taken up by illegally bifurcated spaces with lofted second stories or bedrooms – increasing

the amount of space for more dwellers (and rent-payers).

64. "Rheingold Campaign," *NWB – Neighbors Without Borders*, December 13, 2013, http://www.nwbcommunity.org/camp aign/.

65. Zukin, *Loft Living*, 176.

66. *Ibid.*, 180.

67. Richard Kostelanetz, "All Wrong About Lower Manhattan: Rereading Sharon Zukin," *Hyperallergic*, April 24, 2014, http://hyperallergic.com/122467/all-wrong-about-lower-manhattan-rereading-sharon-zukin/.

68. Zukin, 175.

69. Roslyn Bernstein and Shael Shapiro, *Illegal Living: 80 Wooster Street and the Evolution of SoHo* (Vilnius, Lithuania: Jonas Mekas Foundation, 2010).

70. Zukin, *Loft Living*, 113–15.

71. Lloyd, *Neo-Bohemia*, 14.

72. *Ibid.*, 12.

73. *Ibid.*, 24–25.

74. *Ibid.*, 46.

75. Zukin, *Loft Living*, 59.

76. *Ibid.*, 67–68.

77. Lloyd, *Neo-Bohemia*, 185–86.

78. Zukin, *Loft Living*, 179.

79. Lloyd, *Neo-Bohemia*, 188.

80. *Ibid.*, 215.

81. *Ibid.*, 221.

82. Sophy Bot provides a longform celebration of freelance labor conditions in Bot, *The Hipster Effect*.

83. Lloyd, *Neo-Bohemia*, 248.

84. Lloyd, 245.

85. A selection from *The New York Times* alone reveals a glut of press on both of these companies and their battles with regulatory bodies in New York City and around the world. David Streitfeld, "Companies Built on Sharing Balk When It

Comes to Regulators," *The New York Times*, April 21, 2014, http://www.nytimes.com/2014/04/22/business/companies-built-on-sharing-balk-when-it-comes-to-regulators.html; William Alden, "The Business Tycoons of Airbnb," *The New York Times*, November 25, 2014, http://www.nytimes.com/2014/11/30/magazine/the-business-tycoons-of-airbnb.html; Elizabeth A. Harris, "The Airbnb Economy in New York: Lucrative but Often Illegal," *The New York Times*, November 4, 2013, sec. N.Y. / Region, http://www.nytimes.com/2013/11/05/nyregion/the-airbnb-economy-in-new-york-lucrative-but-often-unlawful.html; David Streitfeld, "Airbnb Listings Mostly Illegal, New York State Contends," *The New York Times*, October 15, 2014, http://www.nytimes.com/2014/10/16/business/airbnb-listings-mostly-illegal-state-contends.html; Nick Wingfield, "A Victory for Airbnb in New York," *The New York Times*, May 13, 2014, http://www.nytimes.com/2014/05/14/technology/judge-quashes-new-york-subpoena-for-airbnb-records.html; Vikas Bajaj, "Who's Profiting From Airbnb?" *Taking Note*, October 17, 2014, http://takingnote.blogs.nytimes.com/2014/10/17/whos-profiting-from-airbnb/; Mike Isaac, "Airbnb Pushes to Modify San Francisco Housing Laws," *Bits Blog*, August 1, 2014, http://bits.blogs.nytimes.com/2014/08/01/airbnb-pushes-to-modify-san-francisco-housing-laws/; David Streitfeld, "New York's Case Against Airbnb Is Argued in Albany," *The New York Times*, April 22, 2014, http://www.nytimes.com/2014/04/23/technology/albany-judge-hears-caseagainst-airbnb.html; Brian X. Chen, "App Maker Uber Hits Regulatory Snarl," *The New York Times*, December 2, 2012, sec. Technology, http://www.nytimes.com/2012/12/03/technology/app-maker-uber-hits-regulatory-snarl.html; Mike Isaac, "Uber Picks David Plouffe to Wage Regulatory Fight," *The New York Times*, August 19, 2014, http://www.nytimes.com/2014/08/20/technology/uber-picks-a-political-insider-to-wage-its-regulatory-battles.html; Mike Isaac, "Uber Flunks the Better Business Bureau Test," *Bits Blog*, October 9, 2014, http://bits.blogs.nytimes.com/2014/10/09/uber-flunks-the-better-business-bureau-test/; David Streitfeld, "Rough Patch for Uber Service's Challenge to Taxis," *The New York Times*, January 26, 2014, http://www.nytimes.com/2014/01/27/technology/rough-patch-for-uber-services-challenge-to-taxis.html.

86. Zukin, *Loft Living*, 51–52.

87. Lloyd, *Neo-Bohemia*, 117.

88. *Ibid.*, 58.

89. Ann Markusen, "Urban Development and the Politics of a Creative Class: Evidence from a Study of Artists," *Environment and Planning A* 38, no. 10 (2006): 1921.

90. Lloyd, *Neo-Bohemia*, 2.

91. *Ibid.*

92. Alexis Soloski, "Bushwick Starr, a Humble Space With Bold Works," *The New York Times*, October 2, 2014, http://www.nytimes.com/2014/10/05/theater/bushwick-starr-a-humble-space-with-bold-works.html.

93. Lloyd, 110–111.

Chapter 5

1. "Press Release: Subway Ridership Surges 2.6% In One Year," *MTA.info*, April 20, 2015, http://www.mta.info/press-release/nyc-transit/subway-ridership-surges-26-one-year.

2. Pete Donohue, "Oh, L, Not Enuf Trains!" *Daily News (New York)*, July 7, 2006, http://www.skyscrapercity.com/showthread.php?t=371385.

3. Henry Reed Stiles, *A History of the City of Brooklyn: Including the Old Town and Village of Brooklyn, the Town of Bushwick, and the Village and City of Williamsburgh*, vol. 2 (Brooklyn, NY: Pub. by subscription, 1867), 339.

4. *Ibid.*, 2:329.

5. Harry Macy, Jr., "Before the Five-Borough City: The Old Cities, Towns and Villages That Came Together to Form 'Greater New York,'" *The NYG & B Newsletter*, Winter 1998, 5.

6. Strickland, "The Neighborhood Name Police."

7. Rebecca Fishbein, "Controversial 'Jefftown' Creator Has Some Words For The Haters," *Gothamist*, May 16, 2014, http://gothamist.com/2014/05/16/jefftown_luv_it_or_leave_it .php.

8. Morgantown residents typically refer to their neighborhood, the industrial park north of Flushing Ave., as Bushwick. On modern city maps, however, the neighborhood of Bushwick ends at Flushing and, therefore, Morgantown is technically part of East Williamsburg. The public often perceives the renaming of a neighborhood as an expression of the power of developers and a harbinger of gentrification.

9. Michelle Higgins, "Crossing Into Queens," *The New York Times*, August 18, 2013, sec. Real Estate.

10. Nick E., "E Williamsburg or Bushwick?" Yelp (January 13, 2007), http://www.yelp.com/list/e-williamsburg-or-bushwi ck-brooklyn.

11. "Bushburg Properties, Inc.," *NYS Department of State: Division of Corporations Entity Information*, October 13, 2000, http://appext20.dos.ny.gov/corp_public/CORPSEARCH.ENT ITY_INFORMATION?p_nameid=2596874&p_corpid=256322 9&p_entity_name=Bushburg&p_name_type=A&p_search_ty pe=BEGINS&p_srch_results_page=0.

12. "Morgantown Management, LLC," *NYS Department of State: Division of Corporations Entity Information*, December 10, 2003, http://appext20.dos.ny.gov/corp_public/CORPSEARCH.ENT ITY_INFORMATION?p_nameid=3007892&p_corpid=298712 9&p_entity_name=Morgantown&p_name_type=A&p_search _type=BEGINS&p_srch_results_page=0.
A Deli with the Morgantown name has been registered since 2010, after the early debates over neighborhood naming.

See: "Morgantown Deli & General Inc.," *NYS Department of State: Division of Corporations Entity Information*, October 27, 2010, http://appext20.dos.ny.gov/corp_public/CORPSEAR CH.ENTITY_INFORMATION?p_nameid=4018649&p_corpi d=4012221&p_entity_name=Morgantown&p_name_type=A &p_search_type=BEGINS&p_srch_results_page=0.

13. Jeff Vandam, "Go East, Young Man," *The New York Times*, June 19, 2005, http://www.nytimes.com/2005/06/19/nyreg ion/go-east-young-man.html.

14. "Bushwick Emerges As City's Next Artist Colony," *Boy in Bushwick*, January 11, 2008, http://boyinbushwick.blog spot.com/2008/01/bushwick-emerges-as-citys-next-artist.html.

15. Rafael Fuchs, "Bushwick Yearbook," accessed October 18, 2015, http://www.bushwickyearbook.com/index.php.

16. Kevin Lindamood of OfficeOps specifically mentioned neighborhood sensitivities around the use of the name Morgantown. (Kevin Lindamood, conversation with the author, April 14, 2014.)

17. This is not unlike the case in DUMBO, where resident artists coined the term in a bid to discourage others from moving to the area.

18. Chris Heuberger, "A Brewing History of Bushwick," *Jane's Walk*, accessed October 14, 2015, http://janeswalk.org/united-states/new-york-city-ny/brewing-history-bushwick/.

19. Montrose Morris, "Walkabout: The Sausage King of Brooklyn, Part 3," *Brownstoner*, December 6, 2012, http://www.brownstoner.com/blog/2012/12/walkabout-the-sausage-king-of-brooklyn-part-3/.

20. During my time living on the fourth floor of the 538 Johnson/75 Stewart Avenue building, the building was occupied on 3 stories by print works and continued to be so as of 2015.

21. "About the Creek," *Newtown Creek Alliance*, accessed October

14, 2015, http://www.newtowncreekalliance.org/about/hist ory/.

22. Nate Lavey, "The Most Radioactive Place in New York City Is Now a Superfund Site," *The New Yorker*, May 8, 2014, http://www.newyorker.com/tech/elements/the-most-radioactive-place-in-new-york-city-is-now-a-superfund-site.

23. Emma Whitford, "Owners Of New Ridgewood Bar Say Neighboring Superfund Site Is No Big Deal," *Gothamist*, June 24, 2015, http://gothamist.com/2015/06/24/blinky_drinks_fre e.php.

24. Emma Turetsky, "Not Even Toxic Waste Can Stop Gentrification: NYC's Superfund Neighborhoods Are Booming," *Gothamist*, August 22, 2014, http://gothamist.co m/2014/08/22/superfund_vs_gentrification.php.

25. Eric, interview by Amanda Wasielewski, e-mail, May 10, 2016.

26. Sullivan, "Psst… Have You Heard About Bushwick?"

27. Bill Driscoll, interview by Amanda Wasielewski, e-mail, October 11, 2015.

28. Eric, interview.

29. Patrick Hedlund, "Life Cafe in East Village Closes After 30 Years," *DNAinfo New York*, September 12, 2011, http://www. dnainfo.com/new-york/20110912/lower-east-side-east-village/life-cafe-east-village-closes-after-30-years.

30. Kathy Kirkpatrick, "Life Café 983 Bushwick to Close June 30, 2012," *Life Café*, June 24, 2012, http://lifecafe.com/tag/closing/.

31. *Ibid*.

32. Sullivan, "Psst… Have You Heard About Bushwick?"

33. Stephen Smith, "Permits Filed: Live/Work Space at 117 McKibben Street, East Williamsburg," *New York YIMBY*, accessed October 18, 2015, http://newyorkyimby.com/ 2014/08/permits-filed-livework-space-at-117-mckibben-street-east-williamsburg.html; Nell Casey, "Brooklyn

Roasting Company Brings Buzz To DUMBO, Beyond," *Gothamist*, accessed October 18, 2015, http://gothamist.com/2011/08/08/dumbo_buzzing_from_newly_opened_bro.php; Andrea Huspeni, "Bushwick Hoping to Break the Cycle with the Loft Law," *Outside the Box*, December 16, 2011, https://outsidetheboxblogs.wordpress.com/2011/12/16/bushwick-hoping-to-break-the-cycle-with-the-loft-law/.

34. "About – Northeast Kingdom," Northeast Kingdom, accessed October 14, 2015, http://www.north-eastkingdom.com/?page_id=1092. [Offline, archived site at archive.org as of April 2017: https://web-beta.archive.org/web/20150312035715/http://www.north-eastkingdom.com/?page_id=1092]

35. Occupancy records for 255 McKibbin: "Property Profile Overview: 255 MC KIBBIN STREET," *NYC Department of Buildings*, May 15, 2014, http://a810-bisweb.nyc.gov/bisweb/PropertyProfileOverviewServlet?requestid=3&bin=3071385&restore=1.
Occupancy records for 248 McKibbin: "Property Profile Overview: 248 MC KIBBIN STREET," *NYC Department of Buildings*, May 15, 2014, http://a810-bisweb.nyc.gov/bisweb/PropertyProfileOverviewServlet?boro=3&houseno=248&street=MC%20KIBBIN%20STREET&requestid=0&s=A03C41B885B461E4F46BD08866A7430E.

36. "Certificate of Occupancy, 248 McKibbin," May 15, 2014, http://a810-cofo.nyc.gov/cofo/B/301/378000/301378364F.PDF.

37. "McKibbin Street Lofts," *Wikipedia, the Free Encyclopedia*, April 18, 2014, http://en.wikipedia.org/w/index.php?title=McKibbin_Street_Lofts&oldid=604793481; "Property Profile Overview: 255 MC KIBBIN STREET."

38. Kevin Lindamood, conversation with the author, April 11, 2014; "Job Overview 248 MC KIBBIN STREET BROOKLYN," *NYC Department of Buildings*, May 15, 2014, http://a810-bisweb.nyc.gov/bisweb/JobsQueryByLocationServlet?reques

tid=1&allbin=3071420&allstrt=MC%20KIBBIN%20STREET&
allnumbhous=248; Katarina Hybenova, "McKibbin Lofts
Veteran Opens a Cafe & Shares a Bunch of Stories," *Bushwick
Daily*, June 10, 2013, http://bushwickdaily.com/2013
/06/mckibbin-lofts-veteran-opens-a-cafe-shares-a-bunch-of-
stories/.

39. David Colon, "9 Things You Should Know before Moving
into McKibbin Lofts," Brokelyn, February 14, 2012, http://
brokelyn.com/9-things-you-should-know-beforemoving-
into-mckibbin-lofts/; Aaron Short, "Can The Loom Spin a
New Scene in Bushwick? » The Bushwick News/
BushwickBK," June 16, 2009, http://bushwickbk.com/2009/06
/16/can-the-loom-spin-a-new-scene-inbushwick/. [Offline,
archived at archive.org as of April 2017: http://bush
wickbk.com:80/2009/06/16/can-the-loom-spin-anew-scene-
in-bushwick/]

40. Cara Buckley, "Young Artists Find a Private Space, Only
Without the Privacy," *The New York Times*, May 7, 2008, sec.
A; Column 0; Metropolitan Desk.

41. *Ibid*.

42. Driscoll, interview.

43. Lee, "Has Billburg Lost Its Cool?"

44. Choire, "Bedbug Population Explodes At Bushwick Hipster
Ground Zero," *Gawker*, accessed October 14, 2015,
http://gawker.com/299467/bedbug-population-explodes-at-
bushwick-hipster-ground-zero; "Bed Bug Report for 248
Mckibben St, Brooklyn, NY," *Bed Bug Registry*, accessed
October 14, 2015, http://bedbugregistry.com/location/NY
/11206-3577/Brooklyn/248-Mckibben-St.

45. KW, "Bed Bug Report for 248 Mckibben St, Brooklyn, NY,"
Bed Bug Registry, April 26, 2007, http://bedbugregistry.com
/location/NY/11206-3577/Brooklyn/248-Mckibben-St.

46. David Colon, "McKibbin Loft Bans Parties, the Only
Reason to Live There," *Brokelyn*, March 14, 2013,

http://brokelyn. com/mckibbin-loft-bans-parties-the-only-reason-to-live-there/.

47. "255 MC KIBBIN STREET – ECB Query By Location," *NYC Department of Buildings*, accessed October 15, 2015, http://a810-bisweb.nyc.gov/bisweb/ECBQueryByLocation Servlet?requestid=1&allbin=3071385.

48. Buckley, "Young Artists Find a Private Space, Only Without the Privacy."

49. "Rooftop Films," *Wikipedia, the Free Encyclopedia*, April 8, 2014, http://en.wikipedia.org/w/index.php?title=Rooftop_Films&o ldid=596536384; Rachel Hartman, "Rooftop Films," *WNYC*, June 10, 2011, http://www.wnyc.org/story/140043-rooftop-films/?utm_source=sharedUrl&utm_media=metatag&utm_c ampaign=sharedUrl; Loris Jones-Randolph, "R.I.P. To McKibbin Loft's Roof Access," *Bushwick Daily*, August 28, 2015, http://bushwickdaily.com/bushwick/categories/news/ 3275-r-i-p-to-mckibbin-lofts-roof-access; Colon, "9 Things You Should Know before Moving into McKibbin Lofts."

50. "The History of Rooftop Films," *Rooftop Films: Underground Movies Outdoors*, May 15, 2014, http://rooftopfilms.com /2014/info/about_history.

51. Occupancy records for 57 Thames Street: "Property Profile Overview: 57 THAMES STREET," *NYC Department of Buildings*, May 15, 2014, http://a810-bisweb.nyc.gov/bis web/PropertyProfileOverviewServlet?boro=3&houseno=57& street=THAMES%20STREET&requestid=0&s=A03C41B885B 461E4F46BD08866A7430E.

52. "Overview for Complaint #:3160120 = RESOLVED," *NYC Department of Buildings*, June 13, 2005, http://a810-bisweb.nyc.gov/bisweb/OverviewForComplaintServlet?requ estid=2&vlcompdetlkey=0000021298; "Overview for Complaint #:3315913 = RESOLVED," *NYC Department of Buildings*, August 18, 2009, http://a810-bisweb.nyc.gov/bis web/OverviewForComplaintServlet?requestid=2&vlcom-

pdetlkey=0001206153; "Overview for Complaint #:3314140 = RESOLVED," *NYC Department of Buildings*, August 3, 2009, http://a810-bisweb.nyc.gov/bisweb/OverviewForComplaint Servlet?requestid=2&vlcompdetlkey=0001200177.

53. Kevin Lindamood, conversation with the author, April 14, 2014.

54. Kevin Lindamood, "Office Ops in Williamsburg NY is innovating its role as property managers," *The Journal of Aesthetics & Protest*, no. 3 (June 2004), http://www.joaap.org/new3/lindamood.html.

55. "CLASSICAL MUSIC AND DANCE GUIDE – June 6, 2003," *The New York Times*, June 6, 2003, sec. Section E; Part 1; Column 1; Movies, Performing Arts/Weekend Desk.

56. "CLASSICAL MUSIC AND DANCE GUIDE – June 4, 2004," *The New York Times*, June 4, 2004, sec. Section E; Part 1; Column 1; Movies, Performing Arts/Weekend Desk.

57. "The Listings: Oct. 6 – Oct. 12," *The New York Times*, October 6, 2006, sec. Section E; Part 1; Column 1; Movies, Performing Arts/Weekend Desk.

58. Occupancy records for 304 Boerum Street: "Property Profile Overview: 304 BOERUM STREET," *NYC Department of Buildings*, May 15, 2014, http://a810-bisweb.nyc.gov/bisweb/ PropertyProfileOverviewServlet?boro=3&houseno=304&stre et=Boerum+Street&go2=+GO+&requestid=0.

59. Sullivan, "Psst… Have You Heard About Bushwick?"

60. Gia Kourlas, "Grab a Beer and Watch Dance Grow in Brooklyn," *The New York Times*, April 9, 2006, sec. Section 2; Column 2; Arts and Leisure Desk; DANCE.

61. "About – CPR," *Center for Performance Research NYC*, accessed October 16, 2015, http://www.cprnyc.org/about/.

62. Lynne Miller, "Brooklyn 'Green' Development To House Dance Center," *The New York Sun*, October 18, 2007, sec. Real Estate.

63. Choire Sicha, "Village People," *Bookforum*, Sept/Oct/Nov

2015, 4.

64. Sullivan, "Psst... Have You Heard About Bushwick?"

65. Nicole Carter, "Ask a broker: Corcoran's Williamsburg Specialist Tom Le," *NY Daily News*, April 15, 2011, http://www.nydailynews.com/life-style/real-estate/broker-corcoran-williamsburg-specialist-tom-le-article-1.1045709.

66. Occupancy records for 119 Ingraham: "Property Profile Overview: 119 INGRAHAM STREET."

67. Occupancy records for 56 Bogart: "Property Profile Overview: 56 BOGART STREET," *NYC Department of Buildings*, May 15, 2014, http://a810-bisweb.nyc.gov/bisweb/PropertyProfileOverviewServlet?boro=3&houseno=56&street=Bogart&go2=+GO+&requestid=0.

68. Thomas Burr Dodd, conversation with the author, May 3, 2014.

69. Prices were collected based on advertisements in the Listings Project (http://www.listingsproject.com) which is another example of an artist entrepreneurial project. Stephanie Diamond, the creator of the project, collects listings from artists for rooms, studios and apartments and sends out an e-mail once a week. She charges a fee per listing. The prices above were listed on April 9, 2014, March 26, 2014, and January 14, 2014 respectively.

70. Powhida, "Bushwick Don't Worry."

71. Katarina Hybenova, "Last Call! Brooklyn Fire Proof East is Closing After 8 Years in the Neighborhood," *Bushwick Daily*, November 25, 2014, http://bushwickdaily.com/2014/11/brooklyn-fire-proof-closing/.

72. Driscoll, interview.

Chapter 6

1. Driscoll, interview.

2. Jordan Pearson, "MakerBot Just Laid Off 20 Percent of Its Staff," *Motherboard*, April 17, 2015, http://motherboard.vi

ce.com/read/makerbot-just-laid-off-20-percent-of-its-staff; Sean O'Kane, "MakerBot Lays off 20 percent of its staff for the second time this year," *The Verge*, October 8, 2015, http://www.theverge.com/2015/10/8/9477999/makerbot-layoffs-employees-lawsuit.

3. "MakerBot Opens a New, Bigger Brooklyn Factory," *MakerBot*, July 22, 2015, https://www.makerbot.com/media-center/2015/07/22/opening-new-bigger-brooklyn-factory.

4. For another example of American-based "lean" manufacturing at work, see the example of hoodie maker American Giant (a favorite of hoodie-wearing Valley wunderkinds): Farhad Manjoo, "American Giant Hoodie: This Is the Greatest Sweatshirt Known to Man," December 4, 2012, http://www.slate.com/articles/technology/technology/2012/12/american_giant_hoodie_this_is_the_greatest_sweatshirt_known_to_man.html; Hayley Peterson, "This hoodie is so insanely popular you have to wait months to get it," *Business Insider*, December 5, 2013, http://uk.businessinsider.com/this-hoodie-is-so-insanely-popular-you-have-to-wait-months-to-get-it-2013-12.

5. "All-Star Lineup Invests in MakerBot," *MakerBot*, accessed October 10, 2015, http://www.makerbot.com/blog/2011/08/23/all-star-lineup-invests-in-makerbot.

6. Zach Hoeken, "MakerBot vs. Open Source – A Founder Perspective," September 21, 2012, http://www.hoektronics.com/2012/09/21/makerbot-and-open-source-a-founder-perspective/.

7. "MakerBot Opens a New, Bigger Brooklyn Factory."

8. Tyler Woods, "New 3D-printing factory opens in Bushwick. Meet Voodoo Manufacturing," *Technical.ly*, October 7, 2015, https://technical.ly/brooklyn/2015/10/07/voodoo-manufacturing-3d-printing-factory-bushwick/.

9. Allegra Hobbs, "Tech, tech, boom! Developers banking on Bushwick as next big startup hub," *The Brooklyn Paper*,

October 8, 2015, http://www.brooklynpaper.com/stories/38 /41/dtg-office-buildings-in-bushwick-2015-10-09-bk.html.

10. Sarah Bernard, "Business Plan? What Business Plan?" *NYMag.com*, August 3, 2008, http://nymag.com/arts/art /features/48924/.

11. Occupancy records for 195 Morgan Avenue: "Property Profile Overview: 195 MORGAN AVENUE," *NYC Department of Buildings*, May 15, 2014, http://a810-bisweb.nyc.gov/bisweb/PropertyProfileOverviewServlet?bor o=3&houseno=195&street=Morgan&go2=+GO+&requestid=0.

12. Pechin, "All That We've Met."

13. *Ibid.*

14. Tricia Romano, "Put a Cork in It: Bottle Service Corrupts the Soul of New York City Nightlife," *The Village Voice*, December 12, 2006, http://www.villagevoice.com/2006-12-12/nyc-life/ put-a-cork-in-it/.

15. "3rd Ward offers no refunds, owner was a 'selfish, duplicitous crook' with a history of being an unorganized slumlord," *Free Williamsburg*, October 11, 2013, http://freewilliamsburg.com/3rd-ward-members-will-not-get-refunds-owner-had-history-of-being-an-unorganized-slumlord/.

16. Bernard, "Business Plan? What Business Plan?"; Mostafa Heddaya, "Blessed Are the Makers: The Rise and Fall of 3rd Ward," *Hyperallergic*, May 16, 2014, http://hyperallergic.com /88183/blessed-are-the-makers-the-rise-and-fall-of-3rd-ward/.

17. E. Vincent, "UPDATED: Art Fakes Times Square," *In Love With Mony*, June 19, 2012, http://inlovewithmony.word press.com/2012/06/19/art-fakes-times-square/.

18. See.Me, accessed May 15, 2014, https://www.see.me/.

19. Heddaya, "Blessed Are the Makers"; "3rd Ward offers no refunds, owner was a 'selfish, duplicitous crook' with a history of being an unorganized slumlord."

20. Liz Spikol, "Brooklyn's 3rd Ward Opens in Philadelphia,"

Philadelphia Magazine, March 1, 2013, http://www.philly
mag.com/property/2013/03/01/brooklyns-3rd-ward-has-
chosen-philadelphia-for-its-second-location/; Marguerite
Preston, "3rd Ward Gets Approval for Kitchen Incubator,"
Eater NY, June 5, 2013, http://ny.eater.com/archives
/2013/06/3rd_ward_gets_approval_for_kitchen_incubator_at
_1000_dean_street.php.

21. Melena Ryzik, "The Arts Collective 3rd Ward Thrives in
Bushwick, Brooklyn," *The New York Times*, July 2, 2010, sec.
Arts / Art & Design, http://www.nytimes.com/2010/07/03/
arts/design/03third.html.

22. Anderson, *Makers*.

23. Jenn Godbout, "Jason Goodman: On Maker Culture, Hands-
On Learning & the D.I.Y. Movement," *99U by Behance*, 2012,
http://99u.com/articles/7197/jason-goodman-on-maker-
culture-hands-on-learning-the-diy-movement.

24. Spikol, "Brooklyn's 3rd Ward Opens in Philadelphia."

25. Jeff Gordinier, "At Roberta's, Pizza and a Broken
Partnership," *The New York Times*, March 31, 2015,
http://www.nytimes.com/2015/04/01/dining/at-robertas-
pizza-and-a-broken-partnership.html.

26. It is unclear when this structure was built but actions under
its BIN number with the DOB suggest that it was newly built
in either 1919 or 1933, though subsequent alterations
occurred regularly over the years. See: "Actions: 272 SEIGEL
STREET," *NYC Department of Buildings*, May 15, 2014,
http://a810-bisweb.nyc.gov/bisweb/ActionsByLocation
Servlet?requestid=1&allbin=3071483.

27. Lori Waxman, "The Banquet Years: FOOD, A SoHo
Restaurant," *Gastronomica: The Journal of Food and Culture* 8,
no. 4 (November 1, 2008): 27, doi:10.1525/gfc.2008.8.issue-4.

28. Rachel Wharton, "Roberta's: A slacker pizza shop stumbles
into greatness," *Edible Brooklyn*, October 2, 2009,
http://www.ediblebrooklyn.com/magazine/back_of_the_hou

se-2/.

29. Gordinier, "At Roberta's, Pizza and a Broken Partnership."

30. Lizzie Widdicombe, "Roberta's," *The New Yorker*, July 11, 2011, http://www.newyorker.com/magazine/2011/07/11/robertas.

31. Waxman, "The Banquet Years," 32.

32. *Ibid.*, 27.

33. Gordinier, "At Roberta's, Pizza and a Broken Partnership."

34. Marguerite Preston, "Roberta's Owners Battling Over $5.4 Million in Nasty Split," *Eater NY*, February 27, 2015, http://ny.eater.com/2015/2/27/8119807/robertas-owners-battling-over-5-4-million-in-nasty-split; Dai, Serena, "Billionaire Tisch Family Drops Roberta's Buyout Plan," *Eater NY*, March 21, 2017, http://ny.eater.com/2017/3/21/15003620/tisch-robertas-sale-update.

35. John Marzulli, "Bushwick Pizzeria Sued over Cheated Overtime Wages," *NY Daily News*, accessed October 18, 2015, http://www.nydailynews.com/new-york/brooklyn/bushwick-pizzeria-sued-cheated-overtime-wages-article-1.2291342; Devra Ferst, "Roberta's Kitchen Staffer Slaps Restaurant With Lawsuit Alleging Unpaid Overtime," *Eater NY*, July 14, 2015, http://ny.eater.com/2015/7/14/8958349/robertas-kitchen-staffer-slaps-restaurant-with-lawsuit-alleging.

36. Rebecca Fishbein, "It Appears That Roberta's Owes $480K In Unpaid Taxes," *Gothamist*, August 19, 2015, http://gothamist.com/2015/08/19/robertas_bushwick_taxes.php.

37. Benjamin Wallace, "You Can Do Anything in Bushwick," *NYMag.com*, September 26, 2010, http://nymag.com/news/features/establishments/68498/.

38. Wharton, "Roberta's: A slacker pizza shop stumbles into greatness."

39. "Chris Parachini & Brandon Hoy: Locavore Leaders," *Food & Wine*, May 15, 2014, http://www.foodandwine.com/articles/

40-big-food-thinkers-under-40-chris-parachini-brandon-hoy.

40. Wharton, "Roberta's: A slacker pizza shop stumbles into greatness."

41. Sullivan, "Psst… Have You Heard About Bushwick?"

42. Ashlie Stevens, "Techies Want to Reinvent How We Cook," *MUNCHIES*, October 6, 2015, http://munchies.vice.com/articles/techies-want-to-reinvent-how-we-cook.

43. New and Classic Flavors | Empire Mayonnaise," accessed October 21, 2015, http://www.empiremayo.com/ [Offline, archived at archive.org as of April 2017: https://web-beta.archive.org/web/20161221045945/https://www.empiremayo.com/]; Parowpryo, "The Divisiveness of Artisanal Mayo," *F'd in Park Slope*, May 2, 2012, http://www.fuckedin-parkslope.com/home/the-divisiveness-of-artisanal-mayo.html. [Offline, archived at archive.org as of April 2017: https://web-beta.archive.org/web/20120518043033/http://www.fuckedinparkslope.com:80/home/the-divisiveness-of-artisanal-mayo.html]

44. Mark Hay, "Why Mayonnaise Matters in the Gentrification Debate," *GOOD Magazine*, June 5, 2015, http://magazine.good.is/articles/empire-mayonnaise-gentrification-brooklyn.

45. "Brooklyn Flea," *Brooklyn Flea*, accessed October 21, 2015, http://brooklynflea.com/about/.

46. "About | Smorgasburg | A Brooklyn Flea Food Market," accessed October 21, 2015, http://www.smorgasburg.com/about/.

47. "Food Artisans: Maiden Preserves," accessed October 21, 2015, http://newyork.seriouseats.com/2011/09/food-artisans-maiden-preserves.html; Benjamin Wallace, "The Twee Party," *NYMag.com*, April 15, 2012, http://nymag.com/news/features/artisanal-brooklyn-2012-4/.

48. "Brooklyn Sesame – All-Natural Artisanal Halva Spread," accessed October 21, 2015, http://www.brooklynsesame.com.

49. "Brooklyn Soda Works – artisanal, handmade sodas made

with fresh ingredients," *Kickstarter*, February 24, 2010, https://www.kickstarter.com/projects/1427166211/brooklyn-soda-works-artisanal-handmade-sodas-ma; Natasha Singer, "Brooklyn Soda Works, Inspired by Its Founders' Day Jobs," *The New York Times*, March 5, 2011, http://www.nytimes.com/2011/03/06/business/06stream.html.

50. Ana Nicole Rodriguez, "Faces Behind the Food: Caroline Mak of Brooklyn Soda Works," *The High Line*, August 15, 2013, http://www.thehighline.org/blog/2013/08/15/faces-behind-the-food-caroline-mak-of-brooklyn-soda-works.

51. Singer, "Brooklyn Soda Works, Inspired by Its Founders' Day Jobs."

52. KC Ifeanyi, "Meet The Actress Who Chucked A Successful Career To Start An Organic Ice-Cream Company," *Fast Company*, October 23, 2014, http://www.fastcompany.com/3037418/most-creative-people/meet-the-actress-who-chucked-a-successful-career-to-start-an-organic-ic.

53. *Ibid.*

54. "About Us – Brooklyn Baking Barons," *The Brooklyn Baking Barons*, accessed October 21, 2015, http://bkbarons.com/about-us/.

55. "How Kismet and Cake Turned a Baking Hobby Into a Budding Business," *Edible Brooklyn*, accessed October 21, 2015, http://www.ediblebrooklyn.com/2015/05/14/brooklyn-baking-barons/.

56. "About – Sunny Bang Private Label," accessed October 21, 2015, http://sunnybangprivatelabel.com/about/. [Offline, archived site at archive.org as of April 2017: https://web-beta.archive.org/web/20160206202700/http://sunnybangprivatelabel.com:80/about/]

57. "NYC's Hot Sauce Tasting Room by HEATONIST," *Kickstarter*, accessed October 21, 2015, https://www.kickstarter.com/projects/943136380/nycs-hot-sauce-tasting-room-by-heatonist.

58. Nell Casey, "An Artisanal Hot Sauce NOT Made In NYC's Most Branded Borough," *Gothamist*, July 23, 2015, http://gothamist.com/2015/07/23/bronx_hot_sauce.php.

59. Frederic Lardinois, "Nest's Tony Fadell Talks Thermostats, Apple, Kickstarter And Hardware Startups At LeWeb," *TechCrunch*, accessed October 21, 2015, http://social.techc runch.com/2012/12/04/nests-tony-fadell-talks-thermostats-apple-kickstarter-and-hardware-startups-at-leweb/; "Tony Fadell Archives – StrictlyVC, LLC," December 13, 2013, http://www.strictlyvc.com/tag/tony-fadell/.

60. Hatch, *The Maker Movement Manifesto*, 1.

61. Deirdre Gaquin, "Artists in the Workforce: 1990–2005" (Washington DC: Office of Research & Analysis, National Endowment for the Arts, May 2008), 7–8.

62. "Digest of Education Statistics, 1995 – Table 242. Bachelor's, master's, and doctor's degrees conferred by institutions of higher education, by sex of student and field of study: 1991–92," 1995, http://nces.ed.gov/programs/digest/d95/dtab 242.asp.

63. "Digest of Education Statistics, 2013 – Table 318.30. Bachelor's, master's, and doctor's degrees conferred by postsecondary institutions, by sex of student and discipline division, 2011–12," accessed October 22, 2015, http://nces.ed. gov/programs/digest/d13/tables/dt13_318.30.asp.

64. Ashley Zelinskie, "Reverse Abstraction," *Kickstarter*, August 2, 2011, https://www.kickstarter.com/projects/azelinskie /reverse-abstraction.

65. *Ibid*.

66. Regine, "Interview with Marisa Olson," *We Make Money Not Art*, March 28, 2008, http://we-make-money-not-art.com /archives/2008/03/how-does-one-become-marisa.php#. Viot3qJXBJk.

67. It should be noted that many of those invested in so-called New Media art have questioned the relevance of the term in

recent years, including Lev Manovich, author of *The Language of New Media* (Lev Manovich, *The Language of New Media*, Cambridge, MA: The MIT Press, 2001). See: Michael Connor, "What's Postinternet Got to do with Net Art?" Rhizome.org, November 1, 2013, http://rhizome.org/editorial/2013/nov/1/postinternet/.

Claire Bishop attracted criticism in 2012 for her assertion that artists were not working thematically with the digital, to the dismay of the splinter New Media art world that has often been excluded from the commercial gallery system. (See: Claire Bishop, "Digital Divide," *Artforum International* 51, no. 1 (2012): 434–441.)

68. Bishop, "Digital Divide," 354.

69. Artie Vierkant, "The Image Object Post-Internet," *Jstchillin*, 2010, http://jstchillin.org/artie/pdf/The_Image_Object_Post-Internet_a4.pdf. See also, Lauren Cornell and Ed Halter, *Mass Effect: Art and the Internet in the Twenty-First Century* (MIT Press, 2015); Omar Kholeif, *You are Here: Art After the Internet* (Cornerhouse, 2014); DIS, *9th Berlin Biennale Fur Zeitgenossische Kunst: The Present in Drag* (Berlin: Distanz Verlag, 2016).

Bibliography

"3rd Ward offers no refunds, owner was a 'selfish, duplicitous crook' with a history of being an unorganized slumlord." *Free Williamsburg*, October 11, 2013. http://freewilliamsburg.com /3rd-ward-members-will-not-get-refunds-owner-had-history-of-being-an-unorganized-slumlord/.

"255 MC KIBBIN STREET – ECB Query By Location." *NYC Department of Buildings*. Accessed October 15, 2015. http://a810-bisweb.nyc.gov/bisweb/ECBQueryByLocationServlet?requestid =1&allbin=3071385.

"About – CPR." *Center for Performance Research NYC*. Accessed October 16, 2015. http://www.cprnyc.org/about/.

"About – Northeast Kingdom." *Northeast Kingdom*. Accessed October 14, 2015. http://www.north-eastkingdom.com/?page_id=1092. [Offline, archived site at archive.org as of April 2017: https://web-beta.archive.org/web/20150312035715/http://www.north-eastkingdom.com/?page_id=1092]

"About | Smorgasburg | A Brooklyn Flea Food Market." Accessed October 21, 2015. http://www.smorgasburg.com/about/.

"About – Sunny Bang Private Label." Accessed October 21, 2015. http://sunnybangprivatelabel.com/about/. [Offline, archived site at archive.org as of April 2017: https://web-beta.archive. org/web/20160206202700/http://sunnybangprivatelabel.com:80/about/]

"About the Creek." *Newtown Creek Alliance*. Accessed October 14, 2015. http://www.newtowncreekalliance.org/about/history/.

"About Us – Brooklyn Baking Barons." *The Brooklyn Baking Barons*. Accessed October 21, 2015. http://bkbarons.com/about-us/.

"Actions: 272 SEIGEL STREET." *NYC Department of Buildings*, May 15, 2014. http://a810-bisweb.nyc.gov/bisweb/ActionsByLocation Servlet?requestid=1&allbin=3071483.

Alden, William. "The Business Tycoons of Airbnb." *The New York*

Times, November 25, 2014. http://www.nytimes.com/2014/11/30/magazine/the-business-tycoons-of-airbnb.html.

"All-Star Lineup Invests in MakerBot." *MakerBot*. Accessed October 10, 2015. http://www.makerbot.com/blog/2011/08/23/all-star-lineup-invests-in-makerbot.

Altman, Mitch. "Mitch Altman – It's official. I'm greatly saddened that I won't be…" *Facebook*, April 3, 2012. https://www.facebook.com/photo.php?fbid=10150649823645918&set=a.92403175917.100186.540310917&type=1&theater.

"An Old Art Revived and Advanced by Modern Science." *The Craftsman* II, no. 4 (July 1902).

Anderson, Chris. "20 Years of Wired: Maker movement." *Wired UK*, February 5, 2013. http://www.wired.co.uk/magazine/archive/2013/06/feature-20-years-of-wired/maker-movement.

———. *Makers: The New Industrial Revolution*. New York: Crown Business, 2012.

———. *The Long Tail: Why the Future of Business Is Selling Less of More*. New York: Hyperion, 2006.

Avakian, Talia. "American's Most Expensive Cities For Renters." *Business Insider*, August 25, 2015. http://www.businessinsider.com/americas-20-most-expensive-cities-for-renters-2015-8.

Avanessian, Armen. "A Questionnaire on Materialisms." *October* no. 155 (Winter 2016): 8–10. doi:10.1162/OCTO_a_00243.

Aytar, Volkan and Jan Rath. *Selling Ethnic Neighborhoods: The Rise of Neighborhoods as Places of Leisure and Consumption*. New York, NY: Routledge, 2012.

Baichtal, John, ed. *Maker Pro*. Sebastopol, CA: Maker Media, 2015.

Baird-Remba, Rebecca. "Permits Filed: Hotel And Medical Offices At 25 Stewart Avenue, Bushwick." *New York YIMBY*, May 20, 2015. http://newyorkyimby.com/2015/05/permits-filed-hotel-and-medical-offices-at-25-stewart-avenue-bushwick.html.

Bajaj, Vikas. "Who's Profiting From Airbnb?" *Taking Note*, October 17, 2014. http://takingnote.blogs.nytimes.com/2014/10 /17/whos-profiting-from-airbnb/.

Bal, Alexandra, Jason Nolan, and Yukari Seko. "Mélange of Making: Bringing Children's Informal Learning Cultures to the Classroom." In *DIY Citizenship: Critical Making and Social Media*, edited by Matt Ratto and Megan Boler, 157–68. Cambridge, MA: MIT Press, 2014.

Barbrook, Richard and Andy Cameron. "The Californian Ideology." In *Proud To Be Flesh: A Mute Magazine Anthology of Cultural Politics after the Net*, edited by Josephine Berry Slater and Pauline Van Mourik Broekman, 27–34. London; Brooklyn, NY: Mute Pub. in association with Autonomedia, 2009.

"Bed Bug Report for 248 Mckibben St, Brooklyn, NY." *Bed Bug Registry*. Accessed October 14, 2015. http://bedbugregistry.com/location/NY/11206-3577/Brooklyn/248-Mckibben-St.

Bennett, Jane. *Vibrant Matter: A Political Ecology of Things*. Durham: Duke University Press, 2010.

Bernard, Sarah. "Business Plan? What Business Plan?" *NYMag.com*, August 3, 2008. http://nymag.com/arts/art/features/48924/.

Bernstein, Roslyn and Shael Shapiro. *Illegal Living: 80 Wooster Street and the Evolution of SoHo*. Vilnius, Lithuania: Jonas Mekas Foundation, 2010.

Beuys, Joseph. "Introduction." In *Joseph Beuys*, by Caroline Tisdall. New York: Solomon R. Guggenheim Museum, 1979.

Bishop, Claire. "Digital Divide." *Artforum International* 51, no. 1 (2012): 434–441.

Bonneuil, Christophe and Jean-Baptiste Fressoz. *The Shock of the Anthropocene: The Earth, History and Us*. New York: Verso, 2016.

Bot, Sophy. *The Hipster Effect: How the Rising Tide of Individuality Is Changing Everything We Know about Life, Work and the Pursuit of Happiness*. Sophy Bot, 2012.

Brand, Stewart. "Spacewar: Fanatic Life and Symbolic Death Among the Computer Bums." *Rolling Stone* 7 (1972): 50–57.

Brand, Stewart. "We Owe It All to the Hippies." *Time*, March 1, 1995. http://content.time.com/time/magazine/article/0,9171,982602,00.html.

"Brooklyn Flea." *Brooklyn Flea*. Accessed October 21, 2015. http://brooklynflea.com/about/.

"Brooklyn Sesame – All-Natural Artisanal Halva Spread." Accessed October 21, 2015. http://www.brooklynsesame.com.

"Brooklyn Soda Works – artisanal, handmade sodas made with fresh ingredients." *Kickstarter*, February 24, 2010. https://www.kickstarter.com/projects/1427166211/brooklyn-soda-works-artisanal-handmade-sodas-ma.

Brooks, David. *Bobos in Paradise: The New Upper Class and How They Got There*. New York: Simon & Schuster, 2000.

Brown, Deborah. "Luhring Augustine Arrives on The Scene." *Bushwick Daily*, February 20, 2012. http://bushwickdaily.com/2012/02/luhring-augustine-arrives-on-the-scene/.

Bryant, Levi R., Nick Srnicek, and Graham Harman, eds. *The Speculative Turn: Continental Materialism and Realism*. Melbourne: Re.press, 2011.

Buckley, Cara. "Young Artists Find a Private Space, Only Without the Privacy." *The New York Times*, May 7, 2008, sec. A; Column 0; Metropolitan Desk.

Burnett, D. Graham. "A Questionnaire on Materialisms." *October* no. 155 (Winter 2016): 19–20. doi:10.1162/OCTO_a_00243.

"Bushburg Properties, Inc." *NYS Department of State: Division of Corporations Entity Information*, October 13, 2000. http://appext20.dos.ny.gov/corp_public/CORPSEARCH.ENTITY_INFORMATION?p_nameid=2596874&p_corpid=2563229&p_entity_name=Bushburg&p_name_type=A&p_search_type=BEGINS&p_srch_results_page=0.

"Bushwick Emerges As City's Next Artist Colony." *Boy in Bushwick*, January 11, 2008. http://boyinbushwick.blogspot.com/2008/01/bushwick-emerges-as-citys-next-artist.html.

Carlson, Jen. "Galapagos's Robert Elmes Discusses Move From Brooklyn To Detroit." *Gothamist*, December 9, 2014. http://gothamist.com/2014/12/09/robert_elmes_galapagos.php.

Carta, Maurizio. *Creative City: Dynamics, Innovations, Actions*. Actar

Coac Assn Of Catalan Arc, 2007.

Carter, Nicole. "Ask a broker: Corcoran's Williamsburg Specialist Tom Le." *NY Daily News*, April 15, 2011. http://www.nydailynews.com/life-style/real-estate/broker-corcoran-williamsburg-specialist-tom-le-article-1.1045709.

Casey, Nell. "An Artisanal Hot Sauce NOT Made In NYC's Most Branded Borough." *Gothamist*, July 23, 2015. http://gothamist.com/2015/07/23/bronx_hot_sauce.php.

———. "Brooklyn Roasting Company Brings Buzz To DUMBO, Beyond." *Gothamist*. Accessed October 18, 2015. http://gothamist.com/2011/08/08/dumbo_buzzing_from_newly_opened_bro.php.

Castrataro, Daniela. "A social history of crowdfunding." *Social Media Week*, December 12, 2011. http://socialmediaweek.org/blog/2011/12/a-social-history-of-crowdfunding/.

"Certificate of Occupancy, 248 McKibbin," May 15, 2014. http://a810-cofo.nyc.gov/cofo/B/301/378000/301378364F.PDF.

Chapman, Owen and Kim Sawchuk. "Creation-as-Research: Critical Making in Complex Environments." *RACAR: Revue D'art Canadienne/Canadian Art Review* 40, no. 1 (2015): 49–52.

Chau, Joanna. "Millennials Are More 'Generation Me' Than 'Generation We,' Study Finds." *The Chronicle of Higher Education*, March 15, 2012. http://chronicle.com/article/Millennials-Are-More/131175/.

Chen, Brian X. "App Maker Uber Hits Regulatory Snarl," *The New York Times*, December 2, 2012, sec. Technology. http://www.nytimes.com/2012/12/03/technology/app-maker-uber-hits-regulatory-snarl.html.

"Chris Parachini & Brandon Hoy: Locavore Leaders." *Food & Wine*, May 15, 2014. http://www.foodandwine.com/articles/40-big-food-thinkers-under-40-chris-parachini-brandon-hoy.

Clarke, Arthur C. *Profiles of the Future; an Inquiry into the Limits of the Possible*. New York: Harper & Row, 1962.

"CLASSICAL MUSIC AND DANCE GUIDE – June 4, 2004." *The*

New York Times, June 4, 2004, sec. Section E; Part 1; Column 1; Movies, Performing Arts/Weekend Desk.

"CLASSICAL MUSIC AND DANCE GUIDE – June 6, 2003." *The New York Times*, June 6, 2003, sec. Section E; Part 1; Column 1; Movies, Performing Arts/Weekend Desk.

Cobden-Sanderson, TJ. *The Arts and Crafts Movement*. Hammersmith, England: Hammersmith Pub. Society, 1905.

Colon, David. "9 Things You Should Know before Moving into McKibbin Lofts." *Brokelyn*, February 14, 2012. http://brokelyn .com/9-things-you-should-know-before-moving-into-mckibbin-lofts/.

———. "McKibbin Loft Bans Parties, the Only Reason to Live There." *Brokelyn*, March 14, 2013. http://brokelyn.com/mckibbin-loft-bans-parties-the-only-reason-to-live-there/.

Connor, Michael. "What's Postinternet Got to do with Net Art?" *Rhizome*.org, November 1, 2013. http://rhizome.org/editorial/20 13/nov/1/postinternet/.

Corbett, David Peters. "Visual culture and the history of art." In *Dealing with the Visual: Art History, Aesthetics and Visual Culture*, edited by Caroline van Eck and Edward Winters, 17–36. Farnham, Surrey: Ashgate Publishing, 2005.

Cornell, Lauren and Ed Halter. *Mass Effect: Art and the Internet in the Twenty-First Century*. MIT Press, 2015.

Corris, Michael. "Systems Upgrade." In *Proud To Be Flesh: A Mute Magazine Anthology of Cultural Politics after the Net*, edited by Josephine Berry Slater and Pauline Van Mourik Broekman, 107–20. London; Brooklyn, NY: Mute Pub. in association with Autonomedia, 2009.

Crary, Jonathan. *24/7: Late Capitalism and the Ends of Sleep*. London, New York: Verso, 2013.

Cumming, Elizabeth and Wendy Kaplan. *The Arts and Crafts Movement*. New York, NY: Thames and Hudson, 1991.

Curran, Ted. "'Own the Means of Production': What Karl Marx Knew about Opportunity in the Digital Economy." *Ted*

Curran.net. Accessed December 7, 2014. http://tedcurran.net/20 13/04/09/own-the-means-of-production-what-karl-marx-knew-about-opportunity-in-the-digital-economy/.

Cush, Andy. "The Campaign to Keep Chains Out of Bushwick." *Animal New York*. Accessed December 7, 2014. http://animal-newyork.com/2012/the-campaign-to-keep-chains-out-of-bushwick/.

Dai, Serena. "Bushwick Coffee Shops Skip Names for Mysterious Vibe." *DNAinfo New York*. Accessed December 7, 2014. http://www.dnainfo.com/new-york/20140728/bushwick/bushwick-coffee-shops-skip-names-for-mysterious-vibe/.

Dailey, Jessica. "It's More Expensive to Rent In Brooklyn Than Ever Before." *Curbed NY*, September 17, 2015. http://ny.curbed.com /2015/9/17/9920468/its-more-expensive-to-rent-in-brooklyn-than-ever-before.

"Dale Dougherty – O'Reilly Radar," March 16, 2015. http:// radar.oreilly.com/dale.

"DARPA Mentor Award to Bring Making to Education." *Make: DIY Projects and Ideas for Makers*, January 19, 2012. http://makezine.com/2012/01/19/darpa-mentor-award-to-bring-making-to-education/.

Debord, Guy. *La Société du spectacle*. Paris: Buchet/Chastel, 1967.

———. *The Society of the Spectacle*. New York: Zone Books, 1994.

Deutsche, Rosalyn and Cara Gendel Ryan. "The Fine Art of Gentrification." *October* 31 (December 1, 1984): 91–111.

"Digest of Education Statistics, 1995 – Table 242. Bachelor's, master's, and doctor's degrees conferred by institutions of higher education, by sex of student and field of study: 1991–92," 1995. http://nces.ed.gov/programs/digest/d95/dtab242.asp.

"Digest of Education Statistics, 2013 – Table 318.30. Bachelor's, master's, and doctor's degrees conferred by postsecondary institutions, by sex of student and discipline division, 2011–12." Accessed October 22, 2015. http://nces.ed.gov/programs/digest/d13/tables/dt13_318.30.asp.

DIS. *9th Berlin Biennale Fur Zeitgenossische Kunst: The Present in Drag*. Berlin: Distanz Verlag, 2016.

"Discussion from the Hackers' Conference, November 1984." *Whole Earth Review*, May 1985.

Doctorow, Cory. *Makers*. New York: Tor, 2009.

Donohue, Pete. "Oh, L, Not Enuf Trains!" *Daily News (New York)*. July 7, 2006. http://www.skyscrapercity.com/showthread .php?t=371385.

Doyle, James E. and Biljana Mickov, eds. *The Creative City: Vision and Execution*. London: Routledge, 2016.

Driscoll, Bill. Interview by Amanda Wasielewski, e-mail, October 11, 2015.

Dugan, Andrew. "Americans Most Likely to Say They Belong to the Middle Class." *Gallup*. Accessed May 29, 2016. http://www. gallup.com/poll/159029/americans-likely-say-belong-middle-class.aspx.

Dunbar-Hester, Christina. "Radical Inclusion? Locating Accountability in Technical DIY." In *DIY Citizenship: Critical Making and Social Media*, edited by Matt Ratto and Megan Boler, 75–88. Cambridge, MA: MIT Press, 2014.

Duve, Thierry de. "Joseph Beuys, or The Last of the Proletarians." *October* 45 (July 1, 1988): 47–62. doi:10.2307/779043.

E., Nick. "E Williamsburg or Bushwick?" Yelp, January 13, 2007. https://www.yelp.com/list/E922wMGcubD_wKM5SD0DwQ

Evans, Graeme. *Cultural Planning: An Urban Renaissance?* London: Routledge, 2001.

Falguières, Patricia. "A Questionnaire on Materialisms." *October* no. 155 (Winter 2016): 38–40. doi:10.1162/OCTO_a_00243.

Fensterstock, Ann. *Art on the Block: Tracking the New York Art World from SoHo to the Bowery, Bushwick and Beyond*. Macmillan, 2013.

Ferst, Devra. "Roberta's Kitchen Staffer Slaps Restaurant With Lawsuit Alleging Unpaid Overtime." *Eater NY*, July 14, 2015. http://ny.eater.com/2015/7/14/8958349/robertas-kitchen-staffer-slaps-restaurant-with-lawsuit-alleging.

Fishbein, Rebecca. "Controversial 'Jefftown' Creator Has Some Words For The Haters." *Gothamist*, May 16, 2014. http://gothamist.com/2014/05/16/jefftown_luv_it_or_leave_it.php.

———. "It Appears That Roberta's Owes $480K In Unpaid Taxes." *Gothamist*, August 19, 2015. http://gothamist.com/2015/08/19/robertas_bushwick_taxes.php.

Florida, Richard. *The Rise of the Creative Class: And How It's Transforming Work, Leisure, Community and Everyday Life*. New York: Basic Books, 2002.

Florida, Richard L. *Cities and the Creative Class*. New York: Routledge, 2005.

———. *The Rise of the Creative Class, Revisited*. New York: Basic Books, 2012.

———. *Who's Your City?: How the Creative Economy Is Making Where to Live the Most Important Decision of Your Life*. New York: Basic Books, 2008.

Fomina, Angelina. "The Cost of Living in the Top 25 Startup Cities," September 18, 2015. https://tech.co/cost-living-top-25-startup-cities-2015-09.

"Food Artisans: Maiden Preserves." Accessed October 21, 2015. http://newyork.seriouseats.com/2011/09/food-artisans-maiden-preserves.html.

Freeman, Veronica. *The Poetization of Metaphors in the Work of Novalis*. New York: Peter Lang, 2006. http://catalog.hathitrust.org/api/volumes/oclc/58546089.html.

Fuchs, Rafael. "Bushwick Yearbook." Accessed October 18, 2015. http://www.bushwickyearbook.com/index.php.

Furfaro, Danielle. "Bushwick residents rally against gentrification." *The Brooklyn Paper*, October 16, 2014. http://www.brooklyn-paper.com/stories/37/43/dtg-rent-stabilization-law-anti-gentrification-rally-2014-10-24-bk_37_43.html.

Gaquin, Deirdre. "Artists in the Workforce: 1990–2005." Washington DC: Office of Research & Analysis, National

Endowment for the Arts, May 2008.

García, Beatriz. "Cultural Policy and Urban Regeneration in Western European Cities: Lessons from Experience, Prospects for the Future." *Local Economy* 19, no. 4 (November 1, 2004): 312–26. doi:10.1080/0269094042000286828.

———. "Urban Regeneration, Arts Programming and Major Events." *International Journal of Cultural Policy* 10, no. 1 (March 2004): 103–18.

Gieseking, Jen Jack. "Queering the Meaning of 'Neighbourhood': Reinterpreting the Lesbian-Queer Experience of Park Slope, Brooklyn, 1983–2008." In *Queer Presences and Absences*, edited by Yvette Taylor, 178–200. New York: Palgrave Macmillan, 2013.

Godbout, Jenn. "Jason Goodman: On Maker Culture, Hands-On Learning & the D.I.Y. Movement." *99U by Behance*, 2012. http://99u.com/articles/7197/jason-goodman-on-maker-culture-hands-on-learning-the-diy-movement.

Goldstein, Daniel. "Brooklyn now even hotter than Manhattan when it comes to rentals." *MarketWatch*, September 28, 2015. http://www.marketwatch.com/story/brooklyn-now-even-hotter-than-manhattan-when-it-comes-to-rentals-2015-09-28.

Gooch, Brad. "The New Bohemia." *New York*, June 22, 1992.

Gordinier, Jeff. "At Roberta's, Pizza and a Broken Partnership." *The New York Times*, March 31, 2015. http://www.nytimes.com/2015/04/01/dining/at-robertas-pizza-and-a-broken-partnership.html.

Greif, Mark, Kathleen Ross, and Dayna Tortorici. *What Was the Hipster?: A Sociological Investigation*. New York: N+1 Foundation, 2010.

Hansen, Suzy. "How Zara Grew Into the World's Largest Fashion Retailer." *The New York Times*, November 9, 2012. http://www.nytimes.com/2012/11/11/magazine/how-zara-grew-into-the-worlds-largest-fashion-retailer.html.

Harman, Graham. *The Quadruple Object*. Washington DC: Zero Books, 2011.

Harris, Elizabeth A. "The Airbnb Economy in New York: Lucrative but Often Illegal." *The New York Times*, November 4, 2013, sec. N.Y. / Region. http://www.nytimes.com/2013/11/05/nyregion/the-airbnb-economy-in-new-york-lucrative-but-often-unlawful.html.

Hartman, Rachel. "Rooftop Films." *WNYC*, June 10, 2011. http://www.wnyc.org/story/140043-rooftop-films/?utm_source=sharedUrl&utm_media=metatag&utm_campaign=sharedUrl.

Harvey, David. *Paris, Capital of Modernity*. New York: Routledge, 2003.

Hatch, Mark. "Democratization of Tools and Information." In *The Maker Movement Manifesto: Rules for Innovation in the New World of Crafters, Hackers, and Tinkerers*. New York: McGraw-Hill Education, 2014.

Hay, Mark. "Why Mayonnaise Matters in the Gentrification Debate." *GOOD Magazine*, June 5, 2015. http://magazine.good.is/articles/empire-mayonnaise-gentrification-brooklyn.

Heddaya, Mostafa. "Blessed Are the Makers: The Rise and Fall of 3rd Ward." *Hyperallergic*, May 16, 2014. http://hyperallergic.com/88183/blessed-are-the-makers-the-rise-and-fall-of-3rd-ward/.

Hedlund, Patrick. "Life Cafe in East Village Closes After 30 Years." *DNAinfo New York*, September 12, 2011. http://www.dnainfo.com/new-york/20110912/lower-east-side-east-village/life-cafe-east-village-closes-after-30-years.

Hertz, Garnet. "Interview with Matt Ratto." In *Critical Making: Conversations*, edited by Garnet Hertz, 1–10. Hollywood, CA: Telharmonium Press, 2012. http://conceptlab.com/critical-making/.

———. "Making Critical Making." In *Critical Making: Introduction*, edited by Garnet Hertz, 1–10. Hollywood, CA: Telharmonium Press, 2012. http://conceptlab.com/critical-making/.

Heuberger, Chris. "A Brewing History of Bushwick." *Jane's Walk*.

Accessed October 14, 2015. http://janeswalk.org/united-states/new-york-city-ny/brewing-history-bushwick/.

Higgins, Michelle. "Crossing Into Queens." *The New York Times*, August 18, 2013, sec. Real Estate.

———. "Priced Out of Brooklyn? Try Manhattan." *The New York Times*, May 8, 2015. http://www.nytimes.com/2015/05/10/realestate/priced-out-of-brooklyn-try-manhattan.html.

Hobbs, Allegra. "Tech, tech, boom! Developers banking on Bushwick as next big startup hub." *The Brooklyn Paper*, October 8, 2015. http://www.brooklynpaper.com/stories/38/41/dtg-office-buildings-in-bushwick-2015-10-09-bk.html.

Hoeken, Zach. "MakerBot vs. Open Source – A Founder Perspective," September 21, 2012. http://www.hoektronics.com/2012/09/21/makerbot-and-open-source-a-founder-perspective/.

Hoffman, Meredith. "Controversial Bushwick Rezoning to Add High Rises, Streets and Retail." *DNAinfo New York*, June 20, 2013. http://www.dnainfo.com/new-york/20130620/bushwick/controversial-bushwick-rezoning-add-high-rises-streets-retail/.

Horning, Rob. "The Death of the Hipster." In *What Was the Hipster?: A Sociological Investigation*, edited by Mark Greif, Kathleen Ross, and Dayna Tortorici, 78–84. New York: N+1 Foundation, 2010.

"How Kismet and Cake Turned a Baking Hobby Into a Budding Business." *Edible Brooklyn*. Accessed October 21, 2015. http://www.ediblebrooklyn.com/2015/05/14/brooklyn-baking-barons/.

Howkins, John. *The Creative Economy: How People Make Money from Ideas*. London: Penguin, 2002.

Hudson, James R. *The Unanticipated City: Loft Conversions in Lower Manhattan*. University of Massachusetts Press, 1987.

Huspeni, Andrea. "Bushwick Hoping to Break the Cycle with the Loft Law." *Outside the Box*, December 16, 2011. https://outside-theboxblogs.wordpress.com/2011/12/16/bushwick-hoping-to-break-the-cycle-with-the-loft-law/.

Hybenova, Katarina. "Last Call! Brooklyn Fire Proof East is Closing After 8 Years in the Neighborhood." *Bushwick Daily*, November 25, 2014. http://bushwickdaily.com/2014/11/brooklyn-fire-proof-closing/.

———. "McKibbin Lofts Veteran Opens a Cafe & Shares a Bunch of Stories." *Bushwick Daily*, June 10, 2013. http://bush wickdaily.com/2013/06/mckibbin-lofts-veteran-opens-a-cafe-shares-a-bunch-of-stories/.

Ifeanyi, KC. "Meet The Actress Who Chucked A Successful Career To Start An Organic Ice-Cream Company." *Fast Company*, October 23, 2014. http://www.fastcompany.com/3037418/most-creative-people/meet-the-actress-who-chucked-a-successful-career-to-start-an-organic-ic.

Ingold, Tim. *Making: Anthropology, Archaeology, Art and Architecture.* Routledge, 2013.

Isaac, Mike. "Airbnb Pushes to Modify San Francisco Housing Laws." *Bits Blog*, August 1, 2014. http://bits.blogs.nytimes .com/2014/08/01/airbnb-pushes-to-modify-san-francisco-housing-laws/.

———. "Uber Flunks the Better Business Bureau Test." *Bits Blog*, October 9, 2014. http://bits.blogs.nytimes.com/2014/10/09/uber-flunks-the-better-business-bureau-test/.

———. "Uber Picks David Plouffe to Wage Regulatory Fight." *The New York Times*, August 19, 2014. http://www.nytimes.com/ 2014/08/20/technology/uber-picks-a-political-insider-to-wage-its-regulatory-battles.html.

Jayne, Mark. *Cities and Consumption*. London; New York: Routledge, 2006.

Jenson, Jennifer, Negin Dahya, and Stephanie Fisher. "Power Struggles: Knowledge Production in a DIY News Club." In *DIY Citizenship: Critical Making and Social Media*, edited by Matt Ratto and Megan Boler, 169–78. Cambridge, MA: MIT Press, 2014.

"Job Overview 248 MC KIBBIN STREET BROOKLYN." *NYC Department of Buildings*, May 15, 2014. http://a810-

bisweb.nyc.gov/bisweb/JobsQueryByLocationServlet?requestid=1&allbin=3071420&allstrt=MC%20KIBBIN%20STREET&allnumbhous=248.

Johnson, Paddy and Whitney Kimball. "Jules de Balincourt Issues Call to Arms Against Bushwick Gentrification." *Art F City*, June 9, 2013. http://artfcity.com/2013/06/09/jules-de-balincourt-issues-call-to-arms-against-bushwick-gentrification-on-facebook/.

Johnston, Casey. "Between Kickstarter's frauds and phenoms live long-delayed projects." *Ars Technica*, June 26, 2015. http://arstechnica.com/information-technology/2015/06/worth-the-wait-inside-kickstarters-world-of-delays/.

Jones, Caroline A. *Machine in the Studio: Constructing the Postwar American Artist*. Chicago: University of Chicago Press, 1996.

Jones-Randolph, Loris. "R.I.P. To McKibbin Loft's Roof Access." *Bushwick Daily*, August 28, 2015. http://bushwickdaily.com/bushwick/categories/news/3275-r-i-p-to-mckibbin-lofts-roof-access.

Kamer, Foster. "The Apocalypse and End of Williamsburg's 'Cool' Factor Has Arrived (Video)." *Runnin' Scared*. Accessed December 7, 2014. https://www.villagevoice.com/2010/10/08/the-apocalypse-and-end-of-williamsburgs-cool-factor-has-arrived-video/

Keen, Andrew. *The Cult of the Amateur: How Today's Internet is Killing Our Culture*. New York: Doubleday/Currency, 2007.

Kelly, Kevin. "1,000 True Fans." *The Technium*, March 4, 2008. http://kk.org/thetechnium/1000-true-fans/.

Kholeif, Omar. *You are Here: Art After the Internet*. Cornerhouse, 2014.

Kirkpatrick, Kathy. "Life Café 983 Bushwick to Close June 30, 2012." *Life Café*, June 24, 2012. http://lifecafe.com/tag/closing/.

Kostelanetz, Richard. "All Wrong About Lower Manhattan: Rereading Sharon Zukin." *Hyperallergic*, April 24, 2014. http://hyperallergic.com/122467/all-wrong-about-lower-manhattan-rereading-sharon-zukin/.

Kourlas, Gia. "Grab a Beer and Watch Dance Grow in Brooklyn." *The New York Times*, April 9, 2006, sec. Section 2; Column 2; Arts and Leisure Desk; DANCE.

Krauss, Rosalind. "Sculpture in the Expanded Field." *October* 8 (April 1, 1979): 31–44.

Krisel, Jonathan. "Cops Redesign." *Portlandia*. IFC, February 3, 2012.

———. "Farm." *Portlandia*. IFC, January 21, 2011.

KW. "Bed Bug Report for 248 Mckibben St, Brooklyn, NY." *Bed Bug Registry*, April 26, 2007. http://bedbugregistry.com/location /NY/11206-3577/Brooklyn/248-Mckibben-St.

Landry, Charles. *The Art of City Making*. London: Earthscan, 2006.

———. *The Creative City: A Toolkit for Urban Innovators*. London: Earthscan, 2000.

Landry, Charles and Franco Bianchini. *The Creative City*. London: Demos, 1995.

Lardinois, Frederic. "Nest's Tony Fadell Talks Thermostats, Apple, Kickstarter And Hardware Startups At LeWeb." *TechCrunch*. Accessed October 21, 2015. http://social.techcrunch.com/20 12/12/04/nests-tony-fadell-talks-thermostats-apple-kickstarter-and-hardware-startups-at-leweb/.

Latour, Bruno. *Reassembling the Social: An Introduction to Actor-Network-Theory*. Oxford; New York: Oxford University Press, 2005. http://site.ebrary.com/id/10233636.

Lavey, Nate. "The Most Radioactive Place in New York City Is Now a Superfund Site." *The New Yorker*, May 8, 2014. http://www. newyorker.com/tech/elements/the-most-radioactive-place-in-new-york-city-is-now-a-superfund-site.

Lee, Denny. "Has Billburg Lost Its Cool?" *The New York Times*, July 27, 2003, sec. 14; Column 2; The City Weekly Desk.

Lefebvre, Henri. *Critique de la vie quotidienne*. Paris: Éditions Bernard Grasset, 1947.

Levy, Steven. *Hackers: Heroes of the Computer Revolution*. Garden City, NY: Anchor Press/Doubleday, 1984.

Ley, David. "Artists, Aestheticisation and the Field of Gentrification." *Urban Studies* 40, no. 12 (November 1, 2003): 2527–44. doi:10.1080/0042098032000136192.

———. "Liberal Ideology and the Postindustrial City." *Annals of the Association of American Geographers* 70, no. 2 (1980): 238–58.

———. *The New Middle Class and the Remaking of the Central City*. Oxford; New York: Oxford University Press, 1996.

Lindamood, Kevin. "Office Ops in Williamsburg NY is innovating its role as property managers." *The Journal of Aesthetics & Protest*, no. 3 (June 2004). http://www.joaap.org/new3/lindamood.html.

Livingston, Jay. "Why Rich People Think They're Middle Class." *Sociological Images*, April 22, 2015. https://thesocietypages.org/socimages/2015/04/22/is-chris-christie-middle-class-class-and-self-perception/.

Lloyd, Richard. *Neo-Bohemia: Art and Commerce in the Postindustrial City*. Routledge, 2010.

Lutz, Ashley. "Zara Has Fundamentally Changed Fashion And There's No Going Back." *Business Insider*, November 10, 2012. http://www.businessinsider.com/how-zara-is-changing-fashion-forever-2012-11.

MacCannell, Dean. *The Tourist: A New Theory of the Leisure Class*. New York: Schocken Books, 1976.

Macy, Jr., Harry. "Before the Five-Borough City: The Old Cities, Towns and Villages That Came Together to Form 'Greater New York.'" *The NYG & B Newsletter*, Winter 1998, 3–6.

Mailer, Norman, Jean Malaquais, and Ned Polsky. *The White Negro*. San Francisco: City Lights Books, 1957.

"MakerBot Opens a New, Bigger Brooklyn Factory." *MakerBot*, July 22, 2015. https://www.makerbot.com/media-center/2015/07/22/opening-new-bigger-brooklyn-factory.

Malina, Roger. "Informant No 11: 100 Years of Scientific Making in Celebration of Frank Malina." In *Critical Making: History*, edited by Garnet Hertz, 1–10. Hollywood, CA: Telharmonium Press, 2012. http://conceptlab.com/criticalmaking/.

Manjoo, Farhad. "American Giant Hoodie: This Is the Greatest Sweatshirt Known to Man," December 4, 2012. http://www.slate.com/articles/technology/technology/2012/12/american_giant_hoodie_this_is_the_greatest_sweatshirt_known_to_man.html.

Manovich, Lev. *The Language of New Media*. Cambridge, MA: The MIT Press, 2001.

Markoff, John. *What the Dormouse Said: How the Sixties Counterculture Shaped the Personal Computer Industry*. New York: Viking, 2005.

Markusen, Ann. "Urban Development and the Politics of a Creative Class: Evidence from a Study of Artists." *Environment and Planning A* 38, no. 10 (2006): 1921.

Marx, Karl and Frederick Engels. *Manifesto of the Communist Party*. PDF. Marxists Internet Archive, 2014. https://www.marxists.org/archive/marx/works/1848/communist-manifesto/.

Marzulli, John. "Bushwick Pizzeria Sued over Cheated Overtime Wages." *NY Daily News*. Accessed October 18, 2015. http://www.nydailynews.com/new-york/brooklyn/bushwick-pizzeria-sued-cheated-overtime-wages-article-1.2291342.

"McKibbin Street Lofts." *Wikipedia, the Free Encyclopedia*, April 18, 2014. http://en.wikipedia.org/w/index.php?title=McKibbin_Street_Lofts&oldid=604793481.

McLuhan, Marshall. *The Gutenberg Galaxy: The Making of Typographic Man*. Toronto: University of Toronto Press, 1962.

— — —. *Understanding Media: The Extensions of Man*. New York: McGraw-Hill, 1964.

Mele, Christopher. *Selling the Lower East Side: Culture, Real Estate, and Resistance in New York City*. University of Minnesota Press, 2000.

Miles, Malcolm. "Interruptions: Testing the Rhetoric of Culturally Led Urban Development." *Urban Studies* 42, no. 5–6 (May 1, 2005): 889–911.

Miles, Steven. *Spaces for Consumption*. 1st edition. Thousand Oaks,

CA: SAGE Publications Ltd, 2010.

"Millennial Generation Money-Obsessed And Less Concerned With Giving Back, Study Finds." *Huffington Post*, March 16, 2012. http://www.huffingtonpost.com/2012/03/16/millennial-generation-study-fame-money_n_1354028.html.

Miller, Lynne. "Brooklyn 'Green' Development To House Dance Center." *The New York Sun*, October 18, 2007, sec. Real Estate.

Moore, Peter. "YouGov | Poll Results: Middle Class." *YouGov: What the World Thinks*, May 28, 2015. https://today.yougov.com /news/2015/05/28/poll-results-middle-class/.

"Morgantown Deli & General Inc." *NYS Department of State: Division of Corporations Entity Information*, October 27, 2010. http://appext20.dos.ny.gov/corp_public/CORPSEARCH.ENTIT Y_INFORMATION?p_nameid=4018649&p_corpid=4012221&p_ entity_name=Morgantown&p_name_type=A&p_search_type=B EGINS&p_srch_results_page=0.

"Morgantown Management, LLC." *NYS Department of State: Division of Corporations Entity Information*, December 10, 2003. http://appext20.dos.ny.gov/corp_public/CORPSEARCH.ENTIT Y_INFORMATION?p_nameid=3007892&p_corpid=2987129&p_ entity_name=Morgantown&p_name_type=A&p_search_type=B EGINS&p_srch_results_page=0.

Morozov, Evgeny. "Making It." *The New Yorker*, January 6, 2014. http://www.newyorker.com/magazine/2014/01/13/making-it-2.

Morris, Montrose. "Walkabout: The Sausage King of Brooklyn, Part 3." *Brownstoner*, December 6, 2012. http://www.brownstoner .com/blog/2012/12/walkabout-the-sausage-king-of-brooklyn-part-3/.

Morris, William. *Hopes and Fears for Art*. New York: Longmans, Green, and Co., 1901.

Moynihan, Colin. "Galapagos Art Space Will Make Detroit Its Home." *The New York Times*, December 7, 2014. http://www. nytimes.com/2014/12/08/arts/galapagos-art-space-will-make-detroit-its-home.html.

Murphy, Doyle and Philip Caulfield. "'Greedy Infiltrators': Bushwick coffee shop bashed after anti-Semitic rant." *NY Daily News*, December 7, 2014. http://www.nydailynews.com/new-york/brooklyn/greedy-infiltrators-bushwick-coffee-shop-bashed-anti-semitic-online-rant-article-1.1961070.

"New and Classic Flavors | Empire Mayonnaise." Accessed October 21, 2015. http://www.empiremayo.com/. [Offline, archived at archive.org as of April 2017: https://web-beta .archive.org/web/20161221045945/https://www.empiremayo. com/]

Newport, Frank. "Fewer Americans Identify as Middle Class in Recent Years." *Gallup*, April 28, 2015. http://www.gallup.com /poll/182918/fewer-americans-identify-middle-class-recent-years.aspx.

"No, Brooklyn is not more expensive than Manhattan – but it's getting closer." *Brick Underground*, October 8, 2015. http://www .brickunderground.com/blog/2015/10/brooklyn_market_report.

Nonko, Emily. "How Bloomberg Changed New York Real Estate." *NewYork.com*, August 29, 2013. http://www.newyork. com/articles/real-estate/how-bloomberg-changed-new-york-real-estate-99465/.

Novalis, and Margaret Mahony Stoljar. *Philosophical Writings*. Albany, NY: State University of New York Press, 1997.

"NYAB Venue – The Active Space." *NY Art Beat*. Accessed October 24, 2015. http://www.nyartbeat.com/venue/00E394AC.

"NYC's Hot Sauce Tasting Room by HEATONIST." *Kickstarter*. Accessed October 21, 2015. https://www.kickstarter.com/pr ojects/943136380/nycs-hot-sauce-tasting-room-by-heatonist.

OfficeOps. Accessed May 15, 2014. http://www.officeops.org.

O'Kane, Sean. "MakerBot Lays off 20 percent of its staff for the second time this year." *The Verge*, October 8, 2015. http://www.theverge.com/2015/10/8/9477999/makerbot-layoffs-employees-lawsuit.

Oldenburg, Ray. *The Great Good Place: Cafés, Coffee Shops, Community*

Centers, Beauty Parlors, General Stores, Bars, Hangouts and How They Get You Through the Day. New York: Paragon House, 1989.

O'Reilly, Tim. "Mitch Altman – It's Official. I'm greatly saddened that I won't be…" *Facebook*, April 3, 2012. https://www.facebook.com/photo.php?fbid=10150649823645918&set=a.92403175917.100186.540310917&type=1&theater.

Orland, Kyle. "On Kickstarter, everyone is Peter Molyneux." *Ars Technica*, February 13, 2015. http://arstechnica.com/gaming/2015/02/on-kickstarter-everyone-is-peter-molyneux/.

"Overview for Complaint #:3160120 = RESOLVED." *NYC Department of Buildings*, June 13, 2005. http://a810-bisweb.nyc.gov/bisweb/OverviewForComplaintServlet?requestid=2&vlcompdetlkey=0000021298.

"Overview for Complaint #:3314140 = RESOLVED." *NYC Department of Buildings*, August 3, 2009. http://a810-bisweb.nyc.gov/bisweb/OverviewForComplaintServlet?requestid=2&vlcompdetlkey=0001200177.

"Overview for Complaint #:3315913 = RESOLVED." *NYC Department of Buildings*, August 18, 2009. http://a810-bisweb.nyc.gov/bisweb/OverviewForComplaintServlet?requestid=2&vlcompdetlkey=0001206153.

Owens, Craig. "Commentary: The Problem with Puerilism." *Art in America* 72, no. 6 (1984): 162–163.

Palmeri, Tara. "New hipsters fight old hipsters in Bushwick." *New York Post*, December 2, 2013. http://nypost.com/2013/12/02/new-hipsters-fight-old-hipsters-over-luxury-bushwick-digs/.

Parowpryo. "The Divisiveness of Artisanal Mayo." *F'd in Park Slope*, May 2, 2012. http://www.fuckedinparkslope.com/home/the-divisiveness-of-artisanal-mayo.html. [Offline, archived at archive.org as of April 2017: https://web-beta.archive.org/web/20120518043033/http://www.fuckedinparkslope.com:80/home/the-divisiveness-of-artisanal-mayo.html]

Peacock, Thomas Love, Herbert Francis Brett Brett-Smith, Percy Bysshe Shelley, and Robert Browning. *Four Ages of Poetry,*

Shelley's Defense of Poetry, Browning's Essay on Shelley. Boston: Houghton Mifflin, 1921.

Pearson, Jordan. "MakerBot Just Laid Off 20 Percent of Its Staff." *Motherboard,* April 17, 2015. http://motherboard.vice.com/read/makerbot-just-laid-off-20-percent-of-its-staff.

Pechin, Pauline. "Jason Goodman Relates Failure to Progress." *All That We've Met,* March 17, 2011. http://www.allthatwevemet.org/2011/03/jason-goodman-relates-failure-to.html. [Offline]

Peterson, Hayley. "This hoodie is so insanely popular you have to wait months to get it." *Business Insider,* December 5, 2013. http://uk.businessinsider.com/this-hoodie-is-so-insanely-popular-you-have-to-wait-months-to-get-it-2013-12.

Piketty, Thomas. *Capital in the Twenty-First Century.* Translated by Arthur Goldhammer. Cambridge, MA: Belknap Press of Harvard University Press, 2014.

Plato, and CDC Reeve. *Republic.* Indianapolis: Hackett Pub. Co., 2004.

Powhida, William. "Bushwick Don't Worry," May 15, 2014. http://williampowhida.com/wordpress/archives/476.

———. "The Yellow Building," May 15, 2014. https://docs.google.com/document/d/1dLl0V_7AejNr2eSPgZyZ5Vd3IrSZPgvROMlEW5Jd-EI/.

"Press Release: Subway Ridership Surges 2.6% In One Year." *MTA.info,* April 20, 2015. http://www.mta.info/press-release/nyc-transit/subway-ridership-surges-26-one-year.

Preston, Marguerite. "3rd Ward Gets Approval for Kitchen Incubator." *Eater NY,* June 5, 2013. http://ny.eater.com/archives/2013/06/3rd_ward_gets_approval_for_kitchen_incubator_at_1000_dean_street.php.

———. "Roberta's Owners Battling Over $5.4 Million in Nasty Split." *Eater NY,* February 27, 2015. http://ny.eater.com/2015/2/27/8119807/robertas-owners-battling-over-5-4-million-in-nasty-split.

"Property Profile Overview: 56 BOGART STREET." *NYC*

Department of Buildings, May 15, 2014. http://a810-bisweb.nyc.gov/bisweb/PropertyProfileOverviewServlet?boro=3&houseno=56&street=Bogart&go2=+GO+&requestid=0.

"Property Profile Overview: 57 THAMES STREET." *NYC Department of Buildings*, May 15, 2014. http://a810-bisweb.nyc.gov/bisweb/PropertyProfileOverviewServlet?boro=3&houseno=57&street=THAMES%20STREET&requestid=0&s=A03C41B885B461E4F46BD08866A7430E.

"Property Profile Overview: 119 INGRAHAM STREET." *NYC Department of Buildings*, May 15, 2014. http://a810-bisweb.nyc.gov/bisweb/PropertyProfileOverviewServlet?boro=3&houseno=119&street=ingraham&go2=+GO+&requestid=0.

"Property Profile Overview: 195 MORGAN AVENUE." *NYC Department of Buildings*, May 15, 2014. http://a810-bisweb.nyc.gov/bisweb/PropertyProfileOverviewServlet?boro=3&houseno=195&street=Morgan&go2=+GO+&requestid=0.

"Property Profile Overview: 248 MC KIBBIN STREET." *NYC Department of Buildings*, May 15, 2014. http://a810-bisweb.nyc.gov/bisweb/PropertyProfileOverviewServlet?boro=3&houseno=248&street=MC%20KIBBIN%20STREET&requestid=0&s=A03C41B885B461E4F46BD08866A7430E.

"Property Profile Overview: 255 MC KIBBIN STREET." *NYC Department of Buildings*, May 15, 2014. http://a810-bisweb.nyc.gov/bisweb/PropertyProfileOverviewServlet?requestid=3&bin=3071385&restore=1.

"Property Profile Overview: 304 BOERUM STREET." *NYC Department of Buildings*, May 15, 2014. http://a810-bisweb.nyc.gov/bisweb/PropertyProfileOverviewServlet?boro=3&houseno=304&street=Boerum+Street&go2=+GO+&requestid=0.

Ratto, Matt. "Critical Making: Conceptual and Material Studies in Technology and Social Life." *The Information Society* 27, no. 4 (2011): 252–260.

———. "Critical Making." In *Open Design Now: Why Design*

Cannot Remain Exclusive, 202–9. Amsterdam: BIS Publishers, 2011. http://opendesignnow. org.

———. "Textual Doppelgangers: Critical Issues in the Study of Technology." In *DIY Citizenship: Critical Making and Social Media*, edited by Matt Ratto and Megan Boler, 227–36. Cambridge, MA: MIT Press, 2014.

Ratto, Matt and Stephen Hockema. "FLWR PWR: Tending the Walled Garden." *Walled Garden*, 2009, 51–60.

Ratto, Matt and Megan Boler, eds. *DIY Citizenship: Critical Making and Social Media*. Cambridge, MA: MIT Press, 2014.

Regine. "Interview with Marisa Olson." *We Make Money Not Art*, March 28, 2008. http://we-make-money-not-art.com/archives/2008/03/how-does-one-become-marisa.php#.Viot3qJXBJk.

"Rheingold Campaign." *NWB – Neighbors Without Borders*, December 13, 2013. http://www.nwbcommunity.org/campaign/.

Rodriguez, Ana Nicole. "Faces Behind the Food: Caroline Mak of Brooklyn Soda Works." *The High Line*, August 15, 2013. http://www.thehighline.org/blog/2013/08/15/faces-behind-the-food-caroline-mak-of-brooklyn-soda-works.

Romano, Tricia. "Put a Cork in It: Bottle Service Corrupts the Soul of New York City Nightlife." *The Village Voice*, December 12, 2006. http://www.villagevoice.com/2006-12-12/nyc-life/put-a-cork-in-it/.

"Rooftop Films." *Wikipedia, the Free Encyclopedia*, April 8, 2014. http://en.wikipedia.org/w/index.php?title=Rooftop_Films&oldid=596536384.

Rosler, Martha. *Culture Class*. Berlin: Sternberg Press, 2013.

Rosner, Daniela K. and Miki Foster. "Woven Futures: Inscribed Material Ecologies of Critical Making." In *DIY Citizenship: Critical Making and Social Media*, edited by Matt Ratto and Megan Boler, 189–99. Cambridge, MA: MIT Press, 2014.

Ruskin, John. *Modern Painters*, Vol. 2, 2 vols. New York: CE Merrill, 1891.

———. *Sesame & Lilies; The Two Paths & The King of the Golden*

River. London: Dent; New York: Dutton, 1907.

— — —. *The Stones of Venice*, Vol. 2, 3 vols. New York: J. Wiley, 1867.

Russeth, Andrew. "'Williamsburg Is Over,' Says Art Writer James Kalm." *New York Observer*. Accessed December 7, 2014. http://observer.com/2011/09/williamsburg-is-over-says-art-writer-james-kalm/.

Ryzik, Melena. "The Arts Collective 3rd Ward Thrives in Bushwick, Brooklyn." *The New York Times*, July 2, 2010, sec. Arts / Art & Design. http://www.nytimes.com/2010/07/03/arts/design/03third.html.

Schiller, Friedrich. *On the Aesthetic Education of Man*. Translated by Reginald Snell. Mineola, NY: Dover Pub., 2004.

Schreier, Jason. "*Unsung Story* Is A $660,000 Kickstarter Disaster." *Kotaku*, September 22, 2015. http://kotaku.com/unsung-story-is-a-660-000-kickstarter-disaster-1732312002.

See.Me. Accessed May 15, 2014. https://www.see.me/.

Seifer, Marc J. *Wizard: The Life and Times of Nikola Tesla: Biography of a Genius*. New York: Citadel Press, 1998.

Shelley, Percy Bysshe, Zachary Leader, and Michael O'Neill. *Percy Bysshe Shelley: The Major Works*. Oxford: Oxford University Press, 2009.

Short, Aaron. "Can The Loom Spin a New Scene in Bushwick? » The Bushwick News/BushwickBK," June 16, 2009. http://bushwickbk.com/2009/06/16/can-the-loom-spin-a-new-scene-in-bushwick/. [Offline, archived at archive.org as of April 2017: http://bushwickbk.com:80/2009/06/16/can-the-loom-spin-a-new-scene-in-bushwick/]

Sicha, Choire. "Bedbug Population Explodes At Bushwick Hipster Ground Zero." *Gawker*. Accessed October 14, 2015. http://gawker.com/299467/bedbug-population-explodes-at-bushwick-hipster-ground-zero.

Sicha, Choire. "Village People." *Bookforum*, Autumn 2015.

Sidney, Philip and Ben Jonson. *Sir Philip Sydney's Defense Of Poetry:*

And Observations On Poetry And Eloquence Of Ben Jonson. Kessinger Publishing, LLC, 2009.

Silk, Michael L. and David L. Andrews. *Sport and Neoliberalism: Politics, Consumption, and Culture.* Philadelphia: Temple University Press, 2012.

Singer, Natasha. "Brooklyn Soda Works, Inspired by Its Founders' Day Jobs." *The New York Times*, March 5, 2011. http://www.nytimes.com/2011/03/06/business/06stream.html.

Sleigh, Andrew. "John Ruskin: Grandfather of the Maker Movement? The Lamp of Life, The Lamp of Truth, 7 Lamps in the Hackerspace." *Medium*, October 12, 2015. https://medium.com/@andrewsleigh/john-ruskin-grandfather-of-the-maker-movement-853706eb2bd.

Small, Irene V. "Site and Sociality: Joseph Beuys and the Relics of Modernist Sculpture." *Yale University Art Gallery Bulletin*, January 1, 2009, 86–88.

Smith, Adam. *An Inquiry into the Nature and Causes of the Wealth of Nations.* London: W. Strahan and T. Cadell, 1776.

Smith, Neil. "New City, New Frontier: The Lower East Side as Wild, Wild West." In *Variations on a Theme Park: The New American City and the End of Public Space*, edited by Michael Sorkin. New York: Macmillan, 1992.

———. *The New Urban Frontier: Gentrification and the Revanchist City.* London; New York: Routledge, 1996.

Smith, Stephen. "Permits Filed: Live/Work Space at 117 McKibben Street, East Williamsburg." *New York YIMBY.* Accessed October 18, 2015. http://newyorkyimby.com/2014/08/permits-filed-livework-space-at-117-mckibben-street-east-williamsburg.html.

Snavely, Andrew. "Is the Millennial Generation Really Lazy, Entitled, and Selfish? A CNN Comic Strip by Matt Bors." Accessed May 16, 2014. http://www.primermagazine.com/2013/live/is-the-millennial-generation-really-lazy-entitled-and-selfish-a-cnn-comic-strip-by-matt-bors.

Soloski, Alexis. "Bushwick Starr, a Humble Space With Bold

Works." *The New York Times*, October 2, 2014. http://www.ny
times.com/2014/10/05/theater/bushwick-starr-a-humble-space-
with-bold-works.html.

Spikol, Liz. "Brooklyn's 3rd Ward Opens in Philadelphia."
Philadelphia Magazine, March 1, 2013. http://www.phillymag
.com/property/2013/03/01/brooklyns-3rd-ward-has-chosen-
philadelphia-for-its-second-location/.

Spirou, Costas. *Urban Tourism and Urban Change: Cities in a Global
Economy*. 1st edition. New York: Routledge, 2010.

Steinhauer, Jillian. "Bushwick Artists Ponder Ways to Fight
Gentrification." *Hyperallergic*, June 21, 2013. http://hyperal-
lergic.com/73855/bushwick-artists-ponder-ways-to-fight-gentri-
fication/.

Stevens, Ashlie. "Techies Want to Reinvent How We Cook."
MUNCHIES, October 6, 2015. http://munchies.vice.com/art
icles/techies-want-to-reinvent-how-we-cook.

Stiles, Henry Reed. *A History of the City of Brooklyn: Including the Old
Town and Village of Brooklyn, the Town of Bushwick, and the Village
and City of Williamsburgh*. Vol. 2. Brooklyn, NY: Pub. by
subscription, 1867.

Stone, Madeline. "San Francisco Is More Expensive Than New York
City," September 17, 2014. http://www.businessinsider.com/san-
francisco-is-more-expensive-than-new-york-city-2014-9.

Streitfeld, David. "Airbnb Listings Mostly Illegal, New York State
Contends." *The New York Times*, October 15, 2014.
http://www.nytimes.com/2014/10/16/business/airbnb-listings-
mostly-illegal-state-contends.html.

———. "Companies Built on Sharing Balk When It Comes to
Regulators." *The New York Times*, April 21, 2014.
http://www.nytimes.com/2014/04/22/business/companies-built-
on-sharing-balk-when-it-comes-to-regulators.html.

———. "New York's Case Against Airbnb Is Argued in Albany."
The New York Times, April 22, 2014. http://www.nytimes
.com/2014/04/23/technology/albany-judge-hears-case-against-

airbnb.html.

———. "Rough Patch for Uber Service's Challenge to Taxis." *The New York Times*, January 26, 2014. http://www.nytimes.com/2014/01/27/technology/rough-patch-for-uber-services-challenge-to-taxis.html.

Strickland, Julie. "The Neighborhood Name Police: East Williamsburg." *Brooklyn Based*, July 14, 2012. http://brooklyn-based.com/blog/2012/07/24/the-neighborhood-name-police-east-williamsburg/.

Sull, Donald and Stefano Turconi. "Fast Fashion Lessons." *Business Strategy Review*, Summer 2008.

Sullivan, Robert. "Psst... Have You Heard About Bushwick?" *The New York Times*, March 19, 2006, sec. Section 6; Column 3; Magazine.

Terranova, Tiziana. "Free Labor: Producing Culture for the Digital Economy." *Social Text* 18, no. 2 (Summer 2000): 33–58.

"The American Middle Class Is Losing Ground." *Pew Research Center's Social & Demographic Trends Project*, December 9, 2015. http://www.pewsocialtrends.org/2015/12/09/the-american-middle-class-is-losing-ground/.

"The art and craft of business." *The Economist*, January 4, 2014. http://www.economist.com/news/business/21592656-etsy-starting-show-how-maker-movement-can-make-money-art-and-craft-business.

"The History of Rooftop Films." *Rooftop Films: Underground Movies Outdoors*, May 15, 2014. http://rooftopfilms.com/2014/info/about_history.

"The Listings: Oct. 6 – Oct. 12." *The New York Times*, October 6, 2006, sec. Section E; Part 1; Column 1; Movies, Performing Arts/Weekend Desk.

"The Prehistory of Maker Culture: the arts and crafts movement." Accessed June 30, 2016. https://wiki.p2pfoundation.net/Maker_Movement#The_Prehistory_of_Maker_Culture:_the_arts_and_c rafts_movement.

"Tony Fadell Archives – StrictlyVC, LLC," December 13, 2013. http://www.strictlyvc.com/tag/tony-fadell/.

Tortorici, Dayna. "You Know It When You See It." In *What Was the Hipster?: A Sociological Investigation*, edited by Mark Greif, Kathleen Ross, and Dayna Tortorici, 122–35. New York: N+1 Foundation, 2010.

Tsai, Mu-Ming. *Maker*. Documentary, 2014.

Turetsky, Emma. "Not Even Toxic Waste Can Stop Gentrification: NYC's Superfund Neighborhoods Are Booming." *Gothamist*, August 22, 2014. http://gothamist.com/2014/08/22/superfund_vs_gentrification.php.

Turner, Fred. *From Counterculture to Cyberculture: Stewart Brand, the Whole Earth Network, and the Rise of Digital Utopianism*. Chicago: University of Chicago Press, 2006.

Vandam, Jeff. "Go East, Young Man." *The New York Times*, June 19, 2005. http://www.nytimes.com/2005/06/19/nyregion/go-east-young-man.html.

Varnelis, Kazys. "The Rise of Network Culture," May 15, 2014. http://varnelis.net/the_rise_of_network_culture.

Vartanian, Hrag. "Is Ridgewood Breaking Away from the Bushwick Scene?" *Hyperallergic*, May 8, 2012. http://hyperallergic.com/51210/actually-its-ridgewood/.

Vierkant, Artie. "The Image Object Post-Internet." *Jstchillin*, 2010. http://jstchillin.org/artie/pdf/The_Image_Object_Post-Internet_a4.pdf.

Vincent, E. "UPDATED: Art Fakes Times Square." *In Love With Mony*, June 19, 2012. http://inlovewithmony.wordpress.com/2012/06/19/art-fakes-times-square/.

Wallace, Benjamin. "The Twee Party." *NYMag.com*, April 15, 2012. http://nymag.com/news/features/artisanal-brooklyn-2012-4/.

———. "You Can Do Anything in Bushwick." *NYMag.com*, September 26, 2010. http://nymag.com/news/features/establishments/68498/.

Wasielewski, Amanda. "Grains of Gold in All This Shit." *Hz Journal*

16 (March 2011). http://www.hz-journal.org/n16/wasielews ki.html.

Waxman, Lori. "The Banquet Years: FOOD, A SoHo Restaurant." *Gastronomica: The Journal of Food and Culture* 8, no. 4 (November 1, 2008): 24–33. doi:10.1525/gfc.2008.8.issue-4.

Wharton, Rachel. "Roberta's: A slacker pizza shop stumbles into greatness." *Edible Brooklyn*, October 2, 2009. http://www.edible-brooklyn.com/magazine/back_of_the_house-2/.

Whitford, Emma. "Owners Of New Ridgewood Bar Say Neighboring Superfund Site Is No Big Deal." *Gothamist*, June 24, 2015. http://gothamist.com/2015/06/24/blinky_drinks_free.php.

Whyte, William H. *The Organization Man*. New York: Simon and Schuster, 1956.

Wicks, Erin. "The Coffee Shop: Bushwick's Newest and Most Aptly Named Spot for a Cup O' Joe." *Bushwick Daily*, July 7, 2014. http://bushwickdaily.com/2014/07/the-coffee-shop-bushwicks-newest-and-most-adeptly-named-spot-for-a-cup-o-joe/.

Widdicombe, Lizzie. "Roberta's." *The New Yorker*, July 11, 2011. http://www.newyorker.com/magazine/2011/07/11/robertas.

Wingfield, Nick. "A Victory for Airbnb in New York." *The New York Times*, May 13, 2014. https://www.nytimes.com/2014/05/14/technology/judge-quashes-new-york-subpoena-for-airbnb-records.html.

"Wired Editor-in-Chief Chris Anderson Steps Down to Run Robotics Startup." *Wired*, November 2, 2012. http://www.wired.com/2012/11/wired-editor-in-chief-chris-anderson-steps-down/.

Woods, Tyler. "New 3D-printing factory opens in Bushwick. Meet Voodoo Manufacturing." *Technical.ly*, October 7, 2015. https://technical.ly/brooklyn/2015/10/07/voodoo-manufac-turing-3d-printing-factory-bushwick/.

Yencken, David. "The Creative City." *Meanjin* 47, no. 4 (Summer 1988): 597.

Zelinskie, Ashley. "Reverse Abstraction." *Kickstarter*, August 2,

2011. https://www.kickstarter.com/projects/azelinskie/reverse-abstraction.

Zukin, Sharon. *Loft Living: Culture and Capital in Urban Change.* Baltimore: Johns Hopkins University Press, 1982.

———. *Naked City: The Death and Life of Authentic Urban Places.* Oxford; New York: Oxford University Press, 2010.

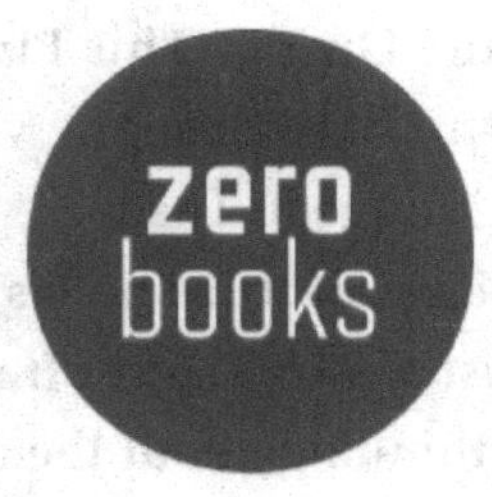

Zero Books

CULTURE, SOCIETY & POLITICS

Contemporary culture has eliminated the concept and public figure of the intellectual. A cretinous anti-intellectualism presides, cheer-led by hacks in the pay of multinational corporations who reassure their bored readers that there is no need to rouse themselves from their stupor. Zer0 Books knows that another kind of discourse – intellectual without being academic, popular without being populist – is not only possible: it is already flourishing. Zer0 is convinced that in the unthinking, blandly consensual culture in which we live, critical and engaged theoretical reflection is more important than ever before.

If you have enjoyed this book, why not tell other readers by posting a review on your preferred book site.

Recent bestsellers from Zero Books are:

In the Dust of This Planet
Horror of Philosophy vol. 1
Eugene Thacker
In the first of a series of three books on the Horror of
Philosophy, *In the Dust of This Planet* offers the genre of horror
as a way of thinking about the unthinkable.
Paperback: 978-1-84694-676-9 ebook: 978-1-78099-010-1

Capitalist Realism
Is there no alternative?
Mark Fisher
An analysis of the ways in which capitalism has presented itself
as the only realistic political-economic system.
Paperback: 978-1-84694-317-1 ebook: 978-1-78099-734-6

Rebel Rebel
Chris O'Leary
David Bowie: every single song. Everything you want to know,
everything you didn't know.
Paperback: 978-1-78099-244-0 ebook: 978-1-78099-713-1

Cartographies of the Absolute
Alberto Toscano, Jeff Kinkle
An aesthetics of the economy for the twenty-first century.
Paperback: 978-1-78099-275-4 ebook: 978-1-78279-973-3

Malign Velocities
Accelerationism and Capitalism
Benjamin Noys
Long listed for the Bread and Roses Prize 2015, *Malign
Velocities* argues against the need for speed, tracking
acceleration as the symptom of the ongoing crises of capitalism.
Paperback: 978-1-78279-300-7 ebook: 978-1-78279-299-4

Meat Market
Female flesh under Capitalism
Laurie Penny
A feminist dissection of women's bodies as the fleshy fulcrum
of capitalist cannibalism, whereby women are both consumers
and consumed.
Paperback: 978-1-84694-521-2 ebook: 978-1-84694-782-7

Poor but Sexy
Culture Clashes in Europe East and West
Agata Pyzik
How the East stayed East and the West stayed West.
Paperback: 978-1-78099-394-2 ebook: 978-1-78099-395-9

Romeo and Juliet in Palestine
Teaching Under Occupation
Tom Sperlinger
Life in the West Bank, the nature of pedagogy and the role of a
university under occupation.
Paperback: 978-1-78279-637-4 ebook: 978-1-78279-636-7

Sweetening the Pill
or How we Got Hooked on Hormonal Birth Control
Holly Grigg-Spall
Has contraception liberated or oppressed women? *Sweetening
the Pill* breaks the silence on the dark side of hormonal
contraception.
Paperback: 978-1-78099-607-3 ebook: 978-1-78099-608-0

Why Are We The Good Guys?
Reclaiming your Mind from the Delusions of Propaganda
David Cromwell
A provocative challenge to the standard ideology that Western
power is a benevolent force in the world.
Paperback: 978-1-78099-365-2 ebook: 978-1-78099-366-9

Readers of ebooks can buy or view any of these bestsellers by
clicking on the live link in the title. Most titles are published
in paperback and as an ebook. Paperbacks are available in
traditional bookshops. Both print and ebook formats are
available online.

Find more titles and sign up to our readers' newsletter
at http://www.johnhuntpublishing.com/culture-and-politics

Follow us on Facebook
at https://www.facebook.com/ZeroBooks

and Twitter at https://twitter.com/Zer0Books